EXISTENCE AND ANALOGY

EXISTENCE AND ANALOGY

A SEQUEL TO "HE WHO IS"

by

E. L. MASCALL

Student and Tutor of Christ Church, Oxford
University Lecturer in the Philosophy of Religion
Priest of the Oratory of the Good Shepherd

Modicum ibi, modicum ibi
Isa. xxviii, 10

LONGMANS, GREEN AND CO
LONDON ⋄ NEW YORK ⋄ TORONTO

LONGMANS, GREEN AND CO LTD
6 & 7 CLIFFORD STREET LONDON W 1
ALSO AT MELBOURNE AND CAPE TOWN

LONGMANS, GREEN AND CO INC
55 FIFTH AVENUE NEW YORK 3

LONGMANS, GREEN AND CO
215 VICTORIA STREET TORONTO 1

ORIENT LONGMANS LTD
BOMBAY CALCUTTA MADRAS

First published 1949

PRINTED IN GREAT BRITAIN
BY WESTERN PRINTING SERVICES LTD. BRISTOL

REGINAE   COELI
DEIPARAE

CONTENTS

PREFACE

ANYONE who confronts the theological and philosophical public with a book bearing such a title as that of the present work will, I think, be prudent if he takes the earliest opportunity of explaining why he has chosen it. For, as the wise man of the Old Testament aptly remarked, if the serpent bite before it be charmed, then is there no advantage in the charmer.

From one point of view, this book may be considered as a sequel or a supplement to an earlier work entitled *He Who Is: A Study in Traditional Theism*, which was published in 1943. Several reviewers of that book, while treating it upon the whole with what I cannot now help feeling was a somewhat undeserved indulgence, did me the service of pointing out that perhaps its chief deficiency lay in the fact that, while it made repeated reference to the doctrine of analogy, it nowhere contained an adequate account of what the doctrine of analogy is. The present work originated in an attempt to fill that gap, but as the task went on it became more and more clear to me that there is another doctrine of equal importance for the construction of any sound scheme of rational theology, namely the doctrine of existence, and indeed that the two are very intimately connected. What emerged in the end was a more or less independent survey, and it is this that is now in the reader's hands. Except upon a few minor points I do not think that I have come substantially to modify the opinions expressed in the earlier work, though I have come to recognize many of its imperfections and its need for amplification. I have therefore, as far as possible, refrained from simply repeating what is contained in it, and for this reason I venture to suggest that, if the reader is not already acquainted with it, he may find that at least an occasional reference to the earlier volume will make the discussion upon which I am now hoping to launch him somewhat less obscure than it would otherwise be.

Natural theology, Lord Macaulay tells us in the essay on von Ranke, is not a progressive science. Neither the evidence that lies before the philosopher's eyes nor the problems that perplex him are any different from what they were in the days of Thales or Socrates. And in a sense the great Whig historian is perfectly right. As Dr. Farrer remarks in the Introduction to his striking work *Finite and Infinite*, it is absurd to propose new grounds for belief in the existence of God. Nevertheless —and no one has done more than Dr. Farrer to show it—there are three tasks which demand the labours of natural theologians in any age: namely, to dispel misunderstandings as to what the grounds of belief actually are, to state them in a way which is relevant to the intellectual outlook of the time, and to answer contemporary objections to their validity. Personally I find the first of these tasks the easiest; at any rate I am sure that the second of them is the most difficult; for the present-day climate of thought, both among professional intellectuals and among people in general, is such as to make any reference of the world of human experience to a transcendent cause seem not merely precarious but also uninteresting. I should feel inclined to doubt whether it was in fact possible to present the case for theism in terms that were intelligible to modern philosophers, were it not that in the work to which I have just referred Dr. Farrer has succeeded in doing it. I have confined myself in the present book to the lowlier task of presenting the traditional case as clearly as I can, in the hope that some readers at least may come to recognize that it is not precisely what they thought it was and that there is still something to be said for it.

And here I should like to state quite categorically my conviction that the rational case for theism is as strong to-day as it was in the first or in the thirteenth century. The late Professor Laird legitimately castigated what he described as "the fallacious practice of reviving discredited demonstrations as if they were near-proofs that should incline towards assent although they do not coerce an enlightened judgment."[1] In all ages there have been people who have ignored or disputed the fundamental assertions of religion, though it is, I think,

[1] *Theism and Cosmology*, p. 294.

almost certain that their number has never been proportion-
ately as large as it is in civilized countries at the present day.
Certainly a thinker such as St. Thomas Aquinas, who denied
explicitly that the existence of God is self-evident and who
expounded not only arguments for the existence of God but
also objections against it, was far from holding that it was
impossible for a thinking man to deny it. But I can think of
hardly any worse service to the cause of religion than is performed by some of its apologists to-day, who seem to make
the implicit assumption that any arguments which are widely
disputed or neglected are *ipso facto* shown to have only a
probable conclusion. For myself I can only say that I find it
difficult to conceive how any argument could show that the
existence of God was merely probable. I can understand that
an argument which claimed to prove that God exists might be
invalid. I can also understand that, if most people who had
examined it thought it was valid but a small number who had
examined it thought it was invalid, then someone who had
never examined it at all might form the initial hypothesis that
it was more probably valid than not. And I should then
expect him to examine it for himself. But what I cannot
understand is the widespread assumption that because most
people to-day who have heard that there are arguments for
the existence of God, whether they have examined them or
not, seem to be unconvinced of God's existence, therefore the
arguments themselves cannot prove anything more than that
the existence of God is probable. What I am pleading, in
short, is that the traditional approaches to the existence of
God need restating and re-examining; and this task seems to
me to be all the more important because of the very prevalent
misunderstanding of their nature which is to be found among
both the supporters and the opponents of theism.

I strongly suspect that theism has, as a matter of fact, been
discredited not so much by its opponents as by some of its
advocates. And among these I am thinking not so much of
those who have been content simply to repeat in so many words
the Five Ways of St. Thomas while failing to penetrate to the
metaphysical depths of St. Thomas's thought, as of those who
have over-hastily attempted to bring under tribute to theism

the discoveries of modern science. It would be easy to give examples of this from twentieth-century writers, but I shall content myself with mentioning a book which, just because it was of a popular kind, exerted very considerable influence at the time when science was entering upon its modern heyday; I mean *The Orbs of Heaven*, by the American astronomer, O. M. Mitchel, which was first published in 1848 and was reissued at intervals throughout the latter half of the nineteenth century. This writer seemed to be completely obsessed by the religious significance of large numbers. The existence of a nebula six thousand million miles in diameter sent him into theological rhapsodies, but his final transports were reserved for Maedlar's theory that the centre of the astral system is the star Alcyone, the light from which, travelling at 186,000 miles a second, takes no less than 537 years to reach the sun.

"Comprehend if you can," he exhorts his readers, "the vast dimensions of our sun. Stretch outward through his system, from planet to planet, and circumscribe the whole within the immense circumference of Neptune's orbit. This is but a single unit out of the myriads of similar systems. Take the wings of light, and flash with impetuous speed, day and night, and month and year, till youth shall wear away, and middle age is gone, and the extremest limit of human life has been attained; count every pulse, and at each, speed on your way a hundred thousand miles; and when a hundred years have rolled by, look out, and behold! the thronging millions of blazing suns are still around you, each separated from the other by such a distance that in this journey of a century you have only left half a score behind you."[1]

And again:

"God has computed the mutual perturbations of millions of suns, and planets, and comets, and worlds, without number, through the ages that are passed, and throughout the ages which are yet to come, not approximately, but with perfect and absolute precision. The universe is in motion, system rising above system, cluster above cluster, nebula above nebula, all majestically sweeping around under the providence of God,

[1] 4th ed. (1853), p. 222.

who alone knows the end from the beginning, and before whose glory and power all intelligent beings, whether in heaven or on earth, should bow with humility and awe."[1]

I am far from wishing to make fun of Professor Mitchel's piety, and I must admit that, on the whole, I prefer his rather uncontrolled fervour to the somewhat cynical attitude of some of the popular scientific writers of the present day. But I am bound to say that the widespread tendency, of which this is a fair example, to suppose that the mere size and complexity of the universe have anything in particular to do with the demonstration of the existence and attributes of God seems to me to have done more harm than good to the cause of religion. Are we to suppose that a smaller and simpler world might have owed its existence to some less exalted agency? I find equal eloquence and far more profundity in Maritain's remark: "If we grant to a speck of moss or to the tiniest ant the value of its ontological reality, we can no longer escape from the terrifying hand which made us."[2]

There is, however, a more serious misconception which I shall illustrate from Mitchel's book. He derives great religious comfort from the consideration of the stability of the planetary system. Having shown, by reference to the theory of perturbations, that any small disturbance to which the solar system might become subject would not increase indefinitely until the system collapsed, but would instead merely cause a rhythmical variation, he concludes as follows:

> "Are we to believe that the Divine Architect constructed this admirably adjusted system to wear out, and to fall in ruins, even before one single revolution of its complex scheme of wheels had been performed? No; I see the mighty orbits of the planets slowly rocking to and fro, their figures expanding and contracting, their axes revolving in their vast periods; but stability is there. Every change shall wear away, and after sweeping through the grand cycle of cycles, the whole system shall return to its primitive condition of perfection and beauty."[3]

There was nothing in the silence of the infinite spaces to frighten Professor Mitchel; but how far we have departed, not

[1] Ibid., p. 223.   [2] *Distinguer pour unir*, p. 212.   [3] Op. cit., p. 125.

only from traditional scholasticism but from the teaching of the Bible itself, when to argue for the perpetuity of the material universe is felt to be a confirmation of theistic belief! There is no *Solvet saeclum in favilla* here; and, as regards God, it is only a step before we shall find ourselves re-echoing *Je n'ai pas besoin de cet hypothèse-là*. Metaphysically, of course, it is supremely unimportant whether the finite world is everlasting or not, and still less important whether part of it, such as the solar system, is; St. Thomas laid that bogy once and for all in his *De aeternitate mundi*. But to a generation which was only too prone to confuse physics and metaphysics such an attitude as I have quoted above was highly misleading. To quote Maritain again: "Leibniz pretended to justify God by showing that the work which proceeded from the hands of that perfect Workman was itself perfect, whereas in reality it is the radical imperfection of every creature which best attests the glory of the Uncreated."[1]

It is thus, I believe, of the greatest importance that theistic apologetic should be put upon a thoroughly sound metaphysical basis. And, however involved our metaphysical arguments may have to become in the discussion of incidental points, the approach itself must be such as can be understood and made by the plain man. The plain man is not, of course, even in this secularized age, entirely devoid of intuitions of a supernatural reality.

"Youths green and happy in first love,
  So thankful for illusion;
And men caught out in what the world
  Calls guilt, in first confusion;

"And almost every one when age,
  Disease, or sorrows strike him,
Inclines to think there is a God,
  Or something very like him."[2]

We can, however, hardly acquiesce in so intermittent and emotional a basis for belief as this. In fact, there has been throughout the history of the human race a direct apprehension of a reality which, however dimly its nature may have been

[1] *Religion and Culture*, p. 40.   [2] A. H. Clough, *Dipsychus*, I, v.

sometimes understood, can be recognized by a Christian theist
as the God in whom he believes. This apprehension, although
direct, is not immediate; it is the apprehension of God as the
ground of finite beings. More accurately, perhaps, it might
be described as the apprehension of finite being in its character
as grounded in God, or simply as the apprehension of God-
and-finite-being in the creator-creature relationship. It is
extremely obscure and opaque, and when it is not reinforced
by a revelation of the divine transcendence, such as that which
is provided by the tradition of Judaism and Christianity, it is
likely to become extremely corrupt. As Dr. C. S. Lewis has
pointed out in his recent book *Miracles*,[1] natural religion when
left to itself almost invariably degenerates into some form of
pantheism. This is easily understandable, for the notion of
transcendence is a highly difficult one to maintain; just because
God is apprehended not in his naked reality but through his
relation to his creatures, it is all too easy for the perfections
which the creatures manifest as God's to be attributed to the
creatures themselves. Nevertheless it is theism and not pantheism that is fundamentally rational, and it is highly significant that Christianity has produced not only a doctrine of
God as revealed, but also the most coherent system of rational
theology of which we have any record.

In spite of the technical character of certain of its parts, the
present work is concerned to defend and clarify the plain man's
apprehension of God in his creatures. As I have already
remarked, this apprehension seems to be abnormally obscure
at the present day. There are, I believe, historical reasons
for this fact into which it is not necessary to enter now. It
provides both peculiar difficulties and peculiar opportunities.
In the book to which I have just referred Dr. Lewis has written
as follows:

> "In the conditions produced by a century or so of Natural-
> ism, plain men are being forced to bear burdens which plain
> men were never expected to bear before. We must get the
> truth for ourselves or go without it. There may be two ex-
> planations for this. It might be that humanity, in rebelling
> against tradition and authority, have made a ghastly mistake;

[1] Ch. xi, "Christianity and 'Religion'."

a mistake which will not be the less fatal because the corrup-
tions of those in authority rendered it very excusable. On the
other hand, it may be that the Power which rules our species
is at this moment carrying out a daring experiment. Could
it be intended that the whole mass of the people should now
move forward and occupy for themselves those heights which
were once reserved only for the sages? Is the distinction
between wise and simple to disappear because all are now
expected to become wise? If so, our present blunderings
would be but growing pains."[1]

I should be sorry to feel that the plain man's burden in the
twentieth century necessarily involved him in attempting to
grapple with the present work; I should be happier if it merely
drove him to Dr. Lewis. But I must emphasize that it is the
plain man's approach to God that I am defending here, and not
some esoteric way reserved for a leisured class of mystical or
philosophical adepts. The defence may call for technicalities
of a high order; what is being defended is as simple as the day.

It would be useless to try to conceal that the general outlook
of this book is one which might be described as that of a
modern Thomism. In many quarters this will be enough to
damn the discussion at the start. I can only plead that if, on
the broad issue and in a number of details, I have had the
temerity to agree with the Angelic Doctor, it is not because
of a nostalgia for the thirteenth century, or because Dominicans
are picturesque, or even in order to scandalize some of my
elders, but simply because, having given a good deal of thought
to these questions, I have come to the conclusion that what
St. Thomas said about them was on the whole correct. I may
of course be mistaken, and if I am I shall be grateful to anyone
who is kind enough to demonstrate this. I would urge only
that the question is one which ought to be decided on its own
merits, and not on the assumption that modern philosophers
must be nearer the truth than St. Thomas simply because
they are later or that Thomism is a kind of pathological or
moral defect. With M. Gilson I would say that I am as fond
of my own intellectual freedom as anyone else, but I want to
be free to agree with somebody when I think that what he

---

[1] C. S. Lewis, *Miracles*, p. 53.

says is right.[1] I am not claiming to be infallible; I am not claiming that St. Thomas is infallible. I have even ventured in the present work to point out at least one point in which it seems to me that St. Thomas's exposition was rather seriously misleading. But having said this, I feel bound to add that the transformation which St. Thomas brought about in natural theology is, as far as my judgment goes, of an importance which it is impossible to exaggerate; in what precisely that transformation consisted will, I hope, become clear in the following pages. It may well be that the Angelic Doctor was some centuries ahead of his time; it would certainly seem that later scholasticism proved incapable of maintaining the radical existentialism of his thought. Had it not been for this decline the *philosophia perennis* would, I think, have been equal to the tasks with which the Renaissance confronted it, and would not have been by-passed as it was by what M. Gilson has called the Modern Experiment. A recovery of authentic Thomism would, I believe, do more than anything else to revitalize present-day philosophy and to bridge the ideological gulf which at the moment yawns so widely between the philosophers and the physical scientists.

However—and here I am afraid I shall lose the sympathy of many of those to whom the name of St. Thomas is most precious—I am convinced that such a recovery of authentic Thomism will require a more thorough attempt than has yet been made to disentangle the essentials of St. Thomas's thought from the accidental forms in which he cast it in order to meet the needs of his own time. That these essentials can be disentangled from the physical theories of the thirteenth century without being mutilated in the process is, I think, generally recognized. But what is perhaps equally necessary is their disentanglement from such of the purely philosophical trappings of thirteenth-century Aristotelianism as are merely accidental. That such a task is not in itself impossible is suggested by the fact that the fundamental principle of St. Thomas's metaphysics—his existentialism—while it completely revolutionized Aristotelianism, did not come from Aristotle at all, however necessary it may have been if Aristotle was to be

[1] *God and Philosophy*, p. xvi.

made really coherent. Such a task of disentanglement cannot, of its very nature, be easy. Some of the apparently accidental Aristotelian elements may in fact turn out to be indispensable to any existential philosophical system. Still more difficult must be the task of reconstructing modern philosophy on Thomist principles; there can be no question of laying down a cut-and-dried programme by the application of which any given philosophical system can be "Thomisticized." What is needed is, first, the extraction of the great conceptions of Thomism from the mass of purely contemporary Aristotelianism in which the Angelic Doctor embedded them, and then a thorough rethinking of our present-day philosophical problems in the light of those conceptions, full use being made in this process of all the relevant material that can be derived from post-Thomist thought. How much Aristotelianism will survive such radical handling it would be hazardous to predict; personally I suspect a good deal. In any case, the reader will be relieved to know that the task is not attempted in the present work; that is concerned with a more restricted problem. But I very much fear that such of my readers as are Thomists will dislike this book for the extent to which it diverges from the general Thomist tradition, while those who are not Thomists will dislike it for the extent to which it adheres to it. That is a risk which I have had to take. There is at any rate nothing un-Thomist in venturing to criticize St. Thomas, for he himself tells us that of all arguments that from authority based on human reason is the weakest.

I have made no reference to arguments for the existence of God drawn from religious experience or from considerations of morality, except in so far as the apprehension of finite being as grounded in God may be considered as falling within the scope of the former, and St. Thomas's Fourth Way as including the latter. I have no desire to imply that such arguments are devoid of value but I do not think that I am specially competent to discuss them, and I am strongly in agreement with Dr. Farrer that they cannot be made a substitute for strictly metaphysical discussion.[1] I have therefore thought it both wise and legitimate to confine myself to this last approach.

[1] *Finite and Infinite*, p. 12.

My indebtedness to other writers will be evident from the references which I have made to their books in the course of my exposition. I have also derived much assistance from conversations with various Roman Catholic friends and it gives me much pleasure to acknowledge this. Apart from my personal limitations, the chief handicap of which I have been conscious while writing this book has been the extreme paucity of any similar writings by authors outside the Roman Communion. I am therefore especially glad to express my gratitude to Dr. A. M. Farrer for the help that I have received from him, both in conversation and through his book *Finite and Infinite*. If more people had been thinking along these lines my task would have been easier. But then in all probability I should not have needed to perform it, for someone else would have done it already.

E. L. M.

Oxford, 1948

Large portions of Chapters V and VII were originally published as an article in *Laudate* for December 1943. Chapter III and part of Chapter VI are based on papers read to the Origen Society at Oxford.

My thanks are due to the following publishers for permission to make use of copyright material:

MM. Beauchesne et ses fils for Père Garrigou-Lagrange's *Dieu, son Existence et sa Nature*; M. J. Vrin for M. Gilson's *Le Thomisme* and *Réalisme Thomiste et Critique de la Connaissance* and for the Abbé Penido's *Le Rôle de l'Analogie en Théologie dogmatique*; M. Fernand Aubier for Père Sertillanges' *L'Idée de Création* and for M. Lossky's *Théologie mystique de l'Église d'Orient*; Messrs. Sheed and Ward, Ltd., for M. Gilson's *God and Philosophy* and for *Essays in Thomism*; the Dacre Press for Dr. A. M. Farrer's *Finite and Infinite*; and Messrs. Macmillan and Co. Ltd., for Miss Dorothy Emmet's *The Nature of Metaphysical Thinking*.

CHAPTER ONE

THE NATURE OF CHRISTIAN THEISM

" En disant ' L'Être même subsistant,' ou ' en lui pas de distinction réelle entre l'essence et l'existence,' le métaphysicien désigne sans le voir l'abîme sacré qui fait trembler les anges d'amour ou de terreur."
J. MARITAIN, *Distinguer pour unir*, p. 457

I

THE primary task of rational theology is to ask what grounds can be found for asserting the existence of God. Before this inquiry can be profitably initiated certain preliminaries are, however, necessary. In particular, it is essential to be clear—or at any rate as clear as by the nature of the case we can be—precisely what meaning the word "God" is to have in this connection. This is imperative for two reasons. In the first place, the word "God" (and its equivalent in languages other than English) has by no means always been used in the same sense, and to ignore the difference between the various senses in which it has been used is almost certain to lead us into ambiguity and confusion. In the second place, the word "God" has a very definite meaning in Christian theology, and the rational theologian, if he is a Christian, has, in consequence, a very special interest in inquiring into the grounds for asserting the existence of the Christian God rather than that of any of the other beings to which the name "God" has been applied. How radically the connotation of the word "God" has in fact been transformed under the influence of Christianity has been made plain by M. Étienne Gilson in more than one of his works and I think we can hardly open our discussion more profitably than by giving attention to his exposition.

In his book *God and Philosophy* Gilson begins by remarking upon two distinct statements which Aristotle makes about the doctrine of Thales of Miletus. Thales, said Aristotle, tells us

B   I

that the first principle, from which all things are born and to which all things return, is water; he also tells us that "all things are full of gods."[1] How are these statements to be reconciled? One way is to say that it is obvious that for Thales water was a god, and indeed the supreme god; another way is to say that for Thales the word "God" means nothing but a metaphysical principle, such as he believed water to be. Students of Greek philosophy can be quoted who have taken each of these courses. The former course theologizes Thales' philosophy; the latter philosophizes his theology. But, Gilson urges, there is not the slightest evidence that Thales himself made any such identification. Similarly, when we come down to the great age of Greek philosophy, Plato never identifies his Idea of the Good with God or with a god, however obvious it may seem to many modern commentators that he ought to have done so. "What makes it so hard for some modern scholars to reconcile themselves to the fact," writes Gilson, "is that after so many centuries of Christian thought it has become exceedingly difficult for us to imagine a world where the gods are not the highest reality, while that which is most supremely real in it is not a god."[2] The assumption that a god, whatever else he may be, must also be a metaphysical principle and that the fundamental metaphysical principle must be a god comes to be taken as a matter of course only after a long period of influence exerted upon philosophical thought by the Judaeo-Christian revelation. "The definition of a Greek god," Gilson says, "should run thus: a god, to any living being, is any other living being whom he knows as lording it over his own life";[3] such a being may be very far from providing a principle of philosophical explanation. For the Greeks the task of reconciling the religious with the philosophical attitude to the world was extremely difficult, if not indeed impossible; and the assumption that if there is a God he must provide not only an object for religion but also a first principle for philosophy is, however little many modern philosophers may have realized it, a direct effect of Christianity.

The absence of this clear identification in even the greatest Greek thinkers is expounded by Gilson in more detail in the

---

[1] Gilson, op. cit., p. 1. Aristotle, *Met.* I, 983b, 20–7; *De Anima*, I, 5, 411a, 8.
[2] Op. cit., p. 27.   [3] Ibid., p. 11.

third chapter of his *Spirit of Mediaeval Philosophy*. For Plato, he points out, "divinity belongs to a class of multiple beings" and "perhaps even to all beings whatsoever in the precise measure in which they are."[1] Even in the *Timaeus* the god who is the cause and father of the universe has rivals in the intelligible order of Ideas and does not exclude the sidereal gods whose author he is, or even the divine character of the world that he fashions; and to say, as has often been said, that the Demiurge of the *Timaeus* is "almost analogous to the Christian God" is only one way of saying that he is not the Christian God at all. To attempt this identification leads merely to confusion in the understanding of Plato's thought: "sometimes the Demiurge of the *Timaeus* is identified with the Idea of the Good in the *Republic*, and the only result of this is that the Demiurge becomes, not Being, but the Good—a thing, by the way, that Plato never made of him."[2]

Turning from Plato to Aristotle, Gilson observes that "the first unmoved mover is very far from occupying in Aristotle's world the unique place reserved for the God of the Bible in the Judaeo-Christian world."[3] Under the first unmoved mover there are forty-nine, or perhaps fifty-five, other movers, all separate, eternal and unmoved and thus all divine. "We cannot say of [Aristotle], as we can of Plato, that he regards all that exists as divine, for he reserves the name of divinity to the order of necessity and pure actuality; but although his First Unmoved Mover is, of all beings, in the highest degree divine and in the highest degree being, he remains nevertheless but one of these 'beings as being.' It cannot possibly be denied that his natural theology has for proper object a plurality of divine beings, and that is enough to distinguish it radically from Christian natural theology." And "even were it granted, in the face of all the texts, that Aristotle's being as being is a unique being, it would still be true that this being is none other than the pure act of thought thinking itself. . . . In good Aristotelian doctrine the first name of God is thought, and pure being is reduced to pure thought; in good Christian doctrine the first name of God is being, and that is why we can refuse to Being neither thought, nor will, nor power, and

[1] Op. cit., p. 44.   [2] Ibid., p. 49.   [3] Ibid., p. 45.

why the attributes of the Christian God overflow the attributes of Aristotle's in every direction. But no one rises to the Christian conception of Being who sets up statues to Zeus and Demeter."[1]

II

I should like to set by the side of M. Gilson's exposition an independent discussion by Mr. M. B. Foster bearing the title "The Christian Doctrine of Creation and the Rise of Modern Natural Science,"[2] which, probably because it appeared in the pages of a technical philosophical journal, is much less familiar to theologians than it deserves to be. If the consideration of it seems to be leading us away from our immediate concern of determining the precise meaning of "God" in Christian philosophy, we shall find in the end that it has in fact set us very far forward on our path. Mr. Foster begins by laying down two assumptions about modern philosophy, which he claims will not be disputed. (Incidentally we should observe that "modern philosophy" in this context is defined as "the philosophy which arose at the end of the Middle Ages and developed along the two main lines of Empiricism and Rationalism from Hobbes to Hume and from Descartes to Leibniz."[3]) The first of these assumptions is that modern philosophy, in so far as it has been concerned with a theory of nature, has been devoted mainly to establishing the possibility or justifying the presuppositions of the modern science of nature; the second is that what distinguishes the modern doctrines of nature from that of Aristotle and of scholasticism is precisely that non-Aristotelian element in them which is the ground of the peculiar distinction between modern natural science and the science of the Greeks and the scholastics. Mr. Foster then asks two questions: (1) What is the source of the un-Greek elements imported into philosophy by the post-Reformation philosophers? (2) What is the source of the un-Greek elements that determine the peculiar character of the modern science of nature? To the first question he answers: the Christian revelation; to the second: the Christian doctrine of creation. Greek science, he goes on to say, assumed that

[1] Op. cit., p. 50. [2] *Mind*, 1934, XLIII, N.S., pp. 446 f. [3] Art. cit., p. 446.

all properties were deducible from essences, and since, for the Greeks, form was the intelligible element in things while matter was the unintelligible, the understanding of nature, so far as that was possible, meant the understanding of forms. This theory presupposes the doctrine that neither matter nor form is created: "If matter were created it would possess a positive being, if form were created it would not be intelligible."[1] "Nature may be conceived as dependent upon a supernatural power for the activity by which its two elements are conjoined, but not for the being of either element."[2] In harmony with this doctrine Greek thought exemplifies three leading theological conceptions:

(1) There is the conception of God as identical with nature, which finds its earliest expression in the deification of natural powers. It is true that the withdrawal of the gods to Olympus in later Greek religion implies a partial distinction between God and nature, in virtue of which sensible objects can henceforth be viewed as *appearances* of the god or as *manifestations* of his activity rather than as being themselves divine. It leads ultimately to the Platonic distinction between the idea and the sensible object which made Greek science possible. Nevertheless, the distinction between God and the universe was never more than partial; and the higher development of modern science depends upon the far deeper distinction between God and nature made by the Christian religion.

(2) There is also in Greek thought the conception of God as the subject of a purely theoretical activity. Aristotle's God, though admittedly transcendent, has no power over the world except that of originating motion, and even of motion he is only the final, and in no way the efficient, cause. Neither form nor matter in natural objects depends on him, and the source of energy in nature is to be found not in God but in the active potency of the form to realize itself. The only activity of which God is capable is the theoretical activity which terminates not upon the world but upon himself.

(3) There is, however, in Greek thought one doctrine of God which does attribute to him a power of efficient causation in the world. This is Plato's doctrine of the Demiurge or

[1] Ibid., p. 456. [2] Ibid.

Artificer, and, writes Mr. Foster, "because this, of all Greek theological doctrines, bears the closest superficial resemblance to the Christian doctrine of Creation it will serve best to throw into relief the essential contrast which still persists between the conception of God as Creator and any conception of the divine activity which is consistent with the presuppositions of Greek natural science."[1] The doctrine *is* essentially non-Christian, because the Demiurge's activity is confined to the imposition of form on a given matter and is directed by the antecedent conception of an end. The form, no less than the matter, must be given to the Demiurge; from his activity it derives not its being but only its embodiment. His work is confined to bringing form and matter into union, but neither element owes its being to him; the doctrine of the Demiurge is thus fully compatible with the characteristically Greek assumption that both forms and matter are eternal. Plato in the *Timaeus* may be unique in asserting that the natural world is the product of a Demiurge, but Aristotle himself says that natural objects are *as though* they were the work of a Demiurge.

Mr. Foster illustrates this doctrine of the Artificer by considering the character of artefacts. If an object is the product of an artificer, it must be capable of definition, for it must be the embodiment of a form that was present in the mind of the artificer before he made it. Once the form has been clearly conceived and defined all the essential properties of the object can be derived from the definition, and the method of this derivation is given by the canons of Aristotelian logic. Now two conditions are necessary for an object to be definable in the Aristotelian sense: (1) its form must be intelligible, and (2) its form must be its real essence. Both these conditions are satisfied by an artefact and both, asserts Mr. Foster, are denied by the Christian doctrine of creation. The intelligibility of the form is denied, because it would involve that the activity of God was purposive in the sense of being directed upon an end which was not itself the product of his activity. The identification of the form with the real essence is denied as inconsistent with God's activity of will. In the view of the world as an artefact any element that is contingent must be

[1] Art. cit., p. 459.

ascribed either to bad workmanship on the part of the artificer or to recalcitrance in the material upon which he works. Now the divine Demiurge cannot be accused of bad workmanship; hence the character of contingency in natural objects must be ascribed to the material element in them. But matter is the object of sensation, as form is the object of intellection. Hence the contingent character of the natural world, which arises from its materiality, cannot be understood; it can only be sensed. It cannot be the object of knowledge, and so the absence of an empirical element in Greek natural science is accounted for. This absence is inevitable so long as the production of the world is viewed as simply the "information" of matter by a Demiurge, whose willing is altogether subjected to the antecedent apprehension of form. In a doctrine in which God is, in the strict sense, a Creator, such a "subordination" does not, however, obtain. It is no defect in a Creator, as it would be in a Demiurge, that his will is not, in the sense described above, "subordinated" to his reason. His activity exceeds determination by reason and it terminates in precisely that element of the creature's being that is contingent. In a world that is *created* and not merely *manufactured*, contingency is not an imperfection in the embodiment of form; it is precisely that which constitutes the creature as a creature. And since the contingent is, as we have seen, the object of the senses, it follows that sensible experience is indispensable to the science of nature, and, moreover, indispensable not merely in the sense that it is a necessary stage on the way to real knowledge, but in the more radical sense that the very element in the creature which constitutes it as a creature, namely its contingency, cannot be an object of the intellect but only of the senses. Now, Mr. Foster remarks, "the reliance upon the senses for evidence, not merely for illustration, is what constitutes the empirical character peculiar to modern natural science; and the conclusion follows that only a created nature is proper object of an empirical science."[1]

Thus, says Mr. Foster, summarizing his argument, modern natural science could begin only when the modern presuppositions about nature had displaced the Greek, and this

[1] Ibid., p. 465.

displacement itself was possible only when the Christian conception of God had displaced the pagan. He adds that by "Christian" here he really means Christian, and not Jewish, for "the Christian doctrine of God derived much from the Greek and thus included within itself, besides much from Jewish sources, much also from the very doctrine which it displaced."[1] He remarks also that "to achieve this primary displacement [of the Greek by the Christian doctrine of God] was the work of Medieval Theology, which thus laid the foundations both of much else in the modern world which is specifically modern, and of modern natural science";[2] the displacement of the Greek by the modern presuppositions about nature was a gradual process, but its crisis occurred at the date of the Reformation. And he brings his discussion to a close by showing how, in modern philosophy, a defect in the doctrine of God is reflected in corresponding defects both in the doctrine of nature and in the theory of natural science. The failure of modern Rationalism was its failure to do justice to the un-Greek element in the Christian doctrine of creation; the failure of modern Empiricism was its failure to do justice to anything else.[3]

I have summarized Mr. Foster's argument at some length not only because of its admirable clarity and cogency, but also because it is of special value coming as it does from one who is by profession a philosopher and not a theologian. How radically the conception of God and his relation to the world has in fact been transformed under the influence of the Christian tradition is shown by the fact that more than one of the statements which Mr. Foster characterizes as inconsistent with Christian doctrine are statements which, so far as their mere wording is concerned, anyone who has come to the terminology of Aristotelian philosophy through the writings of the medieval Aristotelians rather than through the writings of Aristotle himself will have no difficulty in accepting as harmless, and indeed as expressing an important truth. Such are, for example, the statements that form is intelligible and that in the creative

---

[1] Art. cit., p. 465, n. 1.
[2] Ibid., p. 465. Mr. Foster further discusses and develops his theme in an article entitled "Christian Theology and Modern Science of Nature," in *Mind*, XLIV and XLV, N.S. (1935 and 1936).   [3] Art. cit., p. 468.

act the will of God is subordinated to his reason; to both of these a thoroughly respectable interpretation can be given in Christian philosophy, but it is an interpretation radically different from that which came naturally to the Greeks.

The type of universe whose investigation requires the methods of modern science must, I would suggest, have two characteristics: contingency and rationality. If rationality were absent, there would be no laws for science to discover; if contingency were absent, there would be no need for empirical observation and experiment, for every truth about the world could be deduced from first principles. The combination of the two characteristics is precisely correlative to a technique which believes that there are uniformities in nature and yet that these uniformities need to be discovered. Professor Whitehead has, indeed, asserted that it is the belief in uniformity which is the main contribution of the Middle Ages to the formation of the scientific movement: "the inexpugnable belief that every detailed occurrence can be correlated with its antecedents in a perfectly definite manner, exemplifying general principles."[1] The question of priority between the characteristics of rationality and contingency is one that perhaps we need not decide; what is important is to recognize that they are combined in the attitude which produced modern science. Of this attitude, Whitehead tells us that "there seems but one source for its origin. It must come from the medieval insistence on the rationality of God, conceived as with the personal energy of Jehovah and with the rationality of a Greek philosopher."[2] And this, it is needless to add, is the God of the Christian tradition.

III

How, then, are we to characterize the transformation which philosophy underwent at the hands of Christianity? There are no doubt many ways in which it might be expressed, but I am inclined to think that one of the most illuminating is that which M. Gilson has adopted in his recent revision of his

[1] *Science and the Modern World*, ch. i.
[2] Ibid. Dr. C. S. Lewis has drawn attention to this passage in his book *Miracles*, p. 127.

famous work *Le Thomisme*. According to this exposition, the fundamental characteristic of Christian metaphysics, which reaches its most authentic and unambiguous embodiment in the system of St. Thomas Aquinas, is its radical emphasis upon the fact of existence, in contrast to the primacy held in pre-Christian thought by the notion of essence. That the basic fact about God is the fact that he, and he alone, supremely and perfectly exists and that the basic problem with which the world confronts us is the problem of its existence, this is for Gilson the specific contribution which the Christian religion brought into philosophy. It is a contribution which was only imperfectly and partially understood by the pre-Thomist Christian writers, and their understanding of it was hindered rather than helped by their general preference for Platonic and neo-Platonic thought over Aristotelian, for the essentialist attitude is even more markedly congenial to the Platonic than to the Aristotelian type of Greek thought. Even such an intellectual giant as St. Augustine had not altogether shaken off the trappings of essentialism. In St. Thomas, however, existentialism becomes the deliberately and consciously adopted guiding principle of Christian philosophy. And it expresses the specifically Christian doctrine of God and his relation to the world.

I shall postpone to a later chapter a detailed discussion of the existentialism of the Angelic Doctor, and shall now turn to inquire what is the source of this existential character of Christian theism, for this inquiry will bring us back to the main point of this chapter, namely the determination of the precise meaning that is to be given in Christian philosophy to the word "God."

The Christian revelation claims, and always has claimed, to be the fulfilment of the partial and obscurely apprehended revelation given by God to the Jews: "God who at sundry times and in divers manners spake unto the fathers in time past by the prophets hath in these last days spoken unto us by a Son."[1] It is therefore natural to seek in the Old Testament the roots of the Christian conception of God. When we do so we cannot help being specially struck by the third chapter of

[1] Heb. i, 1.

Exodus, for there we are told how God revealed himself to
Moses and declared his name. St. Thomas is only following in
the steps of a long line of Christian writers when he bases his
exposition of the nature of God on this pentateuchal text.
*Dixit Deus ad Moysen: Ego sum Qui Sum. Ait: Sic dices filiis
Israel: Qui est misit me ad vos.*[1] So, the Angelic Doctor tells us,
"He who is" is the most proper name of God.[2] It is important
not to be misled by the use which he makes, in expounding
this text, of the famous phrase in which St. John of Damascus
describes God as "an infinite and unlimited sea of being," for,
however much vestigial Platonic essentialism there may have
been in the thought of the great Greek father, St. Thomas
interprets him in the most existential manner possible;[3] moreover he says explicitly that the first reason why "He who is"
is the most proper name of God is that it signifies "existing
itself" (*ipsum esse*). For St. Thomas, then, the primary element
in the meaning of the word "God" is that of complete and
absolute self-existence, and he claims that this truth has been
revealed by God himself. No doubt, when he goes on to
inquire what the grounds are for believing such a being to
exist, he lays aside all appeal to revelation and formulates
(in the famous Five Ways[4]) an argument of a purely rational
type. Nevertheless, the notion of God which underlies his
inquiry is that which the Mosaic revelation supplies, and
before he expounds this purely rational argument he explicitly
quotes the text from Exodus as a rejoinder to the supposed
objectors who deny that God exists.[5]

Before we can take this notion of God as established we
have, however, to listen to the protests of the Biblical scholars.
It may be true, they say, that St. Thomas bases his notion of

---

[1] Ex. iii, 14. Cf. the LXX: Εἶπεν ὁ Θεὸς πρὸς Μωῦσην λέγων, Ἐγώ εἰμι ὁ Ὤν.
Καὶ εἶπεν, Οὕτως ἐρεῖς τοῖς υἱοῖς Ἰσραήλ, Ὁ Ὤν ἀπέσταλκέ με πρὸς ὑμᾶς.

[2] S. Theol. I, xiii, 11. Cf. I, ii, 3 *sed contra*.

[3] St. Thomas's version of the Damascene is: *Principalius omnibus quae de Deo
dicuntur nominibus est Qui est: totum enim in seipso comprehendens, habet IPSUM ESSE
velut quoddam pelagus substantiae infinitum et indeterminatum* (S. Theol., I, xiii, 11c).
The original is: τὸ εἶναι οἷον τι πέλαγος οὐσίας ἄπειρον καὶ ἀόριστον. (*De Fide Orth.*,
I, ix). Cf. Cajetan's comment on the masculine form of the name: *Neutrum autem
genus, cum informe sit, magis ex parte materiae se tenet; masculinum autem, cum formatum
sit, actualitatem insinuat. Unde, dicendo Qui est, actualitas magis insinuatur existentis, quam
dicendo Quod est* (*In I^m P* ad loc.).

[4] S. Theol., I, ii, 3.   [5] Ibid., *sed contra*.

God upon the Old Testament, or at any rate upon a text
extracted from it, but has he really understood what this text
means? It may be possible to interpret the Latin phrase
Qui est in this existential way, but behind the Latin version
there lies the Septuagint, and the Septuagint phrase is ‘Ο °Ὤν,
which has an unpleasantly essentialist ring. Does not Plato
himself talk about τὸ παντελῶς ὄν? And, whether you interpret
"He who is" existentially or essentially, is there any reason
for supposing that the name of God in the Hebrew means
"He who is" in either sense? It is true we are not altogether
agreed what it does mean, but what God actually said to
Moses (if indeed he actually said anything to Moses at all)
probably meant something like "I will be that I will be"; it
may be that, so far from revealing his name to Moses, he was
refusing to do so.[1] Furthermore, whatever may be the truth
about the text in Exodus, is it not highly precarious to rest our
understanding of the Old Testament conception of God upon
one isolated text, even if we could be sure that our interpretation of that text was accurate? After all, it is notorious that the
Jews were not philosophers, and the doctrine of God that we
find in the Hebrew scriptures is one that is supremely unconcerned with metaphysics and highly interested in ethics. The
God of whom the Bible speaks is not a philosophical first cause
or absolute; he is the living God, who makes himself known to
men in his acts of judgment and salvation. The first verse of
the Bible discloses God in action: "In the beginning God
created the heaven and the earth"; and the climax of this
creative work comes in the making of man. Then we are told
how, when man has rebelled against God and has been
punished by expulsion from Paradise, God sets to work to make
for himself a people in whom and through whom his saving
mercy can be manifested. He chooses one of the nations of the
earth and makes a covenant with them; he repeatedly punishes
them when they sin and forgives them when they repent; he
gives them the promise of a greater redemption and a more

[1] "In Heb. writing of the historical period the name is connected with Heb.
hayah, 'to be,' in the imperf. Now with regard to this verb, *first*, it does not mean
'to be' essentially or ontologically, but phenomenally; and *secondly*, the impf.
has not the sense of a present ('am') but of a fut. ('will be')." (A. B. Davidson
in *H.D.B.*, II, p. 199, s.v. "God (in O.T.)".)

perfect covenant, and he fulfils this promise in an almost
incredible way by sending his Son to be born as one of them.
Finally, when they themselves have put the Son to death, God
raises him from the dead and through his resurrection extends
the covenant and the redemption to all the nations of the
earth, so that membership of Israel, the people of God, is now
thrown open to all men in all places and at all ages. What
could be less like philosophy than this? To those who believed
that God had chosen them to be the recipients of this redemptive act the Christ crucified might indeed be the power and
the wisdom of God, but he was a scandal to the Jew and
foolishness to the Greek. Is not the attempt to approximate
the Gospel of salvation to the philosophizings of men doomed
to failure from the start? Is it possible to reconcile the attitude
of the penitent sinner, humbly receiving mercy from the hand
of God, with that of the detached and judicious philosopher
seeking to understand the world that lies spread out before his
gaze? The Church has never been lacking in Tertullians to
demand what Athens has to do with Jerusalem, the Academy
with the Church, heretics with Christians, and to insist that we
have no need of curious questioning now that we have Christ
Jesus or of inquiry now that we have the Gospel.[1] Nevertheless
the Church has always had its Origens as well as its Tertullians,
and the Scriptures themselves bear evidence of the use of
philosophical categories in order to make plain to men what
the Gospel is. We may indeed admit that the Gospel is too
novel and too divine to be forced into the moulds of humanly
devised systems, but does this necessarily mean that the human
systems cannot themselves be transformed if they are caught
up into the Gospel revelation? The real question is not whether
the Hebrew text of Exodus iii, 14 means what St. Thomas and
many Christian writers before him thought it meant, but
whether what they took it to mean is what is meant by the
Bible as a whole. It is, I think, putting the whole question on
too narrow a basis simply to assert with Gilson that if there is
no metaphysic *in* Exodus there is nevertheless a metaphysic
of Exodus,[2] but it is, I believe, profoundly true to say that

[1] *De Praescr. Haer.*, xiv, 7, 8.
[2] See, e.g., *The Spirit of Mediaeval Philosophy*, ch. iii and iv, with notes.

there is a metaphysic of the Old Testament and that it is substantially expressed by the Exodus text as St. Thomas interprets it. For although the Old Testament is written almost entirely in ethical and hardly at all in metaphysical terms, the declarations which it makes about the activity of God have very far-reaching metaphysical consequences, and however imperfect may have been the attempts of pre-Thomist writers to express in the Exodus text as they understood it the Biblical truth about God, I believe that St. Thomas did succeed in this task through his radically existentialist outlook. If this is so, it will not be the first time that a Christian has succeeded, by a somewhat strained interpretation of a Biblical text, in expressing, not the original meaning of that text considered in isolation, but the meaning of a whole coherent body of Old Testament teaching; St. Matthew is perhaps the most striking instance of this. And when all is said and done, this is a far more important task. The Old Testament taken as a whole bears witness to a twofold truth about God. In the first place, God is altogether transcendent and self-sufficient, he reigns in unspeakable majesty and splendour; in the second place, he has called a world into existence by a sheer act of omnipotent will, and everything that happens in and to the world is a manifestation of his power and love. For the ancient Hebrew, a distinguished Old Testament scholar has said, "God and the world were always distinct. God was not involved in the processes of nature. These processes were caused by God, but he was distinct from them. The Hebrew, however, came down from his thought of God upon the world, he did not rise from the world up to his thought of God. His thought of God explained to him the world, both its existence and the course of events upon it; these did not suggest to him either the existence or the nature of God, these being unknown to him. His contemplation of nature and providence and the life of man was never of the nature of a search after God whom he did not know, but always of the nature of a recognition of God whom he knew." To quote the same writer again, "The Old Testament as little thinks of arguing or proving that God may be known as it thinks of arguing that he exists. . . . The peculiarity, however, of the Old Testament comes out when

the question is raised, *How* is God known? And here the
characteristic conception of the Old Testament is that of
Revelation—if men know God, it is because he has made
himself known to them. . . . God speaks, he appears, man
listens and beholds. God brings himself near to men. He
enters into a covenant with them, he lays commands on them:
they receive him when he approaches, accept his will and obey
his behests. Moses and the prophets are nowhere represented
as thoughtful minds, reflecting on the unseen and ascending
to elevated conceptions of Godhead: the Unseen manifests
itself to them, and they know it. God reveals himself to the
Patriarchs in angelic forms, to Moses in the bush and on the
mount, to the prophets in the spiritual intuitions of their own
minds. The form of manifestation may change, but the reality
remains the same."[1]

IV

The Bible is thus far from being a work on natural theology;
it is a proclamation of the self-revelation of the self-existent
and transcendent God, a self-revelation which reaches its
climax in the Incarnation of his co-eternal Son. The ancient
world had no lack of natural theology: to indulge in that type
of speculation was the peculiar genius of the Greek philosophers,
and that this was so was, we may well believe, included in the
providence of God. But they never wholly managed to overcome the tension between transcendence and creation. Their
philosophy always tended to fall into two irreconcilable parts.
Sometimes they had a transcendent being whose activity was
confined to the contemplation of himself, sometimes they had
a divine artificer who was limited by the recalcitrance of the
material upon which he had to work; in neither case was the
world in its totality the product of his creative act. To combine transcendence and creation in one coherent system was
the work of the great tradition of Christian philosophy. It was
a work which could only be performed over a period of centuries and it was one of extreme complexity and difficulty; we
need not be surprised that the early attempts to achieve it

[1] A. B. Davidson, in *H.D.B.*, II, pp. 196–7, s.v. "God (in O.T.)."

met with only partial success. It involved nothing less than taking the categories of thought and language of the Greek philosophers and turning them inside out in the light of the Biblical revelation. Among other things, this involved an entirely new attitude to the fundamental problem of natural theology. To the Greek, the fundamental problem was how the world of his experience was to be made intelligible; to the Christian, as a philosopher, the fundamental problem was what were the rational grounds for believing that God exists. The Christian was able to ask this last question because he knew, as the Greek did not, what he meant by the word "God," however much there might be about God that he did not know. And he knew it because God had revealed it. It may perhaps, humanly considered, be a misfortune that he tended in his formulation of the revealed fact to lay disproportionate emphasis upon one particular text from the Book Exodus, a text, moreover, which it was only too easy to interpret with a Greek rather than a Biblical emphasis. On the other hand, this very fact is providential, since it provided a point of contact with Greek thought, without which the necessary transformation of Greek thought could hardly have been made. In the end the transformation came about, and the central importance which St. Thomas Aquinas holds in Christian philosophy is due primarily to his clear grasp of the fact that the name of God, "He who is," must be understood in a fully existential sense. He was indeed convinced that the existence of God rendered the world intelligible, but to say so was for him what the modern philosopher would call a synthetic and not an analytic proposition. "God" was not merely a name for the intelligible principle of the world, it was the name of the Being who, according to the Christian Church, had revealed himself to the Patriarchs and Prophets and had become incarnate in Jesus Christ. For St. Thomas, therefore, *Utrum Deus sit* is a precise and definite question; it cannot be evaded by replying "It all depends on what you mean by God." St. Thomas knows what he means by God. God is *ipsum esse subsistens*,[1] and his most proper name is "He who is." Behind these phrases there lies the whole process of

---

[1] *S. Theol.*, I, iv, 2c.

revelation in the Old Testament, with its fulfilment in the New, and the long ages of thought and life which make up the history of the Christian Church. We are thus presented with a truth of fundamental importance which may seem at first sight to be a paradox. Just because the Christian philosopher has a notion of God which comes to him from a source other than the human reason, he can discuss the question of the existence of God as a purely rational problem, with a directness and cogency that are denied to the non-Christian, whose definition of God always remains more or less in suspense. In the last resort the non-Christian can decide to give the name "God" to whatever he discovers the ultimate principle of the universe to be, and whether he decides to confer it or not will be determined more by his general attitude to life than by any rational process. If he is a man of a reverent and pious cast of mind he will ascribe the name of God to something, be it *Deus sive natura*, the *élan vital*, what the world is going to be to-morrow, or "the great companion, the fellow-sufferer who understands"; if, on the other hand, the religious attitude is uncongenial to him, he will cheerfully profess himself an atheist. In either case, whether God exists or not becomes mainly a matter of convention about the use of words.[1] "Some call it evolution, and others call it God." No such way is open to the Christian. He may indeed hope that his subsequent investigation will give him a fuller understanding of the philosophical implications of his notion of God than he possessed to begin with. But the broad fact is plain. He knows what he means by God because the Bible and the Church have told him. He can then institute a purely rational inquiry into the grounds for asserting that God exists.

[1] It is, of course, always possible that a philosopher who is personally a non-Christian may have absorbed so much from the Christian tradition as to refuse to use the word "God" except in the Christian sense; however exceptional in principle, such an instance may in fact be fairly common in a post-Christian society. Furthermore, in view of the roots of Christianity in Judaism and the fact that Islam largely derives from elements in Judaism and Christianity, an exception should perhaps be made for Jewish and Mohammedan philosophers, both of whom believe in a revelation of himself given by God to man. But with such qualifications as these, the statement in the text may be allowed to stand.

C

CHAPTER TWO

THE ESSENTIALIST APPROACH TO THEISM

"If metaphysical speculation is a shooting at the moon, philosophers have always begun by shooting at it; only after missing it have they said that there was no moon, and that it was a waste of time to shoot at it."

E. GILSON, *The Unity of Philosophical Experience*, p. 315.

"The ontological argument for the existence of God has in recent years, largely under Teutonic influence, been relegated to a position of comparative inferiority in the armoury of Christian apologetics."

OPENING PASSAGE (ALLEGED) OF A SERMON TO THE BEDMAKERS
OF THE UNIVERSITY OF CAMBRIDGE

I

I HAVE argued in the last chapter that St. Thomas's affirmation that the most proper name of God is "He who is," and his description of God as *ipsum esse subsistens*, express, when they are taken in the profoundly existential sense which St. Thomas gives them, the fundamental metaphysical truth about God to which the Bible bears witness. To say this is not, of course, to assert that the Bible tells us nothing about God except this truth and such further truths as may be logically deducible therefrom; quite the contrary. Nor is it to imply that whatever further truths about God the Bible tells us are comparatively unimportant. All that is asserted is that, however unmetaphysical its attitude to God and to God's activity in the world may be, the Bible does in fact rest upon a profound metaphysical assumption, namely that of the absolute transcendence and independence of God. It declares this truth in ethical terms, in interpreting to men God's acts and his demands; it is one of the functions of Christian philosophy to penetrate to the metaphysical foundations of the

18

Biblical ethic. And this task was, it would seem, first adequately performed in the great synthesis of Aristotelian and Platonist thought, and their transformation in the light of the Christian revelation, that were brought about in the thirteenth century by the Angelic Doctor.[1]

I would here again emphasize that this identification of the Thomist with the Biblical metaphysic altogether depends upon the Thomist formulae being understood in their full existential meaning. The importance of this can be seen by considering such a typical Thomist statement as that which tells us that in God essence and existence (*essentia* and *esse*) are identical.[2] Understood from the essentialist standpoint, this statement simply affirms that existence is analytically contained in the notion of God's essence, and leads us straight to the ontological argument as that is presented in Descartes' Fifth Meditation. From the existentialist standpoint, on the other hand, it tells us that the fact that God exists in the way in which he does (namely self-existently) is the fact from which every truth about the nature of God can be derived. And this is a very much more full-blooded doctrine. It presents us not just with the super-essential Essence of the pseudo-Areopagite, the Examplar of all other essences, but with the self-existent Being who is the creator of all other beings. We shall return to this point later on. Our present concern is to inquire what rational grounds can be alleged for the existence of a being fulfilling the description that St. Thomas adopts.

It is, in this connection, instructive to notice that the question of proving the existence of God, in the strict sense of the word "prove," hardly seems to have occurred to the pre-scholastic writers. Partly this may be due to the essentialism which dominated their philosophy, however authentically Christian their religion may have been. For essences are expressed in concepts, they are not affirmed, as is existence, in a judgment;[3] and while judgments, which receive formulation in propositions, are fit matter for argumentation, concepts lend

---

[1] "The Thomist philosophy is no mere Aristotelianism revised but a masterly synthesis of both Plato and Aristotle with one another and with Augustine, effected by original insight of the first order" (A. E. Taylor on "St. Thomas as a Philosopher" in *Philosophical Studies*, p. 247).

[2] *S. Theol.*, I, iii, 4.   [3] See p. 50 *infra*.

themselves rather to contemplation. The process by which
St. Augustine, starting from the consideration of creatures and
proceeding by the introspection of his own soul and its faculties,
"arrived in the flash of one trembling glance at That Which
Is"[1] is much more like contemplation issuing in ecstasy than
like rational argument. This can, however, hardly be the full
explanation, for even concepts lend themselves to argumentation of the deductive sort; the vast structure of Greek geometry and the geometrized metaphysics of Descartes and
Spinoza are clear enough examples of this. I would suggest
that a further reason may be found in the fact that it might
well seem faintly ridiculous to take our definition of God from
revelation and then enter upon a purely rational investigation
to discover whether God exists. "We know what we mean by
'God' because God himself has told us; now let us try to find
out whether in fact there is a God." However, the attempt to
prove that God exists is not as absurd as might at first sight
appear. It does not in fact involve us in asserting that belief
in God can only be the result of rational argumentation; St.
Thomas himself makes some very sympathetic remarks about
people who have not the time or the ability or the inclination
to embark upon metaphysics.[2] In spite of this it is both legitimate and useful to investigate whether a conviction which a
Christian holds because he believes that God has spoken can
be established or confirmed by a purely rational inquiry. And
if we put ourselves in the position of an interested non-
Christian we can imagine him saying: "Here is a notion of
God which, if I were convinced that there actually existed a
being that corresponded to it, would revolutionize my outlook
upon the universe. Christians themselves say that they have
acquired this notion because God has revealed himself to them.
I do not know whether they are right in saying this; for all I
know they are the victims of deception. But I can see that it
is very important to know whether such a being does exist,
and I propose, by the use of my reason, to try and find out.
I may succeed in proving that he exists; I may succeed in
proving that he doesn't. I may succeed in proving that the

---

[1] *Conf.*, VII, xvii, 23: *pervenit ad id quod est in ictu trepidantis aspectus.*
[2] *S.c.G.*, I, iv; quoted in *He Who Is*, p. 27, *n.* 2. Cf. *S. Theol.*, II II, ii, 4c.

question is one which the human reason is by its nature
incapable of answering. Or I may simply discover that I am
not clever enough to carry through the investigation. But
anyhow let me try."

It was presumably with such an inquirer in mind that St.
Anselm worked out the famous argument which has come to
be known as the ontological argument for the existence of
God. We must not be misled as to its purely rational nature
by the fact that the work in which it occurs, the *Proslogion*,
bears the sub-title "An Address to God concerning his Existence" and has the form of a prayerful meditation, written in
the first person and spoken to God himself. St. Anselm does
indeed say right at the beginning, "I do not seek to understand
that I may believe, but I believe that I may understand. For
this too I believe, that unless I first believe I shall not understand."[1] But when he comes to ask why it is that the "fool"
in the Psalm "saith in his heart, There is no God,"[2] his answer
is not that the fool has not had the advantage of being brought
up as a Christian or that he is a frivolous or irreligious man,
but that he simply has not understood what the word "God"
means. "He who well understandeth what this is, certainly
understandeth it to be such as cannot even be thought not to
exist."[3] It may very well be the case that nobody but a
Christian would think of defining God as St. Anselm does,
it may be that nobody but a Christian would have thought
of the argument even if the definition of God had been given
him by someone else; it is undoubtedly true that St. Anselm's
own belief in God does not rest on the ontological argument.
But when all this has been said the fact remains that the argument itself professes to be as purely a matter of the human
reason as does Euclid's proof of the theorem of Pythagoras.
For St. Anselm's case is simply that if you define God as he
defines him and then deny that God exists you are led into a
contradiction. The argument is a typical case of the *reductio
ad absurdum*.

Let us remind ourselves how St. Anselm develops his argu-

---

[1] *Proslogion*, i (Migne, P.L., clviii, 223 f.).
[2] *Dixit insipiens in corde suo, Non est Deus*. Ps. lii, 1, Vulg. (E.V., liii, 1).
[3] *Proslogion*, iv.

ment. In the first place, he does not define God precisely as
St. Thomas will later on define him, though St. Thomas himself will admit that St. Anselm does give a valid definition of
God.[1] "We believe," Anselm writes, addressing the Deity,
"that thou art something than which no greater can be
thought," *aliquid quo majus nihil cogitari potest.*[2] Now even the
fool in the psalm when he hears these words understands what
he hears and so has God in his understanding, even if he does
not understand that God really exists. Let the fool then
reflect on what he has heard and he will soon see that God
exists, not only in his understanding but in reality. For what
is the consequence of denying the actual existence of God so
defined? Simply that we can think of a being greater than
God, for we can think of a being possessing all the attributes
of this non-actual God *plus* the additional attribute of actual
existence. Thus the supposition that God has no actual existence
has led us into the absurd situation of claiming that we have
thought of a being greater than any being of which we can
think. And so, by the method of *reductio ad absurdum*, God's
actual existence has been demonstrated.

I have given elsewhere a fairly full discussion of St. Anselm's
argument[3] and I shall not repeat that discussion here. To
summarize it briefly it will be sufficient to remark that the
objections which (as I believe, validly) can be brought against
it fall under three heads.

In the first place, it has not been shown that the definition
which St. Anselm gives of God is itself consistent, and the fact
that several similar definitions have been shown to be self-
contradictory[4] might reasonably lead us to suspect that this
definition may be self-contradictory too. Of course, if we have
independent reasons for knowing that God as so defined
actually exists this will prove that the definition is self-consistent, but St. Anselm needs to know that it is self-consistent
before he can prove that God does actually exist. Unless this
objection can be refuted the whole argument is circular.

Then, secondly, the argument in any case only proves that

---

[1] *S. Theol.*, I, ii, 1 *ad* 2.   [2] *Proslogion*, ii.   [3] *He Who Is*, ch. iv.
[4] Such as the definition of "infinity" as a number than which no greater number
can be conceived.

God, defined as St. Anselm defines him, cannot be thought of except as actually existing, and this is a very different thing from proving that he actually exists. In the later scholastic phrase, it only attributes to God existence *ut signata*, not existence *ut exercita*. And, thirdly, the argument depends upon the assumption that actual existence is a quality that, like other qualities, can be included in the concept of the essence of a being, so that a being which possesses it and a being which does not can be compared in respect of their "greatness."[1]

It is, I think, worth while remarking that these are three distinct objections and not merely the same objection expressed in three different ways. This can be seen by reflecting upon the fact that it would be perfectly possible for anyone who rejected any one of the objections to admit the validity of the others. Thus a man might be convinced that the definition of God proposed by St. Anselm was quite self-consistent and yet deny that actual existence was a quality. Or he might hold that if it was impossible to conceive of God except as existing, God would thereby be proved to exist, and at the same time deny that it was possible to conceive of God as existing at all, on the strength of some private knowledge that St. Anselm's definition of God was self-contradictory. Or, as a third possibility, he might have no difficulty in admitting that existence was a quality and yet see reason to suppose that it was incompatible with the other qualities that the definition entails in God, or that those qualities were incompatible with one another, in the same kind of way as a plane figure cannot be at once square and triangular. And other combinations of affirmation and rejection of the three objections are also conceivable. But in spite of this the objections have this in common, that in one way or another each of them repudiates the fundamentally essentialist character of St. Anselm's argument,

---

[1] This point can be illustrated by a rather trivial example. There is obviously a sense in which we can validly say that a ton of actual coal is "greater" than half a ton of actual coal; and there is obviously a sense in which we can validly say that a ton of merely conceptual coal is "greater" than half a ton of merely conceptual coal. But if we compare a ton of conceptual coal with half a ton of actual coal, which are we to say is the greater? The conceptual coal because there is twice as much of it, or the actual coal because it is actual? If we were interested in heating or cooking, we should, I think, say the latter. As Macaulay observes, an acre in Middlesex is better than a principality in Utopia.

that is to say his attempt to derive an affirmation that God exists from the definition or the concept of his essence. The first one protests that it has not been shown that the essence is one whose actual existence is possible, since it might involve qualities whose actual existences were incompatible; the third one denies that the actual existence of a being can be included within the concept of the essence; the second one simply asserts that the kind of existence, if any, that *can* be included in the concept of the essence is not the kind of existence by which a being actually exists.

It may be added that St. Thomas seems fairly clearly to hold all three objections, though he does not put them in precisely this form. When he says that, even if God's existence is self-evident in itself, it may very well not be self-evident to us, and that we cannot know that it is self-evident until we have proved that God is his own existence, he is voicing what is, to all intents and purposes,[1] the first objection listed above.[2] When he says that, even if all men understand by the word "God" what St. Anselm understands by it, it does not follow that they understand God to exist *in rerum natura* and not merely *in apprehensione intellectus*, he is stating the second objection almost in the same words.[3] And finally, although he does not draw the distinction between existential and attributive propositions in precisely the way in which a modern logician would draw it, we have only to read such a discussion as that in his luminous little work *De Ente et Essentia* to see that he is well aware that existence is fundamentally different from essence.[4]

---

[1] I say "to all intents and purposes," because whereas our objection was that God's existence could not be seen by us to be possible, St. Thomas's is that it cannot be seen by us to be self-evident. It is just conceivable that someone might affirm that even if God's existence was possible, he might for all that not in fact exist; St. Thomas would no doubt rejoin, on the basis of his cosmological argument, that if God did not exist, no existence could be even possible, not even God's. In any case, St. Thomas's objection and ours rest upon the same fundamental assertion that we cannot make a detailed examination of the essence of God.

[2] *S. Theol.*, I, ii, 1c; *S.c.G.* I, xi.   [3] *S. Theol.*, I, ii, 1 *ad* 2; *S.c.G.*, I, xi.

[4] *Patet quod esse est aliud ab essentia vel quidditate, nisi forte sit aliqua res cujus quidditas sit suum esse* (op. cit., cap. iv, E.T., p. 34).

II

The ontological argument is thus, by its very nature, radically defective. Nevertheless its appearance is extremely significant, for it witnesses to the strength of St. Anselm's grasp of the transcendence of the Christian God. If God is altogether independent of all other beings, then there ought to be a proof of his existence which refers to no other being than God. We cannot start from his existence, for that is precisely what we want to prove. But can we not start from his essence and show that his existence follows from it? Such would seem to be the underlying motive of St. Anselm's approach, and, as Gilson has remarked, it is one that could occur only in a Christian setting.[1] So long as God was not identified with being itself, no one could hope to discover whether God exists by simply examining the concept of God, any more than we could hope to discover whether Atlantis exists simply by examining the concept of Atlantis.[2] The main trouble is, however, that the kind of knowledge of God's essence which one would require in order to make the argument valid is one which God's very transcendence would seem to deny us. It could be possessed only by God himself and by those who enjoy the beatific vision; they see that God exists as clearly as we see that a whole is greater than its part, but we cannot see God's essence, we know God only in his effects.[3] How this works itself out can be seen in Descartes' Fifth Meditation, in which the ontological argument takes an even simpler and more direct form than in the *Proslogion*. Descartes defines God as a being supremely perfect, and claims that he has a clear and distinct idea of this

[1] *The Spirit of Mediaeval Philosophy*, p. 59; quoted in *He Who Is*, p. 35.

[2] One of Gaunilo's objections to Anselm's argument—an objection which Anselm never satisfactorily answered—was that, if the argument was valid, it would be possible on the same lines to prove the existence of an island so perfect that no more perfect can be conceived (*Liber pro Insipiente*, Migne, P.L., clviii, 242 f.). An interesting variant which has been pointed out to me is that we could similarly prove the existence of a being so bad that no worse could be conceived. For, if such a being did not exist, we could conceive a similar one which did exist, and this would obviously be worse.

[3] *Sicut nobis per se notum est quod totum sua parte sit majus, sic videntibus ipsam divinam essentiam per se notissimum est Deum esse, ex hoc quod sua essentia est suum esse. Sed quia ejus essentiam videre non possumus, ad ejus esse cognoscendum non per se ipsum sed per ejus effectus pervenimus (S.c.G., I, xi).*

being in his own consciousness. And since it is perfectly plain on examining this idea that unless it was the idea of an existing being it would not be the idea of a supremely perfect one, it inevitably follows that God exists. The consequence is that the Cartesian tradition tends to drift apart into two extremes of agnosticism and anthropomorphism, as Maritain has pointed out.[1] Descartes intends his God to be an infinite God and defines him in accordance with this intention; but since an infinite God surpasses our comprehension this line of development leads to agnosticism. On the other hand, in order to prove God's existence Descartes has to have a clear and distinct idea of him, and a being of whom a man can have a clear and distinct idea cannot very much exceed the man's own stature.[2] St. Anselm, whatever his failings, at least never claimed to have a clear and distinct idea of God and to discern existence as included in it; all that he tried to show was that to deny the existence of God leads to a logical contradiction. St. Anselm takes his definition of God, as he believes, from revelation, and reasons on the basis of his definition; Descartes discovers an idea of God by looking into his own mind and tells us what he sees there. The difference between St. Anselm and Descartes is clear enough, but the difficulty to which I have referred is inherent in the ontological argument in all its forms. "O Lord," writes Anselm, "not only are thou that than which no greater can be thought but thou art something greater than can be thought. For because there may be thought to be something of this kind, if thou are not that something, there may be thought something greater than thee; which is impossible."[3] No doubt Anselm does not intend to say that God cannot be thought about, since all through his work he is in fact thinking about God. What he presumably means is simply that God cannot be conceived or defined. But even so his ontological argument breaks down, since its very starting-

[1] "The Cartesian Proofs of God," in *The Dream of Descartes*, pp. 124 f. (On p. 127, in line 34, "finite" is a misprint for "infinite," as the French original shows.)

[2] Descartes himself denied this: "Pour moi, toutes les fois que j'ai dit que Dieu pouvait être connu clairement et distinctement, je n'ai jamais entendu parler que de cette connaissance finie, et accommodée à la petite capacité de nos esprits" (*I^{res} Réponses*). But to admit this destroys all the evidential force of the argument.

[3] *Proslogion*, xv.

point is a definition of God. Anselm bears towards agnosticism as Descartes bears towards anthropomorphism; and this difference in tendency tells us a lot about the difference between Anselm and Descartes. It does however nothing to meet the fundamental criticism, which is that any ontological argument demands, as the condition of its construction, that we shall have a knowledge of God's nature which the very notion of God denies to us. Does this, then, mean that any attempt to prove that God exists is doomed to failure, as being an attempt to discover the undiscoverable and to know the unknowable? St. Thomas at least did not think so, as we shall see later on. At the moment I shall devote some further attention to the ontological argument.

It is well to notice that St. Anselm's definition of God is by no means independent of all reference to the finite world. When Anselm defines God as something than which nothing greater can be thought, it is necessary, in order to understand the meaning of the definition, to know what is meant by "great." Presumably it includes such characteristics as "powerful," "wise," "good" and so on, which as known by us are qualities which we observe in finite beings, and excludes such other characteristics as "heavy," "voluminous" and the like, which are equally observable in finite beings and are included in certain uses of the word "great." In other words, however clear it may be that St. Anselm believes God to be altogether independent of his creatures, it is equally clear that the form of words which he believes to define God in his most ultimate reality is derived from certain qualities of the created realm. It will, of course, be replied by St. Anselm's partisans that even if this is so, it does not mean that God has no other attributes than those which we discern in the finite realm, but simply that the attribute of "greatness," which formally and eminently applies to God alone, is known by us only in the diversified and finite modes in which creatures are able to participate in it. We must, in fact, distinguish between the *perfectio significata* and the *modus significandi*; even the Thomists, who reject the ontological argument, do this, and they have indeed constructed a portentous theory of analogical predication in order to validate it. This does not alter the fact that Anselm's proof of God's existence does not depend upon the assertion of the existence of finite beings, even if the definition of God which he uses is derived from his experience of them. After all, some reference to the finite world is necessary by the nature of the case, since the mind in which the argument is being thought out is a finite mind; one thing at least St. Anselm was quite clear about, namely that he himself was only a creature. This rejoinder is a good one, as far as it goes, but our point has been worth making, if only to make it plain what are, and what are not, the respects in which the ontological argument claims to be independent of reference to the finite world. The distinguishing feature of the ontological argument, in contrast to arguments which claim to deduce God's existence from the existence of finite beings, is that, in effect, it claims to tell us not merely *that* God exists, but *how* and *why*. However limited our insight into the nature of God may be, it at least, so the argument assures us, extends to this, that we can see that God's nature is one whose existence is logically possible and indeed that it is logically necessary. St. Thomas, on the other hand, will tell us that we have no such insight into the nature of God; according to him we can see that a necessary being exists only because we have experience of certain beings which could not exist unless a necessary being existed too. This contention is the fundamental feature of what has been aptly called "the Thomist agnosticism."

I have taken St. Anselm and Descartes as typical examples of thinkers who have maintained the validity of the ontological argument; but it is important to emphasize that, in spite of this agreement, the argument has an altogether different significance for the eleventh-century scholastic from that which it has for the sixteenth-century mathematician. For Anselm the existence of God is the primary truth in philosophy and theology; for Descartes, however fully he may, as a devout Roman Catholic, have recognized the absolute primacy of the doctrine of God in the sphere of religion, the function of God in the philosophical sphere was simply to guarantee the real existence of the world presented to us by our senses. In the First Meditation he has deliberately adopted the method of universal doubt as being the sole avenue to certain knowledge;

in the Second Meditation he has found, by his famous *Cogito ergo sum*, that one belief at least survives the most radical doubting, namely Descartes' belief that he himself exists at the moment in which he doubts. Then he inquires whether his impression of an external world is proof against his method, and in view of the possibility that that impression might be the work of a mischievous imp, a *malin génie*, he concludes that it can in fact only be relied upon if the existence of God can be proved, since it is unthinkable that God, supposing him to exist, could allow Descartes to be the victim of such a universal delusion. Thus Descartes, as a philosopher, needs God simply in order to guarantee the existence of an external world, and it is for this reason that he is forced to revive the ontological argument. He cannot, like St. Thomas, argue from the existence of the world to the existence of God, for until he has proved the existence of God he cannot be certain that the world exists. But there is a further point involved, of a rather more subtle type, which arises out of Descartes' representative doctrine of perception, that is to say the doctrine that what we directly perceive is not things outside ourselves but ideas within our minds which purport to represent things outside ourselves. The consequence of this doctrine is that, whereas for St. Anselm the ontological argument consists in proving that the essence denoted by the word "God" is such as entails with necessity its own existence, for Descartes it consists in proving that the idea of God which we find in our minds is such as entails with certainty the existence of its objective counterpart. "It is certain," he writes in the Fifth Meditation, "that I no less find the idea of a God in my consciousness, that is, the idea of a being supremely perfect, than that of any figure or number whatever: and I know with not less clearness and distinctness that an actual and eternal existence pertains to his nature than that all which is demonstrable of any figure or number really belongs to the nature of that figure or number." It is thoroughly in accordance with this characteristic Cartesian primacy of thought over being that in the Meditations the ontological argument in this more or less pure form occupies only a secondary place. The first place is given, in the Third Meditation, to two closely related arguments which are based, not upon an examination or analysis of the idea of God itself, but upon a consideration of the facts that the idea of God occurs in Descartes' mind and that Descartes' mind exists as the sort of thing in which the idea of God can and does occur.[1] "By the name of God," he writes, "I understand a substance infinite, eternal, immutable, independent, all-knowing, all-powerful, and by which I myself, and every other thing that exists, if any such there be, were created. But these properties are so great and excellent that the more attentively I consider them the less I feel persuaded that the idea I have of them owes its origin to myself alone. And thus it is absolutely necessary to conclude, from all that I have before said, that God exists: for though the idea of substance be in my mind owing to this, that I myself am a substance, I should not, however, have the idea of an infinite substance, seeing I am a finite being, unless it were given me by some substance in reality infinite." Following the line thus initiated, Descartes refuses to admit that this idea of an infinite being is achieved simply by negating the idea of the finite, or that it arises from a kind of projection, in the sort of way in which some mathematicians have postulated infinity as a number lying "beyond" the endless sequence of finite numbers. On the contrary, he insists, the idea is absolutely clear and distinct, and manifests not a negation of the finite or a perfection that is merely potential, but something far fuller than the finite and altogether actual. It is true, he admits, that "there may be in God an infinity of things that I cannot comprehend, nor perhaps ever compass by thought in any way"—here we see him struggling against the anthropomorphism and univocity inherent in this line of thought— nevertheless the idea of God *is* clear and distinct and contains in itself more "objective reality" (that is to say, ascribes more reality to its *object*) than any other. And the only way to account for the occurrence of such an idea in a finite mind is to suppose that it was placed there by a being who is its exact counterpart, who, to use the technical phrase, possesses in himself *formally* all the reality that the idea of him possesses *objectively*.

Descartes reinforces this argument from the occurrence of the

---

[1] The three arguments are repeated, in a highly mathematical form, at the end of the Reply to the Second Objections (Everyman's ed., App., p. 229).

idea of God in his mind by a further argument which throws
a good deal of light upon his whole outlook. "I am here
desirous," he says, "to inquire further, whether I, who possess
this idea of God, could exist supposing there were no God."
Do I, perhaps, derive my existence from myself? "But if I
were independent of every other existence, and were myself
the author of my being . . . I should have bestowed upon myself
every perfection of which I possess the idea, and I should thus
be God." Do I, then, derive my existence from some being
other than myself? If that other being is God, then God exists,
quod erat demonstrandum. But if that other being is not God,
then it must, like myself, be a thinking being and must itself
possess the idea of God which it communicates to me. And
then the same question arises about its own existence as
originally arose about mine. If it were self-existent it would
be God. "But if it owe its existence to another cause than
itself, we demand again, for a similar reason, whether this
second cause exists of itself or through some other, until, from
stage to stage, we at length arrive at an ultimate cause, which
will be God. And it is quite manifest that in this matter there
can be no infinite regress of causes, seeing that the question
raised respects not so much the cause which once produced
me, as that by which I am at this present moment conserved."

The main interest of this last argument lies in the remarkable
way in which its structure resembles that of the first three of
St. Thomas's Five Ways, with their rejection of the possibility of an infinite regress and their final assertion that the
first cause to which they lead is not merely the initiator, at a
past moment of time, of a temporal process but the source of
a present existence.[1] And Descartes was, of course, familiar
with the Thomist discussion. The radical and highly illuminating difference between St. Thomas and Descartes lies in their
starting-points. Whereas the Angelic Doctor begins with some
characteristic of mobility, dependence or contingency inherent
in the existence of a finite existent as such, Descartes begins
with the occurrence in his own mind of one particular clear and

---

[1] Whether the Five Ways, as St. Thomas states them, prove that God is the
immediate source of the present existence of his creatures is another matter. See
ch. iv *infra.*

distinct idea. Beneath the apparent similarity there lies all the
difference that separates a metaphysic of existence from a
metaphysic of thought. For St. Thomas the existence of finite
beings is a primary datum of experience—*certum est et sensu
constat* . . .—and from any finite existent, no matter what, he
is prepared to argue to the existence of God. For Descartes
there is only one finite existent whose existence is immediately
evident—Descartes himself as a thinking substance having a
clear and distinct idea of God—and until he has argued from
his possession of this idea to God's existence he cannot assert
the existence of anything else. Even when his system is complete he cannot claim to have direct experience of any existent
being; all that he in fact experiences are representative ideas,
idées-tableaux, ideas which purport to be copies of realities and
each of which requires a guarantee of its authenticity. There
is the idea of Descartes himself as a momentary experient,
guaranteed by the *Cogito ergo sum*; there is the idea of God,
guaranteed by the arguments of the Third and Fifth Meditations; there are the ideas of things in an external world and
of Descartes himself as an enduring person with a past history,
guaranteed by the veracity of God. But all these ideas merely
represent their objects, in the sense of standing for them and
being replicas of them; they never *present* their objects, in the
sense of making them present to the mind. This is why it is
that, in spite of their empirical appearance, the psychological
arguments for the existence of an infinite being which occur
in the Third Meditation, no less than the ontological argument
for the existence of a perfect being which occurs in the Fifth
Meditation, are of a basically essentialist type. We must not,
of course, treat Descartes simply as a second Anselm or even
as a second Dionysius. Between the argument of the *Proslogion*
and that of the Fifth Meditation there lies all the difference
that separates the twelfth century from the sixteenth.[1] Never-

---

[1] We may note that Descartes (in his *I^res Réponses*, in reply to Caterus) refused
to admit that his ontological argument was the same as that refuted by St. Thomas.
St. Thomas, he says, was attacking, and rightly, the assertion that God's existence
can be deduced from God's name; his own argument, he insists, is based not
upon the name of God but upon the idea of God, and this is altogether different.
Gilson maintains (*Études sur le Rôle de la Pensée mediévale dans la Formation du Système
cartésien*, IIme P., ch. iv) that Descartes knew Anselm only through St. Thomas's
presentation of him and that in fact Anselm, no less than Descartes, was reasoning

theless, with all their differences, Anselm and Descartes agree in their essentialism. For Descartes our knowledge of God's existence arises neither from our experience of the world nor from God's self-revelation to Moses, but from an innate idea implanted in our minds by God at our creation. He does not start from the consideration of the finite world in order to end with God as the supreme object of philosophy; he introduces God in order to be assured of the existence of a finite world which can be investigated and manipulated by Cartesian mathematics. This is why, in spite of first appearances and in spite of Descartes' own religious practice, the Cartesian philosophy is fundamentally irreligious; it does something worse than deny God, it makes use of him.

That side of Descartes' thought which arises from his representationalist theory of ideas is worked out to its logical conclusion by his avowed disciple Malebranche. The essentialist element, on the other hand, receives its fullest expression in Leibniz and Spinoza and it is to these that I shall now turn.

III

So strongly is Leibniz convinced of the validity of the transition from essence to existence that he constructs what is, to all intents and purposes, an ontological argument to prove, not merely the existence of God, but also the existence of the best possible world, even while he is convinced that its existence can be communicated to it only by the deliberate volition of God. "Each possible world," he says, "[has] the right to claim existence in proportion to the perfection which it involves. And it is this which causes the existence of the best, which God knows through his wisdom, chooses through his goodness, and produces through his power."[1] Many subsequent writers have

---

from the idea of God and not from the mere name. Even if this is the case, it is, I think, clear that a radical difference of outlook between Anselm and Descartes remains, though it is not such as to nullify their common essentialism. My own judgment, for what it is worth, is that Anselm's ontological argument is as much a matter of purely logical ratiocination as an argument could be, but I should be far from asserting that Anselm's own attitude to God is that of a logician. In this respect the second chapter of the *Proslogion* seems to me to conflict rather harshly with the tenor of the work as a whole.

[1] *Monadology*, 54–5 (Everyman's, p. 12).

D

remarked that, in reasoning thus, Leibniz assumes that the notion of a best possible world is not self-contradictory; that is, that there is, in the realm of possible finite essences, one that exceeds all the rest in perfection.[1] St. Anselm would have said that nothing could be "best possible" except God. It is true that Leibniz is perfectly prepared to admit that there may be many worlds of which the human mind can form a notion, but which nevertheless are not possible, because the elements out of which they are compounded are incompatible; he does not assert that the best *thinkable* world exists, but only the best possible. None the less, in saying this he is assuming, first that some worlds *are* possible, and secondly that among these possible worlds one is more perfect than all the others. In support of the former of these assumptions he would no doubt say that, even if all *a priori* arguments in its favour broke down, experience tells us that one particular world exists in actuality and that, in consequence, at least one world is possible.[2] But the second assumption is more difficult to justify. It depends in fact upon two further assumptions, each of which is highly questionable: the first is that there is some common measure of perfection by means of which the various possible worlds can be arranged in increasing order of perfection; the second is that this sequence has a greatest member. It is upon this last assumption that the whole argument finally collapses. It is indeed remarkable that Leibniz did not realize this, for he was quite clear that a precisely similar defect might well vitiate Descartes' ontological argument for the existence of God. And this will bring us back to our main theme.

Leibniz criticizes the argument of Descartes' Fifth Meditation on the ground that, while it proves that if the absolutely perfect being is possible he exists, it does not prove that he is possible.[3] The notion of an absolutely perfect being, he says, might be as self-contradictory as that of a maximum velocity of

---

[1] Cf. *He Who Is*, p. 105. Comparing optimism of the Leibnitian type with the optimism of classical Christian theism, G. K. Chesterton has well written: "One optimism says that this is the best of all possible worlds. The other says that it is certainly not the best of all possible worlds, but it is the best of all possible things that a world should be possible" (*G. F. Watts*, p. 146).

[2] Cf. the Essay on *The Ultimate Origination of Things* (Everyman's, p. 34).

[3] *Nouveaux Essais*, IV, x, 7. Cf. *De la Démonstration cartésienne* (Dutens, II, i, p. 254).

motion.[1] Elsewhere, however, he suggests that the main
defect of Descartes' argument is that it has nowhere been
proved that the various perfections implied in the notion of a
perfect being are mutually compatible.[2] And this is a defect
which he thinks can be easily remedied. For, he argues, the
most perfect being means the being of whom no simple positive
predicate can be denied. Now, no two such predicates can be
mutually incompatible, for, if they were, the second would
have to deny what the first affirmed and so would not itself
be simple and positive.[3] Unfortunately, as A. E. Taylor has
pointed out,[4] this last assertion is by no means unquestionable.
For "red" and "green" are two simple positive predicates,
and yet the propositions "A is red" and "A is green" are
incompatible. The conclusion is that Leibniz's attempt to
rehabilitate the ontological argument is unsuccessful. It only
remains to be added that Leibniz recognizes other arguments
for the existence of God, and in particular that which is based
on the actual existence of the world.[5] For the ontological
argument in its purest form we have to come to Spinoza and
his *Ethica ordine geometrico demonstrata*.

IV

Spinoza, true to the ideal which he has set himself of constructing his metaphysics on the model of Euclid's Elements,
begins his treatise on God by laying down certain definitions.
The first of these is that of *causa sui*. "I understand that to be
cause of itself," he writes, "whose essence involves existence and
whose nature cannot be conceived unless existing." The very
term "cause of itself" provokes our notice. To a Thomist the
very form of words is contradictory if taken *au pied de la lettre*;
causes are *ex hypothesi* metaphysically antecedent to their
effect; we cannot say even that God is the cause of himself, we
can only say that he has no cause and does not require one.
Why Spinoza adopts the term is, however, shown by the

---

[1] *Meditationes de Cognitione, etc.* (Dutens, II, i, p. 14).
[2] *That the Most Perfect Being Exists.* Cf. B. Russell, *Philosophy of Leibnitz*, 2nd ed.,
pp. 174, 287.
[3] Ibid.   [4] *E.R.E.*, XII, p. 272, s.v. "Theism."
[5] See, e.g., the beginning of the Essay on *The Ultimate Origination of Things*
(Everyman's, p. 32).

meaning which he gives it in defining it; a *causa sui* is not strictly speaking a being that causes itself, but one whose essence causes its existence, in the sense of logically entailing it. But the latter part of the definition is more relevant for our consideration, for in the original Latin it conceals a fatal ambiguity, which enables Spinoza to make just that transition from the ideal to the actual order which is the root defect in all argument of the ontological type. *Per causam sui*, the definition runs, *intelligo id cujus essentia involvit existentiam; sive id, cujus natura non potest concipi nisi existens.* The obvious meaning of this would be that the nature of the *causa sui* cannot be conceived except as existing, but it is only too easy to take the form of words as asserting that it cannot be conceived unless it exists. Spinoza's other fundamental definitions are those of "substance" and "God." "I understand *substance* to be that which is in itself and is conceived through itself: I mean that, the conception of which does not depend on the conception of another thing from which it must be formed. . . . *God* I understand to be a being absolutely infinite, that is, a substance consisting of infinite attributes each of which expresses eternal and infinite essence."[1] The argument then takes the following course.

On the basis of eight definitions, of which the three above reproduced are the most important, and of seven axioms, Spinoza builds up a series of propositions, of which the sixth is that one substance cannot be produced by another, with the corollary that a substance cannot be produced by anything else. He then argues (Prop. VII) that existence appertains to the nature of substance and (Prop. VIII) that all substance is necessarily infinite. He then proceeds to prove (Prop. XI) that, since God is a substance and his essence involves existence, God necessarily exists. The climax of the discussion is reached in the assertions that no substance can be granted or conceived except God, and that whatever is is in God and nothing can be or be conceived without God. From this the pantheistic doctrine for which Spinoza is notorious follows. Having in

[1] *Per substantiam intelligo id, quod in se est, et per se concipitur: hoc est id, cujus conceptus non indiget conceptu alterius rei, a quo formari debeat . . . Per Deum intelligo ens absolute infinitum, hoc est, substantiam constantem infinitis attributis, quorum unumquodque aeternam et infinitam essentiam exprimit.*

effect defined substance as that which is self-sufficient, Spinoza is inevitably forced to conclude that anything which is substance is, in some way or another, God. But just as his definition of *causa sui* is ambiguous, so is his definition of substance. *Per substantiam intelligo id quod in se est et per se concipitur.* But what is meant by *id quod in se est*, that which exists as a distinct entity, or that which contains its own explanation? And what is meant by *id quod per se concipitur*, that whose essence can be *conceived* without reference to anything else or that whose existence can be *explained* without reference to anything else? *Hoc est*, he continues, *id cujus conceptus non indigit conceptu alterius rei, a quo formari debeat.* The same point arises again. In fact Spinoza assumes without argument that in each case the two alternatives are identical. He defines substance by an ambiguous formula which in one sense applies to all substances, finite or infinite, and in the other sense applies only to God. Then by confusing the two he claims to have proved that, in spite of appearances, God is the only substance, with the consequence that whatever seems to be another substance must in fact be a mode or appearance of God.

That a philosopher of Spinoza's brilliance should have fallen into so elementary a fallacy can be explained in only one way. The whole trouble is due to his fundamental essentialism. His ideal, he tells us explicitly, is to build up his system on the model of Euclidean geometry—*ordine geometrico*. Now what is the method of geometry as Euclid understood it? Simply the deduction of the logical consequences of definitions, axioms and postulates. *If* we mean by the words we use what the definitions say, *if* the postulates are assumed, and *if* the axioms are true, the consequences asserted necessarily follow, unless there is a sheer slip in the process of reasoning. Thus to achieve the Spinozist ideal of reducing metaphysics to geometry we have somehow to replace the notion of casual efficacy by that of logical implication. God and his creatures must therefore be connected not by an act of creative volition but by a relation of logical necessity. Creatures will then be an aspect or property of God in the same kind of way in which, in Euclidean geometry, the equality of the base-angles is an aspect or property of an isosceles triangle. God's existence must be logically entailed by his definition, and the existence of creatures—in whatever way creatures can be said to "exist"—must be logically entailed by the existence of God.[1]

But how, we naturally ask, can existence be proved in a geometrical system? Is not the method of geometry purely hypothetical? Geometry can indeed prove that, *if* ABC is a triangle in which AB=AC, then, supposing the Euclidean postulates and axioms to hold, the angles at B and C are equal. But no geometrical theorem ever asserts that there is such a thing as a triangle in actual existence. All that geometry ever does is to deduce the consequences of definitions and to display the nature of essences. How, then, can a metaphysic *ordine geometrico demonstrata* prove that anything actually exists? Obviously only by smuggling the notion of existence into the definition; by defining a certain essence as an essence one of whose properties is necessary existence. Then our task will be done for us. Let us define something, be it *causa sui*, substance, or God, in such a way that necessary existence is part of its definition; let us not do this too obviously, so that no one will see the rabbit being slipped into the hat; let us at the right moment seize it by the ears and withdraw it with a triumphant flourish. Then everybody, including (with reasonable luck) ourselves, will say that we have proved the existence of our entity when in fact we have merely postulated it. This is the method of every form of the ontological argument, but nowhere is the conjuring trick done with such an imposing array of patter as in the performance of Spinoza. If you are allowed to conceal your conclusions in your definitions, there is obviously no limit to what you will be able to prove. Spinoza in fact contrives not merely to define God as necessarily existing but as being the only genuine existent; it is therefore not surprising that he is able to demonstrate not merely that God exists, but that nothing else really does. He has really suc-

---

[1] Thus Spinoza writes: *Verum ego me satis clare ostendisse puto, a summa Dei potentia, sive infinita natura, infinita infinitis modis, hoc est, omnia necessario effluxisse, vel semper eadem necessitatem sequi; eodem modo ac ex natura trianguli ab aeterno et in aeternum sequitur, ejus tres angulos aequari duobus rectis* (*Eth.*, I, Prop. xvii, scholium). Whether in fact Euclid's Elements form an example of a perfect deductive system may well be questioned, in view of the work of recent mathematical logicians; the only point that is relevant in the present connection is that the philosophers of the seventeenth century believed them to do so.

ceeded only in proving that if necessarily existent being exists it exists necessarily, and this is a very different matter from proving that it exists.[1]

How light-heartedly Spinoza makes the transition from the logical to the actual order is shown in the subsidiary proof which he attaches to the ontological argument of his eleventh proposition. If God does not exist, he tells us, his existence must be prevented either by something within his nature, or by something outside it. The former alternative is impossible, since if it is granted God is granted. The latter alternative is impossible, since, according to Proposition II, no two substances can have anything in common and so no substance could either give existence to God or withhold it from him. And since there is nothing within God or outside him to prevent his existing, therefore he must exist. Detailed comment is hardly necessary at this point, but it may be worth noting how the confusion between the logical and the real order comes in in the assertion that, if God's existence were prevented by something within God's nature, God would be "granted." Granted in what sense? we inquire. In the logical or in the actual order? In the logical order, presumably. But then the argument falls to the ground. To take a simple comparison, is not the existence of a quadrilateral triangle prevented by something within its nature, namely the incompatibility of having precisely three, and at the same time precisely four, sides? Undoubtedly. Yet nobody would say that, in denying the existence of the quadrilateral triangle, we have been led into a contradiction because we have "granted" the figure whose existence we have denied. It has been "granted" merely as a notional being, an *ens rationis*; and this "grantedness" is perfectly consistent with the non-existence of the figure in the realm of actuality.

To this subsidiary proof Spinoza attaches another. He argues that ability to exist is power, and that God is infinitely

[1] Mr. Joachim expresses the opinion (in his *Study of the Ethics of Spinoza*, pp. 50 f.) that Spinoza in all his arguments intended not to prove God's existence purely *a priori*, but only to prove that the existence of modal or contingent being involves the necessary existence of God. I find this difficult to believe in view of the fact (remarked on in the text below) that in the only place in his proofs where he appeals to the existence of finite beings he explicitly states that this is done simply as a concession to his readers.

powerful. Hence if anything is able to exist, God is able to exist *a fortiori*. But finite beings exist, therefore God exists.[1] We must not be misled, by the reference in this argument to finite beings, into supposing that the argument is really based upon the actual existence of a finite world, for Spinoza immediately goes on to assert that the reference to finite beings is nothing but a concession to his readers. "In this last proof," he writes, "I wished to show the existence of God *a posteriori* so that it might be the more easily perceived, and not because the existence of God does not follow *a priori* from the same basis of argument. For since ability to exist is power, it follows that the more reality anything in nature has, the more power it will have to exist; and accordingly a being absolutely infinite, or God, has an absolutely infinite power of existence from itself, and on that account absolutely exists" (Prop. XI, Scholion). In other words, God being, by definition, a being of infinite power, he must be able to do anything, and therefore *inter alia* to exist. The reference to finite beings is only in order to provide an illustration, but we may note in passing what a remarkable kind of illustration this is. In effect it argues as follows. Either God is powerful enough to cause his own existence, or he is not. If he *is* powerful enough, then he exists. But if he is not, then we know by experience that finite beings exist, and since their existence cannot be caused by God, then it must be caused by themselves. So a finite being is powerful enough to exist by its own power, while an infinite being is not. And this, says Spinoza, is obviously an absurdity. And so God must exist. If we are going to argue in this way, we could, I think, find a very telling reply. We might point out that the difficulty of bringing a being into existence will presumably depend upon the magnitude of the being. It will require infinitely more power to cause an infinite being to exist than to cause a finite one. Now it is quite conceivable that to bring a finite being into existence requires only a finite power, but that to bring an infinite being into existence is more than even an infinite power can do. Fleas can jump many times their own height, but it is possible for a man to be too fat to move. This seems to me to be every bit as good an argument as Spinoza's, but we ought not perhaps to urge it too seriously, since Spinoza, by his own admission, is not too serious at the moment himself. He is, however, absolutely serious when he drops the reference to finite things, and then his incorrigible essentialism asserts itself with all its force. God, we are told, is *ex vi termini* a being so powerful as to be the cause of his own existence. If we interpret "cause" in the only way that makes the argument valid, namely as "logical ground," the only existence that the argument ascribes to God is a purely conceptual one, existence *ut signata*. If, on the other hand, we interpret it in the sense of metaphysical efficacity, the mental image involved is obvious. It is that of a being in a non-existent realm forcing itself into existence.[1] It is sufficient to reply that a non-existent being could not do anything whatsoever. If a moment's flippancy may be allowed, we might exclaim, after the manner of the White King, that we only wish *we* had such eyes, to be able to see Nobody, and at such a distance too! It is difficult not to agree with A. E. Taylor that "the whole of the First Part of the *Ethics* is logically no better than one long *petitio*."[2] Nobody has attempted with more intrepidity than Spinoza to prove the existence of God from his essence, and where Spinoza has failed it is not likely that anyone else will succeed. There is perhaps food for reflection in the fact that the end of the journey is pantheism. I do not think that, in our present connection, any useful purpose would be served by following the vicissitudes of the ontological argument any further. Its history, from its first formulation by St. Anselm, has been summed up in the following words: "It was accepted by Alexander of Hales, praised by St. Bonaventure, rejected by St. Thomas, defended by Duns Scotus, revived in a new dress by Descartes, highly eulogized

---

[1] Gilson remarks that Descartes lays the foundation of the Spinozist doctrines of God as *causa sui* and of God's power as a medium between his essence and his existence, though he has a notion of the transcendence of God which Spinoza lacks. For Descartes the notion of God's *positive essence* is a limiting concept drawn from the concept of efficient cause in somewhat the same way as a circle can be conceived as the limiting case of a regular polygon. See Gilson's very interesting chapter, "Une nouvelle idée de Dieu" (*Études* . . . , IIme P., ch. v).

[2] Art. cit., p. 271.

by Leibniz and Samuel Clarke, opposed by Kant, eagerly supported by Hegel, reconciled with St. Thomas's doctrine by Cardinal Aguirre."[1] For what it is worth, my own judgment upon the essentialist approach to the existence of God might be briefly expressed in the statement that, in the hands of its most authentically Christian exponents, it succeeds in doing almost everything except what it explicitly sets out to do. It provides us with a much needed reminder that God is absolutely unique, that in him and him alone existence and essence are really identical, that he depends upon nothing outside himself, and that if there *is* anything other than himself it must depend entirely upon him. But it fails altogether in its claim to prove to a finite intellect that God exists; and this for two reasons. First, because it postulates an intuition of the divine essence which it is beyond the power of any finite being to acquire.[2] Secondly—and this is the fundamental objection—because it assumes that existence *ut exercita* can be included in the concept of an essence. When St. Thomas says that the proposition "God is" is *per se nota* in itself because the predicate is the same as the subject, although, since we do not know *de Deo quid est*, it is not *per se nota* to us, he must not be taken as implying that in fact, although we cannot see it, God's essence causes his actual existence. He himself says that the reason why the proposition "God is" is *per se nota* is that God is his own *act of existing* (*Deus est suum esse*), not that God is a particular kind of essence.[3] He does not even argue that God is his own essence until he has proved that God exists.[4] And when he maintains that in God essence and existence (*esse*) are identical, his assertion is not that existence is implied by God's essence, but that God's essence is the same as his existence. In finite beings essence is distinct from existence, being related to it as the potential to the actual. In God everything is actual, so everything is existence; therefore God's essence is identical with the act by which he exists. To put the point in a very crude way,

---

[1] Dom Romanos Rios, on "An Anselmian Revival" in the *Dublin Review*, April 1943, p. 132.

[2] In saying this I do not exclude the possibility that God himself may confer upon human beings in the beatific vision (or even in moments of ecstasy in this life) an intuition of himself that they cannot acquire by their own powers. Such an intuition, however, is not part of the subject matter of natural theology.

[3] *S. Theol.*, I, ii, 1c.   [4] *Ibid.*, iii, 3.

the upshot is not that, if we could see fully what sort of being God is, we should see that he was bound to exist, but that, if we could see fully the way in which God exists, we could see that he was bound to be the sort of being that he is. The fundamental truth about God is that he exists self-existently; it is because of this that he is self-existent being. No doubt this antithesis is too sharp; we are perforce speaking *more humano*. Nevertheless the point at issue is a vital one; upon it depends the whole distinction between an essentialist and an existentialist theism. To exist is to *do something*, not in the sense of the Sartrians, according to whom you cannot exist unless you are doing something else, but in the sense that existing is the most fundamental thing that you do. *Operari sequitur esse*, but only because *esse* is itself *actus*. We have, if the argument of this chapter is sound, seen reason to believe that the essentialist approach to the proof of God's existence is bound to fail. Will the existential approach have any greater success? To this question we must shortly turn. But in order to see what the existential outlook really involves I shall devote the next chapter to a discussion of the existentialism of St. Thomas.

CHAPTER THREE

THE EXISTENTIALISM OF ST. THOMAS

*"Une cerise entre les dents contient plus de mystère que toute
la métaphysique idéaliste."*

J. MARITAIN, *Distinguer pour unir*, p. 666

*"The problem facing Christian thinkers from the thirteenth
century and after was the construction of an existential metaphysics.
. . . But whether such an existential metaphysics could be constructed out of the principles of Greek philosophy was precisely* the
problem of the thirteenth century."

A. C. PEGIS in *Essays in Thomism*, p. 156

I

I HAVE given considerable prominence in the first chapter
of this book to the assertion made by M. Gilson that the
fundamental transformation brought about in philosophy under
the influence of the Christian revelation reaches its fullest and
most authentic manifestation in the centrality given by St.
Thomas Aquinas to the notion of existence. "From its earliest
origins," Gilson tells us, "metaphysics had always obscurely
aimed at becoming existential; from the time of St. Thomas
Aquinas it has always been so, and to such an extent that metaphysics has regularly lost its very existence every time it has
lost its existentiality."[1] The importance that Gilson has come
to attribute to this interpretation is most remarkably shown by
a comparison of the new edition (substantially dating from
1941) of his work *Le Thomisme* with the earlier edition of 1925.
It is no exaggeration to say that in recasting and expanding his
work the author has completely revolutionized its perspective.
The great service rendered to philosophy by the Angelic Doctor,
we are told, was to purge it of the essentialism which, ultimately
tracing back to Plato, had hitherto always more or less overlaid

[1] *God and Philosophy*, p. 67.

44

and obscured that emphasis upon concrete reality and factual particularity which is altogether central both to Christianity itself, with its proclamation of the supreme significance of one definite historical Figure and a few definite historical events (*passus sub Pontio Pilato, crucifixus mortuus et sepultus, tertia die resurrexit a mortuis*), and also to the Jewish religion of which Christianity is both the heir and the fulfilment.

Now the word "existentialism"—whatever precise meaning we give to that not always too carefully defined term—is notoriously in the air to-day, and on being confronted with such a remarkable metamorphosis as that to which I have just referred, one might perhaps be pardoned a momentary suspicion that even a scholar of the balance and integrity of M. Gilson had unconsciously allowed himself to be unduly influenced by the climate of the time. Further reflection and examination, however, seem to make it plain that, whatever suggestive power his environment may have exercised, Gilson's new presentation has in fact brought out the true nature of St. Thomas's thought and has given his own exposition a force and a coherence far greater than it had before. If Gilson is right—and I believe he is—we are provided with a complete answer to the common assertion that, because of his use of the pseudo-Areopagite, St. Thomas is only a concealed Platonist or (since any stick will do to beat the Angelic Doctor) that, because of his use of Aristotle, he is only a half-converted Peripatetic. Whatever he may have taken from earlier Christian, semi-Christian or even pagan sources, the remarkable fact is not just where St. Thomas found his material, but what he did with it. Dionysius, Aristotle, even Augustine, all appear in an entirely new light when their thought is transformed by the existentialist outlook and when the notion of essence, instead of being the guiding philosophical principle, falls into a still honourable, but definitely subordinate, place. "Like all Christians, but unlike the Greeks," writes Gilson, "Augustine has a quite clear notion of what it is to create something 'out of nothing.' It is to make it to be. What still remains Greek in Augustine's thought is his very notion of what it is to be. His ontology, or science of being, is an 'essential' rather than an 'existential' one. In other words it exhibits a marked tendency to reduce the existence of a thing to its essence, and to answer the question: What is it for a thing to be? by saying: It is to be that which it is. . . . It was not easy," Gilson adds, "to go beyond St. Augustine, because the limit he had reached was the limit of Greek ontology itself, and therefore just about the very limit which the human mind can reach in matters of metaphysics. When, nine centuries after the death of St. Augustine, a new and decisive progress in natural theology was made, its occasional cause was the discovery of another Greek metaphysical universe by another Christian theologian. This time the metaphysical universe was that of Aristotle, and the name of the theologian was Thomas Aquinas."[1]

I shall not attempt here to give a systematic presentation of Gilson's case, though I would urge upon any who are interested a study of the new chapters which he has added to his work.[2] Instead I shall try, by taking three particular instances from St. Thomas's system, to show the existentialist principle in action, and I hope in so doing to make it plain what the existentialism of St. Thomas is. What relation, if any, it bears to other outlooks claiming the name of Existentialism is another question. It will become apparent in the course of the discussion how much I owe to Gilson's writings, but I should not like to make him responsible for all that I shall say.

My first instance will be from general metaphysical theory, my second from the theory of perception, and my third from the doctrine of human individuation.

II

I shall begin then with St. Thomas's general metaphysical theory or ontology, in order to show how fundamental his existentialism is.

Why is it that in fact a great many people think that Thomist metaphysics is altogether abstract and remote from concrete reality? It is, I believe, because they mistakenly suppose that his fundamental ontological doctrine is to be found in what

[1] *God and Philosophy*, p. 61.
[2] *Le Thomisme*, 5ᵐᵉ éd., Part I, ch. i, ii, iv, vi; ch. iii, § 6; ch. v, §§ 1, 2. Chapters ii to v of Part III are also new.

he says about form and matter, instead of in what he says about essence and existence.

What, after all, is the function of the form-and-matter doctrine in St. Thomas's system? It is not to explain how things come to exist, but how there can be more than one thing of the same kind. Form and matter in union compose a substance (also called an essence or quiddity[1]), but a substance does not by definition exist. A substance or essence is a possible existent, something which *can* exist, and the form-and-matter doctrine is an attempt to explain (or perhaps merely to describe) how it is *possible* for more than one thing of the same kind to exist, not how they actually exist supposing that they do. It may not be an entirely satisfactory doctrine, though it is not altogether easy to see what can be put in its place. In any case St. Thomas takes it over more or less ready-made from Aristotle, though we shall see later on how he deepens and extends it. Perhaps the reason why he does not criticize it more radically than he does is that the problem with which it is concerned is not for him the fundamental one.

[1] More accurately, a distinction can be drawn between the various uses of the terms substance, essence and quiddity according to the following scheme, which is based upon Maritain's *Introduction to Philosophy*:

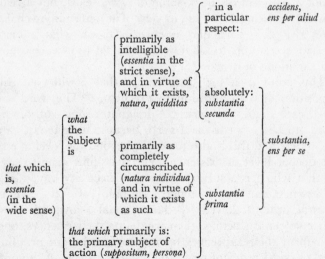

But, in all these nuances, essence as *that which is* is radically contrasted with existence (*esse*) the *act by which* a thing is outside non-existence.

His basic theme is not that essences or substances are composed of matter and form, but that actual beings (what he calls
entia) are composed of essence and existing (*essentia* and *esse*).
It is most important to recognize this. If we start with essences
instead of with *entia* we shall fall into a doctrine of essences
queuing up in some non-existent realm, jockeying for position
and each putting in a claim for existence in virtue of its
existuritio. And before we know where we are we shall have
the best possible world and the whole Leibnitian set-up.

St. Thomas's starting-point, then, is the *ens*, the actual
concrete existent. He does not think of a realm of essences,
some of which achieve existence—that only comes later when,
having proved the existence of God, he explains how all possible beings (even those that never exist in actuality) have ideal
subsistence in the divine mind. He begins with the realm of
diversified finite beings, *entia*, which are apprehended by our
senses, and he sees each of them as the subject and the superject
of an existential act. Now every finite existential act must be
an act of a determinate kind, it must be the existential act of a
particular *essence*, but the essence arises from the existential act
and does not precede it. What is given to us in the finite world
is not a realm of essences, some of which exist, but a realm of
existent acts, each of which, in view of its determinate character,
gives rise to a particular essence. To ask what a being is,
therefore, is simply to ask how it exists, for its essence is nothing
but the mode of its existence.

This point is of such importance that I will give Gilson's
exposition of it in addition to my own. "The word 'being'
[*ens*], as a noun," he writes, "designates some substance; the
word 'to be'—or *esse*—is a verb, because it designates an act.
To understand this is also to reach, beyond the level of essence,
the deeper level of existence. For it is quite true to say that
all that which is a substance must of necessity have also both
an essence and an existence. In point of fact, such is the
natural order followed by our rational knowledge: we first
conceive certain beings, then we define their essences, and last
we affirm their existences by means of a judgment. But the
metaphysical order of reality is just the reverse of the order of
human knowledge: what first comes into it is a certain act of

existing which, because it is *this* particular act of existing, circumscribes at once a certain essence and causes a certain substance to come into being. In this deeper sense, 'to be' is the primitive and fundamental act by virtue of which a certain being actually is, or exists."[1]

Thus what is given in any finite existent (any *ens*) is the composition of existing and essence. This is prior to any question as to whether the essence itself is composed of form and matter. It is well known that in St. Thomas's system there is a whole realm of beings—the angels—in whom the composition of form and matter is altogether absent. This latter composition occurs only when there are a number of beings of the same species, but in St. Thomas's angels, as in any other finite being, there is a real distinction and composition of existing and essence. And in speaking of the distinction and composition of existing and essence one does not mean that existing and essence are two separable things that enter into a sort of chemical union to form a third thing, as hydrogen and oxygen combine to form water; the act of existing is primary, the essence arises simply because any finite act of existing must be an act of existing of some determinate character. Giles of Rome was no true Thomist when he wrote: *Esse et essentia sunt duae res.*[2]

I have used, in the preceding paragraph, the word "existing" rather than "existence," here, so far as the English language permits, following Gilson, who translates St. Thomas's *esse* by the verbal noun "l'exister" and not by the abstract noun "l'existence." "Existence," being an abstract noun, would itself suggest an essence. We cannot too strongly insist that "existing" is not a quality; the recognition of this underlies St. Thomas's rejection of the ontological argument, as well as the modern analysis of the difference between existential

---

[1] *God and Philosophy*, p. 63. It should be noted that in this passage Gilson uses "substance" to mean an existent being or *ens*; his usual use agrees with St. Thomas's and equates substance with individual essence, leaving the question of existence open.

[2] The fundamentally *correlative* character of the various pairs of distinguishable elements in finite being (essence/existence, form/matter, substance/accident, act/potentiality) is, I think, nowhere better expounded than in L. de Raeymaeker's *Philosophie de l'Être*, with its insistence that a *distinctio realis* need not be a *distinctio inter rem et rem*.

E

propositions like "Cats exist" and attributive propositions like "Cats scratch." And, as we have seen, St. Thomas does not normally use the word *existentia*; he uses the verbal noun *esse* or the more emphatic *ipsum esse*.[1]

Thus to use Gilson's words, "the substantial form is only a secondary *quo est*, subordinate to the primary *quo est* which is the very act of existing."[2] And St. Thomas himself writes in the *Contra Gentiles*: "In substances composed of matter and form there is a double composition of act and potentiality: first, that of the substance itself, which is composed of matter and form, and then that of substance so composed with existing."[3] It follows from this that *existing*, not being an essence, cannot be reached in the first act of the intellect, the abstraction of the concept, but only in the second act, the affirmation of the judgment (*compositio*, as St. Thomas calls it).[4] As Gilson points out, it is very hard to expound this doctrine without distorting it, and very few Thomist commentators have succeeded in doing so. "To speak of the distinction of essence and existence is to talk as if existence was itself an essence, the essence of the act of existing. This is to treat an act as if it were a thing."[5] Strictly speaking, I cannot "conceive-a-thing-as-existing," I can only affirm (or deny) that it exists. Or if I do

---

[1] See on this point, Gilson, *Le Thomisme*, 5me éd., p. 44, n. 1.

[2] Ibid., p. 49.

[3] *In substantiis autem compositis ex materia et forma est duplex compositio actus et potentiae: prima quidem ipsius substantiae quae componitur ex materia et forma; secunda vero ex ipsa substantia jam composita et esse* (S.c.G., II, liv). Cf. the following (ad loc.): *In compositis ex materia et forma, dicitur forma esse principium essendi, quia est complementum substantiae cujus actus est ipsum esse;* i.e. the form makes the substance complete as a potential existent. And again: *In compositis ex materia et forma, nec materia nec forma potest dici ipsum quod est nec etiam ipsum esse; forma tamen potest dici quo est, secundum quod est essendi principium. Ipsa autem tota substantia est ipsum quod est; et ipsum esse est quo substantia denominatur ens;* i.e. the whole substance is *what* exists, but it is the act of existing that makes it a *being* (*ens*).

[4] Hume rightly asserted the impossibility of conceptualizing *existing*, but his own explanation how we assert that anything exists is pitifully inadequate (*Treatise of Human Nature*, I, iii, 7; Everyman's ed., vol. I, pp. 96 f.).

[5] *Le Thomisme*, 5me ed., p. 52. Cf. the following: "To exist is an act, it needs therefore an act to express it. To the staticism of the essence corresponds that of the definition, which offers itself as motionless to the intuition of the intellect; to the dynamism of existing corresponds that of the judgment, whose discursive movement imitates the circulation of an existential energy whose act engenders the substance and assures its unity" (ibid., p. 62). The English language being what it is, it is impossible without intolerable clumsiness to avoid the use of the word "existence," but wherever I use it in the sequel, it must be understood in the sense of Gilson's "l'exister." Any sentence containing it can in principle be replaced by one containing instead the verb "to exist."

include existence in a concept it is, to use the jargon of the commentators, only existence *ut signata*, never *ut exercita*. This is why the ontological argument collapses; the concept of God, as St. Anselm defines him, does indeed include existence *ut signata*, but the existence that we want to attribute to him, existence *ut exercita*, cannot be reached in the concept at all. It is thus perfectly possible to hold that God cannot be conceived except as existing, and at the same time to deny that he is thereby shown to exist, since *existing* is not the object of conceptualization but of judgment.[1] For St. Thomas, however noble our concept of God may be it is totally incapable of telling us whether God exists or not; but the actual existence of the most humble and insignificant of actually existing beings is sufficient to demonstrate the existence of self-existent Being itself, *ipsum esse subsistens*. So far is St. Thomas's existentialism from all essentialist metaphysics. It is true that he is usually understood as teaching that not only the actual existence, but even the possible existence, of finite being is sufficient to prove that God exists. We must not, however, be misled into thinking this to be a concession to essentialism. For the Angelic Doctor, *potentia dicitur ad actum*; if finite being is possible, then it might exist, and if it did exist it could do so only because God willed that it should. The possibility of existence here involved is not a mere notional being, but the possibility of being actual. And in any case we only know that finite being *is* possible because we have discovered that some finite beings are actual; *ab esse ad posse valet consequentia*.

I shall not do more than allude in passing to Gilson's highly illuminating discussion of the various views on the relation of essence and existence in such medieval thinkers as Alfarabi, Algazel, Avicenna and Maimonides; it emphasizes the points already made.[2] I will, however, again draw attention to his assertion that St. Thomas's great work as a Christian metaphysician was to purge philosophy of the last traces of Platonic

[1] Cf. A. D. Sertillanges, *St. Thomas d'Aquin*, I, pp. 133–4; Maritain, *The Dream of Descartes*, E.T., pp. 108–9. Strictly speaking, St. Anselm does not say that we can conceive or even "think" (*cogitare*) God, in fact he expressly denies this (*Proslogion*, xv). He does not say that we can think God, but only that we cannot think anything greater. Nevertheless, in his argument the definition of God as *aliquid quo majus nihil cogitari potest* takes the place of a true concept; otherwise the argument could not proceed at all. [2] Op. cit., pp. 55 f.

essentialism and to affirm with complete and deliberate clarity
that God is not merely the *ens perfectissimum*, the Supreme Being
in the order of essences, but *maxime ens*, that which supremely *is*.
Whether or not *Qui est* is an accurate translation of the Hebrew
name of God revealed to Moses in the third chapter of Exodus,
there is, as I have already argued,[1] little doubt that St.
Thomas's radically existential interpretation of *Qui est*, as
signifying not a static perfection but the absolutely unlimited
Act and Energy, is thoroughly in line with Hebrew thought;
it is this that underlies his assertion that God is pure act.[2]
When we turn back from St. Thomas to St. Augustine, one of
the most lovely and haunting features of the great African
doctor is found in the repeated contrast which he draws
between the transience and impermanence of the finite material
realm and the immutability and perfection of God, to enjoy
whom eternally is man's last end. "Being is a term for immutability. For all things that are changed cease to be what
they were, and begin to be what they were not. True being,
pure being, real being has no one save him who does not
change. He has it to whom is said, 'Thou shalt change them
and they shall be changed. But thou are always the self-same.'
What does 'I am who am' mean but 'I am eternal'? What
does 'I am who am' mean but 'I cannot be changed'?"[3]
It is very true and very important and we can find as clear an
insistence upon the eternity and immutability of God in St.
Thomas.[4] But we miss in St. Augustine something of the vigour
and robustness of the Hebrew doctrine of God which we find
again in St. Thomas. And we find it in him, I believe, because
of his conviction that God is primarily Being and pure Act.
St. Thomas's uncompromisingly existential interpretation of
the "sublime truth,"[5] as he calls it, that the most proper name
of God is "He who is," without rejecting whatever is true in
Christian Platonism, brings back into Christian thought a

[1] See pp. 12 f. *supra*.
[2] *Deus est purus actus non habens aliquid de potentialitate* (*S. Theol.* I, iii, 2c., referring
to the First Way in ii, 3c.).
[3] *Serm.* vii, 7. Cf.: *Omnis quippe iste ordo pulcherrimus rerum valde bonarum modis
suis peractis transiturus est; et mane quippe in eis factum est et vespera* (*Conf.*, XIII, xxxv).
*Vacabimus et videbimus, videbimus et amabimus, amabimus et laudabimus, ecce quod erit
in fine sine fine* (*De Civ.* XXII, xxx).
[4] *S. Theol.*, I, ix, x.   [5] *Haec sublimis veritas* (*S.c.G.*, I, xxii).

sense of the divine energy and activity which comes ultimately from the Hebraism of the Bible and which it cannot afford to ignore. I do not think that Luther was the first person to realize this.

III

I shall now pass on to consider St. Thomas's doctrine of perception. For him, as is well known, our knowledge of the external world is acquired through the medium of the senses: *nihil in intellectu quod non prius in sensu*, to quote the famous tag. The sensible species—which to-day we should call the sense-datum—is not just a stimulus which provokes the intellect to turn to the contemplation of an ideal realm of eternal essences, as the Platonists believed. Nor is it, as the sensationalists hold, the terminus of the perceptive act, so that the intellect can acquire an intelligible object only by inferring it from, or constructing it out of, the sense-data. Nor, as I think the Kantians would have it, is the intelligible object something which the mind *makes* intelligible in the very act of apprehending it, so that we can never really tell how far the mind discovers it and how far it creates it. For the Angelic Doctor, to whom the human soul operates on the twofold level of sense and intellect, the sensible species is not the *objectum quod* but the *objectum quo* of the whole perceptive act; it is indeed an impression received by the sense, but an impression which the intellect uses as its instrument in order to grasp, admittedly obscurely and imperfectly and under the mode in which the sensible species presents it, the actually existing extrasubjective being or *ens*. Furthermore, in perception there are not two successive acts, one of sensation and the other of intellection, any more than the percipient himself consists of two beings, one sensitive and the other intelligent; there is one percipient act in which sensation and intellection are intricately combined.

But now the trouble begins. For granted that what is perceived is a finite existent, to what activity of the soul are we to assign the perception of existence? *Est enim sensus particularium, intellectus vero universalium.*[1] Sensation has as its object the

<hr />

[1] *In II de Anima*, lect. 5.

particular, but this is not the actual existent perceived; the sense-datum is only the *objectum quo* of the whole perceptive act, not its *objectum quod*. On the other hand, the intellect, while it penetrates to the actual existent, knows it not in its individual particularity but only under the universal form of a specific essence in the concept which it abstracts from it; and no amount of concept-forming or concept-analysis does anything to tell us whether what is conceived exists outside the mind or not. Existence would thus seem to be radically unknowable, for existence is always of the particular. The sense can receive particulars but cannot know them; while the intellect can know but can know only universals. Hence the intelligible world of the Platonists and neo-Platonists, and as for Aristotle —well, St. Thomas, with the large-hearted generosity with which he always gives people the benefit of the doubt and the cheerful lack of scruple with which he frequently transforms their doctrines in order to be able to do so, would no doubt be easier on him than most Christian philosophers would. Anyhow, it is St. Thomas's Aristotelianism with which we are now concerned, and not Aristotle's. And in seeing how he deals with the difficulty I shall chiefly follow the discussion given by Gilson in Chapters VII and VIII of his *Réalisme Thomiste et Critique de la Connaissance*, which was published in 1939.

The problem of human knowledge, he remarks, must be approached, not just by discussing knowledge in general, but by considering the nature of the knowing subject, the human being. *Non enim proprie loquendo*, writes St. Thomas, *sensus aut intellectus cognoscit, sed homo per utrumque.*[1] Man, as we saw above, does not consist of two beings, one sensitive and the other intelligent; he is one being who both senses and understands. Thus, says Gilson, "we can form a certain knowledge of singulars. By the senses we attain directly to the things known, thanks to our perception of their sensible qualities, and by the intellect we attain to these same things, thanks to the abstract concepts which we form of them. Thus it is the man himself who knows the particular things from the fact that he thinks what he perceives."[2] But, as Gilson goes on to point

---

[1] *De Ver.*, q. 2, a. 6 *ad* 3m.   [2] *Réal. Thom.*, p. 186.

out, this is not precisely our problem. It is true that only particulars exist, but what we want to explain is how we can know that they exist, not how we can know that they are particulars. Is there then some index of existence other than the certitude that accompanies sensation? There is not, Gilson replies, and there cannot be, in a doctrine in which only the singular exists.[1] Intellect and sense are united in the perceiving subject: "in some way man conceives the singular and perceives the universal";[2] and this is directly connected with the fact that the proper object of the human intellect, as the intellect of a being in which soul and body together make up a unity, is not being in general but the being of sensible things.

Now clearly, as soon as one equates the index of existence with the certitude that accompanies sensation one raises the problem of error in an acute form. If this doctrine is true, how can our perceptions ever mislead us, how can we ever have hallucinations or dreams? Gilson does not say very much about this, but I think we can construct his answer for him. And the first point to notice is that the phrase used was not just "certitude" but "the certitude that accompanies sensation."

For, as we have seen, in human perception sensation and intellection are intimately combined, and since it is sensation that indicates both the particularity of the thing perceived and its existence, for an act of perception to give us true information about the external world the mechanism of sensation must be properly functioning. It follows that in the last resort the veridicity of the perceptive act is to be tested not by a mere analysis or scrutiny of the object as presented, which may be precisely the same in a hallucination as in a genuine perception, but by an examination of the sense-organs and their working. And in fact if a man persists in saying that he is seeing pink snakes with green spots we do not content ourselves with asking the man carefully to examine the snakes; we ourselves proceed carefully to examine the man. To say this is not to deny the commonplace and obvious truths that error actually occurs in a false judgment made by the intellect, and that as regards its mere passive reception of a sense-datum the sense cannot be deceived; what we are concerned with is not where error occurs

[1] Ibid., p. 210.   [2] Ibid., p. 211.

but whence it arises and by what kind of investigation it is to be corrected. This is quite a different matter. The point at issue simply is that error about existence can occur in the judgment of the intellect even if existence is not the object of the intellect but of the sense, since, as we have seen, it is not strictly speaking either the intellect that knows or the sense that senses, but the man himself who knows by his intellect and who senses by his sense.[1]

It further follows that to assert that perception gives us no ground for believing in an extrasubjective world, on the strength of the fact that no existential index is to be found in the concepts formed in perception, is altogether beside the point. It is, if I may use a rather crude illustration, like asserting that because I cannot tell by examining a telegram which I have received whether the statement contained in it, that Cambridge has won the Boat Race, is true or false, therefore there is no reason for supposing that the Boat Race took place at all. The truth is that this is to be decided by other methods than scrutinizing the telegram, not that it cannot be decided at all.

It is thus through the senses that both the particularity and the existence of things are manifested. This does not, however, leave us in a nominalism, like that of the radical physicalists, in which no abstract or universal statements are significant, for the intellect plays its part in perception as well as the senses; it both abstracts the universal from the sensible species and also affirms its embodiment in the existent extrasubjective being.

This last assertion leads on to a further point, which I think Gilson would have made even more strongly than he does had he written *Réalisme Thomiste* in 1946 and not in 1939.[2] We

---

[1] It should be remarked in passing that this doctrine of error is no more proof than any other against a universal scepticism. When we examine the man to discover why it is that he is seeing snakes which no one else can see, we have to assume that we are not in error in our perceptions of the man. This cannot, however, be discussed in more detail here.

[2] There is an illuminating discussion of the evolution of Gilson's epistemology in Georges van Riet's *L'Epistémologie Thomiste*, pp. 494–517. It is summed up as follows:

"In 1927 the existence of things is the simplest hypothesis to explain the objectivity of the concept. It is also a simple hypothesis.

"In 1932 it is a sensible self-evidence.

"In 1939 it is a sensitive-intellectual self-evidence.

"In 1942 it is furthermore the object of a judgment."   (Op. cit., p. 509.)

have seen already that existence—or, better, exist*ing*—is not abstracted in the concept but affirmed in the judgment. If then, as we have just said, in the perceptive act the intellect *both* abstracts the universal *and* recognizes its extrasubjective embodiment, both the first and the second operation of the intellect—conceptualization and judging—are involved. The intellect conceives the universal and affirms its actual existence in the particular, and in both these operations it is intimately associated with the senses in the unity of the perceptual act. "The problem of the judgment of existence for St. Thomas," writes Gilson, "meets the analogous problem of the apprehension of the singular."[1] And again: "Realist abstraction . . . is an apprehension of the universal *in* the singular and of the singular *by* [*par*] the universal. The concept, and the judgment which expresses it, are thus for us the substitutes for an intellectual intuition of the singular which is lacking to us, but what we cannot apprehend as a pure spirit would apprehend it, since we are men, we can apprehend as men and approach it as closely as possible at the junction of our intellect and our sensibility."[2] Or once more: "To think as a realist is to think that what is expressed in our definition of 'man,' namely 'rational animal,' is the essence of man, and that what establishes our knowledge as real is, in the essence itself, the existential act which makes it both be and also be what it is."[3] And finally, commenting on the famous definition of truth as "the adequation of the intellect and the thing," Gilson writes: "To give this formula its full realist meaning we must rise above the plane on which the thing is reduced to an essence which in turn is reduced to the quiddity expressed by the definition. All the noetic of St. Thomas invites us to take this step, and he has even gone so far as to state it in so many words, although it was doubtless self-evident to him: it is not the essence, but the act of existing, of a thing that is the ultimate foundation of anything true that we know about it. . . . *Veritas fundatur in esse rei magis quam in ipsa quidditate*.[4]"[5] Clearly if Gilson's interpretation is correct, St. Thomas's existentialism is shown in his theory of perception no less than in his ontology.

---

[1] *Réal. Thom.*, p. 210.   [2] Ibid., p. 212.   [3] Ibid., p. 224.
[4] *In I Sent.*, d. 19, q. 5, a. 1, sol.   [5] *Réal. Thom.*, p. 224.

IV

We must now turn our attention to our third illustration, that from human individuation.

St. Thomas quite contentedly takes over Aristotle's teaching that the soul is the form of a man and the body is his matter. This immediately raises problems for the Christian which do not arise for the pagan. To begin with, this view seems to deny to the individual man that unique personal status which is involved both in the Christian emphasis on human responsibility and in the Christian doctrine of salvation. If the different human beings that exist are merely so many numerically diverse particular instances of the universal "manhood" in the same kind of way as a number of lumps of cooking-salt are so many particular instances of the universal "sodium chloride," I can hardly be considered to have any ultimate significance. Nobody bothers what happens to a lump of salt, so long as another is forthcoming to take its place. Can we say in such a doctrine, "The Son of God loved *me* and gave himself for *me*"? In the second place, what happens to the individual when the body dies? When the salt has been decomposed, where is its saltness? And thirdly, all those personal characteristics and idiosyncrasies which make human beings at once so different and so interesting seem to be reduced to a purely trivial and accidental status. Are the things in which we differ from one another really of as little importance as this?

Now St. Thomas has an answer to all these objections, but as it is only too often expounded it bears, for all its ingenuity, many of the marks of a *tour de force*. There is first the doctrine of the unity of the substantial form, for which the Angelic Doctor contended so stubbornly. Although the soul is united to the body as form to matter, its penetration of the individual does not stop there; as form the soul subsumes into itself all those lower formalities which the body as an organized entity, animate, vegetative and corporeal, already possesses, so that the matter which it ultimately embraces is not merely the body of an animal but the fundamental *materia prima* itself. The soul penetrates to the deepest metaphysical root of the man;

it does not just confer rationality on an ape or galvanize a corpse. Again, we are told the soul does not merely *acquire* a temporary substantiality from its union with a particular parcel of signate matter; it is a form existing *in se*, which *confers* substantiality upon the composite being. And finally, against the Averroists with their denial of personal immortality, we are told that the soul possesses individuality in itself and not from the matter which it informs, though it possesses it in virtue of its aptness to inform matter. "The matter is the passive principle of individuation, but the form is the active principle of individuality."[1]

Now all this is, of course, highly satisfactory from the standpoint of theological orthodoxy; it preserves the three cardinal doctrines of the survival of the soul, of personal immortality and of the resurrection of the body. But it is difficult to feel that, as usually presented, it is satisfactory from the philosophical point of view. After all, it may be objected, this is a philosophy in which only particulars exist and in which, at any rate, as regards corporeal beings, forms are particularized only in union with matter; surely, therefore, the notion that the form can exist when the matter has left it is ridiculous. If, as is asserted, the soul is the form of the body, survival is impossible, we die like cows or cabbages. And even if this objection can be somehow rebutted, the difficulties are by no means over. For if the form goes on existing after it is separated from the body, it must then exist either individualized or not. If it exists in separation individualized, then humanity as a universal has vanished; each soul is a different form and hence a different species, men are angels in disguise, and Descartes was right after all. But if the form exists in separation unindividualized, then personal identity has gone; we merge at death into a universal soul, and the Averroists are vindicated against St. Thomas. So the philosopher will argue, and, however much he may admire the Angelic Doctor's dexterity, he will, I think, feel that for once St. Thomas has allowed his faith not to perfect his reason but to destroy it. And what more heinous crime could a Thomist commit?

I do not see how we can get out of this tangle if we adopt an

[1] Gilson, *Le Thomisme*, 5me éd., p. 267, n. 1.

essentialist standpoint. From such a standpoint we start with
a general doctrine of form as the principle of essence and then
our understanding of the individual is inescapably at the mercy
of the universality inherent in essence and form. Instead of the
rich variety and vitality of a world of actual and active beings
we shall have a shadowy and spectral realm in which bloodless
categories perform their unearthly ballet to the tinny accom-
paniment of the laws of identity and contradiction, and
chimeras bombinate *in vacuo* devouring second intentions. The
particular characteristics of the individual will appear nugatory
and transient, and we shall be able to save something of its
importance only by desperate *ad hoc* expedients. And, like
other exponents of legerdemain, we may perhaps command
admiration but we shall be unlikely to carry conviction.

Something like this did, I think, in fact happen in the
scholasticism of the later Middle Ages. But now let us see
what the situation is when we interpret St. Thomas's teaching
existentially. This time we start with the individual acts of
existing, each of which constitutes a concrete, particular,
actually existing being, an *ens*. Each of these existential acts
is the existential act of a different individual essence, for every
finite existential act must be an act of a determinate type. The
existential act comes first in the metaphysical order, and the
essence that it constitutes arises out of it. Furthermore, the
essence so constituted is loaded not only with its individual
characteristics but, in all probability, with specific characteristics too; and the individual and the specific characteristics
have the same ontological basis, all alike being constituted by,
and wholly by, the existential act. God, we can suppose, might
have made a world in which there were no specific characteristics at all, in which every individual was altogether different
from every other, no two existential acts having any feature in
common except the bare fact of both being existential acts;
indeed, if St. Thomas was reliably informed, this is more or less
true of the realm of pure spirits, each of which is the unique
individual of its kind. (It is not entirely true even here, because
St. Thomas's angels have common quasi-generic characteristics
even if they have no common specific ones; they all have the
characteristic of being an angel and they fall under the Diony-

sian classification of the nine celestial choirs.[1]) At the other extreme, God certainly seems to have made certain classes of entities in which there are practically no individual character- istics, but only specific ones; this is presumably why it is so difficult for the physicist to keep track of an electron. It has hardly any individual characteristics, and those that it has, such as position- and momentum-co-ordinates, are purely accidental and variable; it has a certain very tenuous specific nature but no inherent individual identity.[2] And between these two extremes there is a whole range of species of the most bewildering variety. In some of them the individuals have almost as few individual characteristics as the electrons, in others the individual characteristics preponderate over the specific ones almost as much as in the case of St. Thomas's angels, while in the great majority the individual and the specific characteristics are of comparable importance, though their relative weights and their reciprocal interactions vary in the most baffling way from species to species. Lumps of amor- phous matter (amorphous, that is, in the sense of the physicist, not in that of the metaphysician) would provide an example of the first type, and men of the second; while between them lie all the intermediate species of the mineral, vegetable and animal realms which are the proper objects of physical and biological science: crystals, viruses, bacteria, turnips, sparrows, the rabbit which sports in the fields, and the dog which is the friend of man. Man is a little lower than the angels, but even the sparrow does not fall to the ground without the Father's knowledge; it has its individuality, however humble, and is not all specific. And, paradoxical as the statement might at first sight appear, it is just those species in which the individual counts for most and the species as such for least that are the most noble, for it is only in the individual that the species achieves actuality.

At this point it will be well to anticipate the objection that to expound St. Thomas in this way is to be guilty of the supreme treason of turning him into a nominalist. This, I

---

[1] *S. Theol.*, I, cviii.

[2] I think this is a correct account of the metaphysical status of an electron. But I am not absolutely sure that an electron is not a purely logical or mathe- matical construct.

emphatically reply, is not the case. In an essentialist theory, where everything depends on the duality of form and matter, it is true that you can locate reality in the particular only at the expense of denying reality to the universal. Here, however, we are concerned with the more ultimate duality of essence and existing, and on this level it is just in the case when the individual existent acts are most intense that the species to which the individual belongs acquires most significance, since the specific essence is constituted not by a mere logical anteriority of the universal to the particular, but by a common life generated by the individual existents in their concrete activity.

This, however, is a digression though not an unimportant one; let us return to the main theme. If, as I have urged, our starting-point is to be the individual, not merely conceived as a substance or essence but affirmed as an existent, there is no question of the world having to conform to a predetermined scheme of universals and particulars. On the contrary, our doctrine of universals and particulars will have to conform to the actual world with all the variety and complexity that it contains. Instead of the theory of universals and particulars, of form and matter, being a univocal scheme applying in exactly the same mode to all types of being, from the electron to the angel, it will be a highly analogical one, whose modes will be as manifold and diversified as is the world that God has created and are to be discovered only by the thoroughly empirical method of patiently examining the world in order to see what it is like. And what is man, of whom God is mindful? If the Christian religion is true, he is a being of the most complicated and mysterious kind. A rational animal, yes; a member of the genus *homo* and of its unique species *homo sapiens*, if you will; but at the same time, in his private and incommunicable individuality, a responsible person, created in the image of God, made for eternal beatitude in the vision of the Holy Trinity, and answerable for the use which he makes of the life that God has given him. A composite being, made up of matter and spirit most intimately interpenetrating, so that its very unity can be maintained only by the continual absorption of matter from the lower creation, and yet such that when the material part has fallen into decay the spiritual part continues to exist in its individual reality, awaiting the restoration, in a mysterious eschatological transformation, of its material counterpart. And these are only a selection from the whole constellation of characteristics manifested in the existential act by which a human being is constituted; many of the most important are those individual characteristics which vary from one human being to another and which are the business of the biographer rather than the philosopher. We need hardly be surprised that it is difficult for us to comprehend and formulate the precise analogical mode in which the doctrine of form and matter and the doctrine of essence and existing apply to man. We can, however, at least see something of what is meant by saying that a human being is a *person* and how it is that, as a mere individual, a man exists for the sake of the species, while at the same time it is he, as a person, for whose sake the species exists.[1] And we can, I think, understand what St. Thomas has in mind when he tells us that a person is the most perfect thing in the whole of nature.[2]

The purpose of this rather extended discussion has been twofold: first to make it clear, by giving some examples of its application, what in fact the existentialism of St. Thomas is, and secondly to show that what St. Thomas did with the philosophy of Aristotle was not to plaster it over with a façade of Christian ornamentation, which might serve for a few centuries to conceal its inherent structural defects, but to transform it radically from within by providing it with a guiding principle which had hitherto been lacking but which was absolutely necessary if it was to achieve a real unity and coherence. This principle was the principle of existence, and its source was the Judaeo-Christian revelation of God as the transcendent self-existent Being who confers upon his creatures all that they have and are. There are many other questions upon which it throws light which I have not touched on here. In particular, it can be argued that the analogical transition from finite beings to God can be validly made only in an existential philosophy and that, in an essentialist system,

---

[1] Cf. J. Maritain on "The Human Person and Society," in *Scholasticism and Politics*, ch. iii.

[2] *Persona significat id quod est perfectissimum in tota natura* (*S. Theol.*, I, xxix, 3c.).

analogical discourse is bound to collapse into either agnosticism or anthropomorphism; I have commented on this point elsewhere in this book.[1] Again, it would be interesting to discuss what, if anything, St. Thomas's existentialism has in common with the present-day attitudes which are known by the same name. They have this at least in common, that both are concerned to emphasize the ultimate significance of the individual as an active and willing being, though the Sartrians see him as creating himself by acts of sheer self-asserting unconditioned decision, while for St. Thomas he is a creature deriving his existence from the will of God and therefore morally bound to use his own will in accordance with the end for which God has created him. I shall resist the temptation to follow up this point in any detail here. I shall only suggest that the marked popularity which has come to be enjoyed in recent years, in both Christian and non-Christian circles, by existentialist systems of a markedly voluntaristic and anti-rational type may be due to the virtual oblivion of the fundamentally existential orientation of the thought of St. Thomas Aquinas. It would perhaps be too narrow a definition to say that the specific differentia of Thomist existentialism is its intellectualism, as contrasted with the voluntarism of both non-Christian existentialists like Sartre and non-Thomist Christian existentialists like Kierkegaard; rather it would, I think, be true to say that in St. Thomas both the rational and the volitional elements receive their proper recognition. It will, I hope, have at least become clear that the Thomist philosophy, so far from being, as is too often imagined, couched on beds of amaranth and moly in an essentialist nephelococcygia, is concerned above all else to grapple with the obstinate realities of existential fact. And, having recognized this, we can now go on to consider the existential approach to the knowledge of God's existence.[2]

[1] See pp. 119 f. *infra*.

[2] The present book was completed when M. Maritain's *Court Traité de l'Existence et de l'Existant* and M. Gilson's much longer treatise *L'Être et l'Essence* came into my hands. The reader may perhaps find it interesting to compare M. Maritain's first chapter with the above discussion.

CHAPTER FOUR

THE EXISTENTIAL APPROACH TO THEISM

"Uno itinere non potest pervenire ad tam grande secretum.
SYMMACHUS, *Ep.* x, 3.

"The extreme oddness of existence is what reconciles me to it."
LOGAN PEARSALL SMITH, *All Trivia*, p. 153.

I

I ARGUED in the second chapter of this book that any attempt to prove the actual existence of God—his *existentia ut exercita*—from the consideration of his essence is bound to fail, since essences are grasped by the mind in the formation of concepts, while actual existence is asserted in the affirmation of a judgment. And I illustrated this contention by examining at some length several of the most notable examples of the essentialist approach with which the history of philosophy provides us. Existence, so our thesis runs, cannot be proved from essence, not even the existence of God. How then can it be proved? We might be tempted to suppose that it is immediately apprehended, that if we only look in the right direction we shall see God as plainly as we normally see the beings that compose the finite world. And there is indeed a recurrent strain in Christian thought which asserts that this is in fact the case; it bears the name of "ontologism." God, it asserts, is the primary object of the human intellect; we know him more immediately and more certainly than we know anything else. The persistence of this tendency makes it reasonable to suppose that if it is not actually true it is probably a misunderstanding or a distortion of something that is; and I shall in fact attempt to show that this is so. The grave objection to accepting it as true in fact is that, if it *were* true, God would himself inevitably be proportioned to the human mind. It is noteworthy that

F

ontologism almost invariably issues, either in an immanentism which virtually identifies God with the world or with some one of its characteristics and so denies his transcendence, or else in a view of man as naturally divine which virtually denies man's creatureliness; on this ground as much as on any other it was officially condemned by the Roman Church in 1861.[1] Both logically and historically, it is a natural development of the anthropomorphic element which we have already noticed in Descartes.[2] For if we take Descartes' doctrine that we have a clear and distinct idea of God and then eliminate from it Descartes' representationalism, we shall be left with the view that God himself is the adequate and proportionate object of the human mind. The inevitable outcome of ontologism is a blurring of the distinction between God and his creatures. If, then, God's existence can neither be proved from the examination of his essence nor be immediately apprehended, is there anything else from which it might conceivably be known? There would seem to be only one other possible starting-point, namely, the existence of finite beings. We are thus led to propound this question: Can we, starting from the existence of finite beings, validly affirm the existence of God?

That this question must be answered in the affirmative was the conviction of the dominant school of thought in that great period of Western theology which began with the rejection of the ontological argument by St. Thomas Aquinas and ended with its revival by Descartes. Indeed, most of those Christian philosophers who have accepted the ontological argument have been ready to give to this cosmological approach an honourable, if a subsidiary, place. For the Thomist school, however, it provides the chief, if not indeed the only, foundation for a rational demonstration of the existence of God, and its classical exposition is in the famous Five Ways of the third article of the second question of the First Part of the *Summa Theologica*. St. Thomas's own exposition of the argument was, of course, adapted to the circumstances of his time and was deeply influenced by the sources from which he derived it.[3] For a

---

[1] Denz, 1659 f.   [2] Ch. ii, p. 27, *supra*.
[3] On this point reference may be made to Fr. Hilary Carpenter's article on "The Historical Aspect of the *Quinque Viae*" in the volume *God*, edited by Fr. C. Lattey.

detailed discussion of it I may perhaps be allowed to refer the reader to the relevant sections of my previous book *He Who Is*,[1] though I shall have some more to say about it in the present chapter. I shall begin by recalling, that, although in its structure each of St. Thomas's Five Ways has the form of a hypothetical constructive syllogism, the heart of the argument is found not in the recognition that the conclusion follows from the premisses but in the recognition that the major premiss is true. For example, the Third Way, when reduced to its essentials, argues thus:

If there exists a contingent being there must exist a Necessary Being.

But there do exist contingent beings.

Therefore, there exists a Necessary Being.

(And "this all men speak of as God.")

The truth of the minor premiss is obvious. Contingent beings—beings which come into existence and pass away, and whose existence is therefore not necessary—are known to us in our daily experience. But on what grounds are we able to assert that the existence of such beings involves the existence of a Necessary Being? Not, surely, by a mere logical play upon the words "necessary" and "contingent," but by an intimate metaphysical grasp of what contingency, as our experience reveals it to us, really is. And it is just this grasp that the modern mind, since the days of Hume, finds it so difficult to achieve. As I have written elsewhere, in the book to which I have just referred,

"In practice the argument is either accepted or rejected as a whole, according as we have or have not come to know the things of this world as being what they really are. And this contention is strengthened by the fact that in the hands of St. Thomas the argument does not simply assert that the proposition 'Necessary Being exists' is a logical consequence of the proposition 'Contingent being exists,' but maintains that contingent being derives its own existence from Necessary Being; in other words, that we are not concerned just with logical relations between propositions, but with metaphysical or ontological relations between existent beings.

[1] Ch. v and vi.

"What is necessary, in short, if we are to pass from a belief in the existence of finite beings to a belief in the existence of God is not so much that we should thoroughly instruct ourselves in the laws and procedures of formal logic as that we should thoroughly acquaint ourselves with finite beings, and learn to know them as they really are."[1]

It is, I think, interesting to notice that modern expositors of St. Thomas, while they are very far from belittling the syllogistic form of his argument, have come to lay more and more stress upon the datum which it presupposes, namely the immediate recognition of the very nature of finite being as such. So strict a Thomist as Fr. Garrigou-Lagrange quotes with approval the assertion of Scheeben that "the proof which is necessary for every man in order to attain full certitude is so easy and so clear that one hardly notices the logical procedure which it implies, and that the scientifically developed proofs, so far from giving man his first certitude of the existence of God, only illuminate and consolidate that which already exists."[2] Dom Mark Pontifex, in his recently published Thomist essay on *The Existence of God*, hardly refers to the Five Ways at all, but insists that the direct object of our knowledge is "effect-implying-cause."[3] This does not, it is perhaps needless to say, imply ontologism. "The concept from which we start," he writes, "is effect-implying-cause, and we cannot consider the source of being entirely apart from the creature whose being we are considering. We only know the first cause in and through the created essence, and cannot know it except in this way. . . . We can focus our attention on the idea of the source of being as the element in the background of the double concept, effect-implying-cause, with which we start; but if we try to bring it into the foreground and isolate it and look at it directly, we find ourselves at once looking, not at the first cause as such, but once again at a limited essence with the cause in the background."[4] For this writer, the basis of the argument is the recognition that in finite beings essence and existence are really distinct, that is, that there is nothing in their essence that necessitates their

---

[1] *He Who Is*, p. 73. [2] *Dieu, son existence et sa nature*, p. 233.
[3] Op. cit., p. 31. [4] Ibid., p. 32.

existence.[1] Once this is clearly apprehended all the rest follows, and although the plain man would not express this fundamental fact about finite being in the language of the philosopher, the fact itself is one which he is perfectly capable of grasping, and all the Five Ways are merely different procedures for bringing it into the open. Dr. Sherwood Taylor has pointed out that "before the separation of science and the acceptance of it as the sole valid way of apprehending nature, the vision of God in nature seems to have been the normal way of viewing the world, nor could it have been remarked as an exceptional experience."[2] It may well be that the necessity of approaching the existence of God by the way of argument is the price that we have to pay for our increasing sophistication; if this is so, we must be prepared to foot the bill. In adopting the way of argument we are not, however, claiming access to an approach which is denied to the plain man; we are merely examining that approach in order more confidently to make use of it ourselves. "There is no question," writes Dr. A. M. Farrer in his book *Finite and Infinite*, "of demonstrating God from the creatures by a pure inference. God, being a unique existent, must be apprehended if he is to be known at all. But . . . he must be apprehended in the cosmological relation [that is, his relation to the finite world] and not in abstraction from it."[3] One of the most important features of Dr. Farrer's book consists in the thorough and systematic discussion which he devotes to the question: "What sort of thing would a proof of God's existence be?" as a necessary preliminary to any attempt to provide such a proof. In the case of St. Thomas it must be admitted that no such preliminary investigation is given; before he has come to the end of the second question of his great work he claims to have demonstrated that God exists. It would, however, be quite wrong to conclude that the point is absent from his mind. No one has ever been more constantly aware than St. Thomas

[1] It might perhaps be suggested that to apprehend finite being as effect-implying-cause is to go a stage further than merely to apprehend it as being in which essence does not imply existence. This may possibly be so, in the sense that it requires a more deeply penetrating act of apprehension, but it does not require a different type of apprehensive act.

[2] *The Fourfold Vision*, p. 91.   [3] Op. cit., p. 45.

that God is an absolutely unique being and that in consequence his existence must be proved in an altogether unique
manner. That this is not immediately evident is perhaps
chiefly due to the fact that the form of his argument, though
not its content, is largely derived from pre-Christian sources.

II

There is, I believe, considerable significance to be found in
the fact that St. Thomas assumes without further discussion
that each of his Five Ways demonstrates the existence of the
same being, which is identical with the Christian God. At
first sight this is surprising. First, by what he describes as the
prima et manifestior via, he argues that there must be a first
mover which is itself unmoved; "and this," he serenely observes,
"everyone understands to be God." Next, he tells us there
must be a first efficient cause, itself uncaused, and to this
"everyone gives the name of God." The Third Way argues
to a first necessary being, and again we are told that "this all
men speak of as God." The Fourth Way is the famous and
much discussed argument from degrees of perfection; it claims
to demonstrate the existence of a being which is absolutely
and infinitely perfect, "and this we call God." Lastly, the
finality inherent in the processes of this world is alleged to
show that there is a supreme intelligence which directs all
natural things to their end, and "this being," the argument
concludes, "we call God."

The objection that, even if they are separately valid, the Five
Ways might very well indicate the existence of five different
beings who govern the universe as a kind of celestial committee,[1] is so obvious that many expositors of St. Thomas have
felt it necessary to argue explicitly that these five beings are in
fact identical. Thus Dr. Phillips, in his manual *Modern
Thomistic Philosophy*, writes as follows:

"They [*sc.* the Five Ways] lead us to five attributes which,
in fact, are proper to God; namely: *primum movens, primum
efficiens, primum necessarium, primum et maxime ens, primum gubernans*

[1] The fact of evil might be adduced as suggesting that the committee was not
altogether unanimous.

intelligendo. These attributes can, in fact, only belong to a being whose essence and existence are identical; and the proof of the existence of God is essentially incomplete until this has been shown to be true."[1]

Accordingly, Dr. Phillips proceeds to argue, taking the conclusions of the Five Ways one by one, that they can only apply to a being in which essence and existence are really identical and that, in consequence, since there can only be one such being, the Ways all lead to the same God and not to five different beings each supreme in its own sphere. His argument is not in itself unconvincing, but I find it difficult to believe that it really represents the cast of St. Thomas's own thought. For it seems, to say the least, unlikely that so glaring a gap as this interpretation supposes to exist in the Angelic Doctor's own exposition can have been altogether overlooked by him, or that he can have supposed it to be adequately bridged merely by the repeated assertion that everyone will agree that "this" is what is meant by God. I think that the explanation lies further back and that when it is found it is profoundly revealing. As I see it, the ultimate function of the Five Ways is to make it plain, by calling attention to five outstanding features of finite being, what the fundamental characteristic of finite being is. And that fundamental characteristic is a radical inability to account for its own existence. In other words, finite being is being in which essence and existence are really distinct; in which, therefore, existence is not self-maintained but is received from without and, in the last resort, is received from a being whose existence is not received but is self-inherent. The Five Ways are therefore not so much five different demonstrations of the existence of God as five different methods of manifesting the radical dependence of finite being upon God, of declaring, in Dom Pontifex's phrase, that the very essence of finite being is to be effect-implying-cause. It is only in this way, it seems to me, that a satisfactory understanding can be found of a further point on which I have not so far commented, namely the use that in the first three Ways is made of the impossibility of an infinite regress. In the First Way, for example, it is argued, first, that whatever is "in

[1] Op. cit., II, p. 292. Cf. Garrigou-Lagrange, *Dieu*, pp. 338 f.

motion"[1] must be put in motion by something else, and then that it is impossible to go to infinity, since in that case there would be no first mover and consequently no motion at all. Therefore, St. Thomas concludes, "it is necessary to arrive at some first mover which itself is not moved by anything; and everyone understands this to be God." Now, as it is frequently interpreted, this argument is open to the objection, among others, that it does not necessitate any immediate influence exerted by God upon the being first considered. A is mobile, therefore its motion is derived from B; if B too is mobile, its motion must be derived from C; and so on, until we arrive at God who, himself unmoved and immobile, initiates the whole process. God moves some finite being Z, Z moves Y, and so on, until we come to C moving B, and B moving A. *Ultimately*, therefore, A's own motion would be derived from God, but it would not be derived from him *immediately*; it would in fact be immediately derived from B. Now it is perfectly clear from his thought as a whole that St. Thomas does not envisage God's causal efficacy as being of this remote kind. He is, of course, thoroughly convinced of the real efficacy of secondary causes, and to deny their reality would be, for him, to destroy the very foundation of the argument from finite being to God. But he also sees God's primary causality as exerted immediately upon every one of his creatures and not merely as stimulating the secondary causality of some one of them. Even if we were to suppose that God communicated *motion* purely mediately, we could not suppose this about his communication of *existence*. St. Thomas is explicit that to create (that is, to give *existence*) belongs to God alone,[2] and he repudiates in so many words the view of Peter Lombard[3] that God can communicate to a creature the power of creating. It is clear, therefore, in spite of first appearances, that if the First Way is really an argument for the existence of God it must be something much more than the mere demonstration of a first mover in the order of motion. And this fact has, of course, been almost universally recognized by Thomist commentators, who insist that the first and un-

---

[1] For St. Thomas, it must be remembered, as for Aristotle, "motion" means any kind of change, not merely change of locality.

[2] *S. Theol.*, I, xlv, 5.   [3] Ibid. Cf. Lombard, *Sent.*, l. 4, d. 5.

moved mover cannot merely operate at the beginning of the series but must be active in the series as a whole.[1] The only difficulty about this is that St. Thomas does not say it when he is expounding the argument from motion and that the argument itself, as he develops it, does not seem to imply it. There is no doubt that he believed it, as appears from his whole discussion of the relation of God to the world in the treatise on Creation;[2] our present problem arises from the fact that it does not seem to be involved in what is for him the most important argument for the existence of God. I suspect that the answer is partly to be found in the fact that in the earlier part of the *Summa Theologica* he is making as many concessions as possible to the limitations of the "beginners" for whom the work was written,[3] and that he expects them to deepen their comprehension as their study of the work proceeds. But I also cannot help thinking that he is handicapped by his determination to follow so far as is possible the exposition of Aristotle, though the transformation that Aristotle ultimately undergoes in the process is quite cataclysmic. (In the statement of the argument from motion in the earlier *Summa contra Gentiles* the influence of Aristotle is even more evident.[4]) In any case the question remains: How are we to understand the Prima Via in order to bring it into line with St. Thomas's thought as a whole? In particular how are we to understand the words *Non est procedere in infinitum* ?

The real point of the argument is, I am convinced, not that we *cannot* proceed to infinity, but that it does not get us any nearer the solution of our problem if we do. The problem itself is that of the occurrence of change—motion, in St. Thomas's sense of the word. That the things of the world undergo change is indubitable—*certum est et sensu constat aliqua moveri in hoc mundo*—potentialities are constantly being actualized. Now how is this actualization of potentialities to be accounted for? If it came from the beings themselves all their potentialities would have been actualized from the very first moment of their existence. Every potentiality would be actualized at the start or it never could be actualized at all

---

[1] Cf. Garrigou-Lagrange, *Dieu*, p. 246.   [2] *S. Theol.*, I, xliv–xlix.
[3] Cf. the Prologue.   [4] *S.c.G.*, I, xiii. Cf. *He Who Is*, pp. 40 f.

and so would not in fact be a potentiality. If everything that was needed in order for a seed to become a plant came from the seed itself, then as soon as the seed existed it would be a plant, for everything that the seed itself could provide would be there from the beginning and *ex hypothesi* nothing could come from without. The mere fact of change, then, is an indication that finite beings are not self-contained; they receive influences from outside themselves. Whence, then, do they receive them? Can it be from other finite beings? It may be so, but in that case what are we to say of the changes that the other finite beings undergo? We began with one mutable being, whose mutability we wished to account for; now we have two or more. There is obviously no way out along this road; each problem as it arises is solved only at the expense of raising others of the same kind. *Non est procedere in infinitum*, not in the sense that the infinite regress is impossible but that it leads us no nearer to the solution of our problem. (Similarly the notice "No Thoroughfare" does not necessarily forbid our entering a street, but only informs us that if we do enter it we shall not get any nearer to our destination.) The explanation of motion therefore cannot be found in the realm of mobile beings; it must be sought in a different direction altogether. That is the real lesson which the First Way forces upon us; the first mover must itself be motionless not merely in such a way as to provide the sequence of *moventia* and *mota* with a first term, but in such a way as to maintain the motion which is a feature of the sequence as a whole. It is this last point that the First Way, as St. Thomas actually expounds it, fails to elicit. He does indeed make it plain that the first mover, just because it is itself unmoved, must be of a radically different nature from all the other terms in the series; that it is, in fact, not merely at the beginning of the series, but outside it. The situation is not that indicated by Fig. 1, but that indicated by Fig. 2.

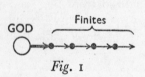

Fig. 1

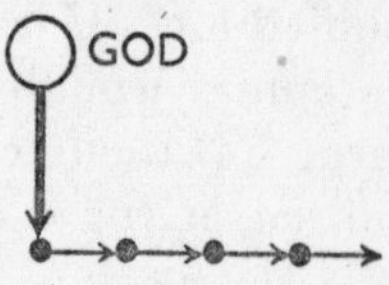

Fig. 2

This, however, is far less than we require and is far less than is involved in St. Thomas's thought as a whole. As the treatise on Creation shows, he does in fact maintain that, without suppressing or superseding the secondary causality of creatures, God's primary causality operates directly upon *every* element of every finite process, englobing as it were all the secondary causes. This is the situation indicated by Fig. 3. The essential

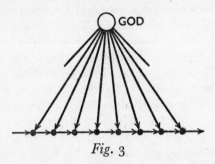

Fig. 3

point is that God does not merely initiate the motion but sustains it, and the weakness of the First Way is that it fails to make this clear.[1]

A criticism which is in all essentials precisely similar to the above may be levelled against the Second and Third Ways, which argue to the existence of a first uncaused efficient cause and a first necessary being respectively, and in both of which the impossibility of an infinite regress is urged. It is of course perfectly true, as has often been pointed out, that all that is

---

[1] The case is not substantially altered if we replace the linear sequence of finite movers by an interrelated network. The essential contrast is that between a view in which God's activity operates directly upon *all* the finite beings, englobing them and their own activities, and a view in which his activity bears upon *some* of them only, leaving the other beings external to it and only mediately affected by it.

It may be added that, in view of Newton's First Law of Motion, according to which no impressed force is needed to sustain a body in uniform rectilinear motion, some modern scholastics have taken the view that St. Thomas's First Way can no longer be applied to the case of local motion. This concession seems to me to rest upon a confusion between metaphysical causality and the purely descriptive causality of the physical sciences. But I should say myself that even if there were no processes of change in the finite world at all, a cosmological argument could be based upon the world's finite character. If this is so, the partial character of the First Way is even more obvious. But in any case, Newton's First Law, conceived as an exact statement, belongs to the pre-Einsteinian era of physical science.

demonstrated is the impossibility of an infinite regress of *essentially* subordinated causes. It is also true that St. Thomas was not concerned to deny the rational possibility that the world had existed for an infinite time; his well-known work *De aeternitate mundi* shows that.[1] The fact remains that any argument based upon the notion of a regress can never prove more than that God acts at the beginning of the sequence, whether that sequence be a temporal sequence or not. We can see from the place that it holds in the *Summa contra Gentiles* the extent to which St. Thomas looked upon the argument from motion as of supreme importance; almost the whole of the subsequent discussion in that work depends upon it. And in the *Summa Theologica* the quite crucial question on the Simplicity of God is explicitly based upon the First Way. And even when we recognize that the other ways are made use of in deducing other divine attributes, the difficulty which was pointed out at the beginning of this discussion remains, that no justification has been given for the assumption that each of the Five Ways in fact proves the existence of the same being. Is there any way out of this tangle?

III

In trying to answer this question we shall, I think, find a pointer in the much discussed Fourth Way, the argument from degrees of perfection. In this St. Thomas argues from the occurrence in nature of perfections which are in ordered relations to one another—"among beings there are some more and some less good, true, noble, and the like"—to the existence of a being in which all these perfections occur without limitation. The commonest objection that is brought against the argument is that it is only the ontological argument in a concealed form. But whatever its weakness it is not that, for it argues not from the mere notion of limited perfections but from their actual concrete existence. I have discussed the Fourth

[1] It is clear that St. Thomas saw nothing repugnant to reason in the notion of an infinite temporal succession of finite beings, though he held, on the ground of revelation, that the world had in fact a beginning in time. On the question of the possibility of an infinite multitude of *simultaneous* beings his thought seems to have somewhat wavered; see Garrigou-Lagrange, *Dieu*, pp. 78 f.; Lallemand, *Le Transfini*, pp. 222 f. In any case the argument in the text is not affected.

Way at some length elsewhere;[1] here I am concerned with it
only for the light which it throws upon the real bearing of the
Five Ways as a whole. And for our present purpose its significance is that it makes no use of the idea of an infinite regress.
The observation that some things are more perfect than others
is not made in order to suggest that in any way the less perfect
receive anything from the more perfect, but in order to emphasize the fact that all of them are limited in their perfection.
When this has been established, the argument goes on to assert
that if a being possesses perfection and yet possesses it only in a
limited degree, it must receive it from a being which possesses
it unconditionally and without limitation. If a being does *not*
receive perfection, then either it cannot possess it at all or it
must possess it without limitation. Thus, the fact that beings
exist with limited perfection declares their immediate dependence upon a being that is absolutely and infinitely perfect.
It would be quite easy to insert an infinite regress here to make
this Way correspond with the first three; the significant fact
is that St. Thomas does not do so. It could quite well be argued
that, if a being has limited perfection, that perfection must be
received from another being, and that if that other being has
limited perfection it must be received from a third being; and
so we could proceed until we came to a being which possessed
perfection fully and completely in its own right. And this, we
should conclude, all men will understand to be God. The fact
that St. Thomas makes no use of such a regress in the Fourth
Way gives, I suggest, strong grounds for holding that its
occurrence in the first three Ways is really little more than a
historical accident. He found the regress-form in Aristotle[2]
and he was, as we know, extremely anxious to show that
Aristotle's arguments, if properly understood, would lead not
to the God of Aristotle but to the God of Christianity. Such a
procedure may have been well adapted to the needs of his
time, but it does not seem to be particularly relevant to those
of the present day. And we have already noticed that modern
exponents of St. Thomas do not for the most part lay very much
stress upon it. This does not, however, mean that the Five
Ways have nothing to teach us. Their primary function, as I

<hr>

[1] *He Who Is*, pp. 52 f.   [2] *Physics*, viii.

believe, is not to provide us with five different proofs of God's existence—viewed as such they are, as we have seen, open to the objection which St. Thomas never directly rebuts, that it is by no means evident that they all terminate in the same God. Their function is to exhibit to us five different characteristics of finite beings, all of which show that it does not account for its own existence. In the last resort St. Thomas has only one datum for an argument for the existence of God, namely the existence of beings whose existence is not necessitated by their essence; that is, beings in which essence and existence are really distinct. The Five Ways are not so much syllogistic *proofs* that finite being is of this type as *discussions* of finite being which may help us to apprehend that it is. Considered as proofs they may well seem to be circular. Anyone who cannot see that the essence of finite beings does not involve their existence is hardly likely to admit that they are contingent in the precise sense that the Third Way requires. Nevertheless, the fact to which the Third Way calls our attention may assist us to understand their true nature. It must be added that even when we have recognized that finite being is of this type, the process by which we go on to affirm the existence of God is hardly to be described as a "proof" in the usual sense of that term. The existence of being in which essence and existence are really distinct does not *logically* imply the existence of a being in which essence and existence are really identical.[1] We can, of course, put the argument from finite to infinite in a syllogistic form, but when we do so we are not so much describing the process by which we have passed from the recognition of the finite to the affirmation of the infinite as convincing ourselves that the transition was not in fact unreasonable. The transition itself was made in the recognition that being whose essence is really distinct from its existence declares by its very existence the creative activity of God. In other words the primary requirement if we are to pass from the recognition of the finite to the affirmation of the infinite is not that we shall be skilled in the manipulation of Aristotelian

---

[1] I do not myself agree with those scholastics who maintain that the passage from the finite to the infinite in the cosmological approach simply involves the use of the "principle of contradiction."

logic but that we shall grasp in its ontological reality the act
by which finite existents exist.   And then we shall affirm God
by recognizing him.   We shall recognize him not, as ontologists
affirm, in his naked reality, but as the primary agent of the
act by which finite beings exist; in Dr. Farrer's phrase, we
apprehend him in the cosmological relation and not in abstraction from it.   There is one act of intellection in which we
recognize both the real distinction of essence and existence in
the finite existent and also its dependence upon the being in
which essence and existence are identical.   In Dom Pontifex's
phrase, the direct object of our experience is "effect-implying-
cause."[1] /The Five Ways are not really five different methods
of proving the existence of God, but five different aids to the
apprehension of God and the creature in the cosmological
relation; they exhibit the cosmological relation under five
different aspects.   And if we understand them so we can see
that they are no longer incoherent with the rest of St. Thomas's
system.   We may not find them very useful to us as twentieth-
century men; we may have other ways of recognizing the
fundamental fact about finite existents.   But they will no
longer be an embarrassment to us.   And the radically existential
nature of St. Thomas's thought will then appear in its fulness.
To exist is not just to lie about the place exemplifying characteristics; it is to *do something*, to be exercising an activity, to be
tending to an end; to make this plain is the real function of
the Fifth Way, the "argument from finality."   And to exist
as a finite being is to be exercising this activity without at the
same time being the ultimate ground for the possibility of
exercising it.   No amount of examination of concepts helps us
to approach God in this way; we can do so only by grasping
an existent being in its existential act.

---

[1] I cannot literally agree with Dr. Farrer when he writes that "the premise of
St. Thomas's *Via Prima* is not 'constat quaedam moveri in hoc mundo' but is the
habit men have of reading into the system of events an absolute agency which
can find its ultimate agent in God alone" (*Finite and Infinite*, p. 10, second italics
mine). I should say that the premiss was not the "habit", but what the habit
discovers, namely the radically dependent character of finite being. And I am
not too happy about the word "habit" in this context anyhow.

IV

In the light of what has been said above we can, I think, account for the attraction which ontologism has had for many Christian thinkers. The whole bearing of our discussion has been to assert that the existence of God is not inferred by a logical process but apprehended in a cognitive act. The ontologist is so carried away by this discovery that he fails to notice that the object of his apprehension is not God in his naked reality but God as manifested in his creative activity in finite being; more accurately, the object is finite being as manifesting God in his creative act. The ontologist is correct in his conviction that he is apprehending God, but he has overlooked the fact that he is apprehending God in the cosmological relation and not in abstraction from it. For this reason there is only a step—and it is a step that is easily taken— between ontologism and pantheism. For since, in their different ways, both God and the creature are apprehended in the same act it is all too easy to confuse them; that is, to mistake the cosmological relation for sheer identity. In itself, pantheism, whether in its sophisticated form or in the more popular guise of polytheistic idolatry, is an error of the most lamentable kind; but, as history shows, it is one into which it is only too easy for men to fall if they are not protected by a revealed religion of a jealously monotheistic type. It is not indeed an error to which present-day Anglo-Saxons are very seriously exposed, but this is not so much because they are firmly attached to monotheism as because they are almost entirely uninterested in religion. Whether they are in better or worse case than the polytheistic idolater is a question which we are not here called upon to decide.

It will be well at this point to observe that, although the preceding discussion has perforce been conducted in technical language, the apprehension of God with which it has been concerned is not one which it requires any philosophical training to achieve. I would repeat Dr. Sherwood Taylor's observation that, in earlier days, "the vision of God in nature seems to have been the normal way of viewing the world, nor

could it have been remarked as an exceptional experience."
The plain man need not be able to analyse systematically the
apprehension of God and the creature in the cosmological
relation; he need not indeed necessarily know that the apprehension of God and the creature in the cosmological relation is
what he is in fact having. What *is* important is that he should
have it. And, as things are at present, it looks as if, in spite
of everything, he is rather more likely to have it than the
philosopher is. For since the time of Hume at any rate, the
assertion that the existence of God can be known from the
existence of the finite world has been, to say the least of it,
unpopular in philosophical circles. Indeed, to assert that the
finite world can be known to "exist" in any sense which would
require an explanation for its existence would be dismissed as
a piece of quaint medieval superstition by most of those who
teach or study philosophy in our modern British universities.
The word "substance" has ceased to denote anything except
a recurrent and persistent pattern of sense-data or a constellation of mental states, and "causality," if the word is used at
all, has come to indicate nothing but a regularity in the
succession of phenomena. It is true that a tendency has
recently become observable to hold that sentences which
purport to be about substances are not logically reducible to
sentences which are wholly about sense-data, but this must
not be interpreted as indicating the revival of a belief that
substances exist; it is equally consistent with the view that
sentences which purport to be about substances are in fact
about nothing at all[1]. In the place of a realist metaphysic
which held the world to be composed of interacting beings we
are offered a radical sensationalism which holds it to be
nothing but a series of phenomenal patterns; indeed there are
many who would go further than this and reduce philosophy
to mere logic, concerned with the logical relations of propositions, or to mere linguistic, concerned with the syntactical
relations of words. For systems such as these, to say that the
fundamental characteristic of finite being is to be effect-
implying-cause is simply to make meaningless noises. It must
be frankly admitted that there can be no possibility of proving

---

[1] See additional note on p. 91.

the existence of God to adherents of these systems on their own terms. A God who was only a regulative principle of the realm of phenomena, or a category of logic, or a linguistic term, would *ex hypothesi* not be the God whose existence the theist is concerned to establish. Unless we can rehabilitate the notions of substance, existence and causality we can neither demonstrate nor even intelligibly affirm the existence of a Being which, itself self-existent, causes the existence of everything else that exists. But in saying this we are not asserting that substance, existence and causality must be taken with the meanings which they are commonly supposed to have. Most of the tragedy of modern philosophy arises, I believe, from the fact that, having rightly rejected certain quite indefensible views about certain fundamental notions, it has assumed that the notions themselves are discredited. I would instance the case of Locke's view of substances as beings of the sensible order with the secondary qualities strained out. No such view could survive criticism, and Berkeley made short work of it. What he left undone was completed by Hume, and since their time little has been heard about substance among philosophers whose approach is fundamentally empirical. Locke's view of substance is, however, by no means the only possible one, and his very invention of it was a concession to the sensationalism which ultimately destroyed it. It was his assumption that perception is nothing but sensation which led him to conclude that the realities which we perceive can have no characteristics that are not of the sensible order. But the refutation of Locke leaves altogether unaffected the doctrine of substances as beings of the intelligible order, grasped by us in a perceptive act which includes intellection as well as sensation. Very few philosophers, however, down to the present day have noticed this, with the exception of a few scholastics to whom no one would listen. Perhaps the most obvious weakness of the positivist school in its rejection of the notions of substance, existence and causality lies in its failure to explain satisfactorily why such notions have been held by intelligent people. There is always something profoundly unsatisfactory in proving that a widely held theory is false if you are not able to explain on your own principles why it has in fact been widely held. The most that the positivists can do to account for the fact that people have universally believed in the existence of a real world of substances causally interacting is to suggest that they have projected into the world of sensible phenomena certain characteristics of their own internal experience. When we shift a heavy object we have a certain feeling in our muscles of overcoming resistance, and so we assume the occurrence of something similar when one heavy object, as we say, "moves" another. But nobody in fact (with the possible exception of Leibniz) has ever held that when two stones come into contact they feel what I feel when I push a stone. Instead of rejecting causality as an illusion, it is far more reasonable to suppose that it is a universal characteristic of the external world, although, by the nature of the case, the causality which I myself exert is the only kind of causality that I can "feel." And when it is alleged that my attribution of substantiality to the external world is only a projection into it of my own psychological coherence, is it not far more reasonable to suppose that I do actually apprehend the world as substantial, although, as must obviously be the case if that is so, my own substantiality is the only substantiality that I can experience as its personal subject?[1]

These rather random remarks will, I fear, do little to convince the positivist, for he has put himself under a self-denying ordinance which prohibits him from recognizing any object that is not purely phenomenal. Even if he admitted the possibility of substance and causality, his own technique would prevent him from apprehending any particular instance of it. With a quite hyper-Cartesian fear of being deluded, he has restricted the realm of philosophy to sense-data and psychological states, and anything that cannot be reduced to these is

[1] Very few people, I think, have had such a vivid apprehension of the reality and actuality of finite beings as the late G. K. Chesterton. It is seen in his discussion of the Thomist attitude to Being in his brilliant little book *St. Thomas Aquinas* (ch. vi). It comes out in quite another form in the following extract from a letter to his fiancée, to which Dr. W. G. Peck has kindly drawn my attention: "I am black but comely at this moment; because the cyclostyle has blacked me. . . . I like the cyclostyle ink; it is so inky. I do not think there is anyone who takes quite such a fierce pleasure in things being themselves as I do. The startling wetness of water excites and intoxicates me: the fieriness of fire, the steeliness of steel, the unutterable muddiness of mud" (Maisie Ward, *Gilbert Keith Chesterton*, p. 97).

ipso facto excluded from his system. This does not, however, prove that nothing else exists; it only proves that if it does exist the positivist cannot see it. Such an excess of caution is in fact not proper to man; we are far more likely to discover the true nature of the world if we use the faculties with which nature has provided us and learn from our mistakes. It is the refusal of so many philosophers to be fully human when they are philosophizing that has led to the general discredit of philosophy at the present day; to the ordinary man it appears as a complicated game played by certain people with a flair for it, instead of as something which may help him in the problems of life. Perhaps the only way in which we can hope to shake the positivist is by assisting him to realize the gulf which separates his philosophizing from his ordinary human activity in the day-by-day business of living. It may be remembered that Hume, the father of all the positivists, could only console himself for the scepticism to which his philosophizing reduced him by the reflection that it was impossible to be a philosopher all the time.[1] The most we can do with the positivist is to catch him off duty; the one thing we must not do is to try to prove our conclusions from his premises.

I shall therefore assume that the notions of causality, substance and existence need not be abandoned, but I must also make it clear that we are not in consequence committed to a revival of all the details of Aristotelian metaphysics. I have argued at some length in this chapter that the highly Aristo-

---

[1] "The *intense* view of these manifold contradictions and imperfections in human reason has so wrought upon me, and heated my brain, that I am ready to reject all belief and reasoning, and can look upon no opinion even as more probable or likely than another. Where am I, or what? From what causes do I derive my existence, and to what condition shall I return? Whose favour shall I court, and whose anger must I dread? What beings surround me? and on whom have I any influence, or who have any influence on me? I am confounded with all these questions, and begin to fancy myself in the most deplorable condition imaginable, environed with the deepest darkness, and utterly deprived of the use of every member and faculty.

"Most fortunately it happens, that since reason is incapable of dispelling these clouds, Nature herself suffices to that purpose, and cures me of this philosophical melancholy and delirium, either by relaxing this bent of mind, or by some avocation, and lively impression of my senses, which obliterate all these chimeras. I dine, I play a game of backgammon, I converse, and am merry with my friends; and when, after three or four hours' amusement, I would return to these speculations, they appear so cold, and strained, and ridiculous, that I cannot find in my heart to enter into them any further" (*Treatise of Human Nature*, Book I, Part IV, *ad fin.* (Everyman's ed., I, p. 253)).

telian form which St. Thomas gives to his argument for the existence of God is not essential to it and moreover that, for us at the present day, it clouds to some extent the real issue. What *is* necessary is the recognition of finite being as being in which there is a real distinction of essence and existence, as something which is *there* and yet need not be there, as perfect in its degree and yet not self-subsistent perfection, as being whose very limitation declares that whatever it is and has it receives from without, as an effect implying a cause that possesses in its own right all that it communicates. There are still people in whom this grasp of finite being in its dependence can be induced by the study of St. Thomas's Five Ways, but for most of us, I think it comes most easily by quietly contemplating any finite being, however humble, in the attitude of wonder.

> "When all my days are ending
> And I have no song to sing,
> I think I shall not be too old
> To stare at everything;
> As I stared once at a nursery door
> Or a tall tree and a swing.
>
> "Wherein God's ponderous mercy hangs
> On all my sins and me,
> Because He does not take away
> The terror from the tree
> And stones still shine along the road
> That are and cannot be."[1]

It is this recognition that things "are which cannot be"— that is, which cannot account for their own occurrence—that is the necessary basis of the cosmological or existential approach to theism. We shall never become theists if we take the world for granted; but so long as we do *not* take it for granted we are within measurable distance of taking it as granted to us by God.

[1] G. K. Chesterton, *A Second Childhood*. He remarks elsewhere how his kindred spirit G. F. Watts was "dominated throughout by a prehistoric wonder" (*G. F. Watts*, p. 146).

v

We are not yet, however, out of the wood. For in order to give rational justification to the assertion that the existence of God can be affirmed on the basis of our apprehension of finite beings, it is not sufficient to convince ourselves that the notions of substance, existence and causality[1] have reference to a real world and that they are not merely regulative notions which are of use for the correlation of sense-data or phenomena. We must also be convinced that they have relevance to God and his activity and not only to the realm of finite being. That is to say, we must be assured not merely of their ontological validity but of their transcendental validity too. The very essence of the cosmological approach to God is that it claims to declare the existence and the activity of a being which is of a radically different order from that of all finite existents and agents. If God were not of this radically different order, then finite beings could themselves be and do all that we have alleged that God is and does, and the cosmological necessity for God would vanish; the ground would be cut away from under our feet. But if we cannot establish the transcendental validity of the notions mentioned, our very assertions about God will be meaningless, and God will have vanished from our grasp at the very moment in which we affirm him. You have already asserted, we shall be told, that the only existence which you can apprehend is that of finite beings; you denied, in so many words, that you were an ontologist. But now you are saying that you have apprehended the existence of a being which is more than finite. Again, you have told us that the causality which God exerts on finite beings is altogether different from any causality which finite beings themselves can exercise; your whole argument for God's existence depends

---

[1] It is, I hope, unnecessary to point out that in using such a phrase as "the notion of existence" I am not forgetting my previous assertion that existence cannot be included in a concept, but am merely conforming to the necessities of the English language. In saying, for example, that the notion of existence has transcendental validity, I mean nothing more than that it can be significantly affirmed that God exists. The abstract noun "existence" is in fact what the modern logicians would call an "incomplete symbol"; any sentence containing it can be reduced to a sentence containing instead some part of the verb "to exist."

upon your assertion that there is something about finite beings, namely their existence, which no finite cause can confer. But since the only causality of which you, as a finite being, can be aware is the causality which finite beings exercise, in attributing causality to God you are using the word "causality" in a sense to which, on your own hypothesis, it is impossible to attach any meaning. You are in fact in an insoluble dilemma. If you assert existence and causality of God in the same sense in which you assert them of finite beings, you are rendering God incapable of fulfilling the very function for whose performance you alleged him to be necessary. But if you assert existence and causality of God in an altogether different sense from that in which you assert them of finite beings, you are making statements about God to which you can, *ex hypothesi*, assign no intelligible content. God therefore is either useless or unthinkable; this would seem to be the conclusion of the matter. We seem to be on the brink of an ontological argument for the non-existence of God.

The objection just made is a serious one, and it is one to which, in many expositions of theism, far too little attention has been paid. In particular, the absence of any adequate discussion of it is one of the most unsatisfactory features of the work of both James Ward and F. R. Tennant. It would, of course, be very strange if the objection was sound, as in that case not only would it follow that the cosmological approach failed to provide a valid demonstration of the existence of God, but it would remain a complete mystery why the existence of finite being should ever have led people to assert that God exists. The logical positivists say that anyone who makes statements about God is simply talking nonsense. But if so, why is this sort of nonsense talked? This rejoinder may not be a valid refutation of the objection, but it may to some extent clear the air.

The objection in effect accuses the cosmological approach of asserting that we are able to conceive a being and an activity which are *ex hypothesi* inconceivable. But does the cosmological approach in fact make this assertion? All that it does assert is (1) that God exists, and (2) that God causes the existence of finite beings. Now we have already argued at considerable length[1] that existence is not contained in a concept, but is affirmed in a judgment. It may, of course, be replied that in making the judgment "God exists" we must have some sort of concept of God if this very judgment is not to be meaningless; that otherwise we are merely saying "X exists" where X has no intelligible content. But in fact neither of these alternatives is true and they are not exhaustive. In saying "God exists" and "God causes the existence of finite beings," all that we mean by God is "that which exists self-existently." God is not defined by forming a concept of him, but by affirming his mode of existence, and existence is not conceptualizable. God is, of course, given to us in a concept, but not in a concept of God; he is given to us in the concept of finite being, which declares its dependence for existence on a transfinite cause. The proposition "God exists" is indeed a very remarkable proposition; it is of an altogether unique type. The process by which God's existence is inferred is also a very remarkable and altogether unique process. But this is only what we should expect, since God, if there be a God, must be an altogether unique being. The one thing that would be quite destructive of theism would be an argument which claimed to demonstrate God's existence in the same way in which we could demonstrate the existence of anything else. We have not started with a clear and distinct idea of God or with a concept of his essence and then proceeded to discover something that corresponds to this idea or this concept. We have, on the contrary, started from the existence of finite being and found it declaring by its very finitude the existence of a being of which we can form no clear and distinct idea and of whose essence we can form no concept. We can define God only in terms of his self-existence; and existence, as we have just said, is not conceptualizable. We have not claimed, as it were, to understand the mechanism by which God exists or by which he creates the world; we have only claimed that unless God existed and did create the world, the world's existence would itself be unintelligible. From this point of view it might appear that the purpose of our whole procedure has been not to prove the existence of God but to provide the world with a

---

[1] See ch. iii *supra*.

principle of rationality. In a sense this is true; we have after all to start from where we are. But the outcome has been the affirmation of the existence of a God who is self-existent and therefore does not exist just in order that the world may be rational. We have in fact, arrived at the God of whom the Old Testament speaks. *Quoad nos* and *in ordine cognoscendi*, God appears primarily as the world's creator, but, in the very process by which we come to recognize him, he is manifested as existing *quoad seipsum* and *in ordine essendi* in his own right and not for our convenience. The only being who *could* create a world is one for whom a world is unnecessary; only a self-existent being can confer existence.[1] At the beginning of our search, what is given to us is the existence of the world, and the existence of God is problematical. But when we have come to see that the world can only exist if God wills that it should, the ultimate problem is seen to be not whether God exists but why a self-existent God should create anything outside himself. This is the final mystery, and by the nature of the case it is one to which God alone can know the answer.

I must make it plain at this point that the remarks in which I have just been indulging in the last paragraph are not to be considered as an argument for the existence of God. Whether we describe the cosmological approach itself as an argument depends mainly on how the word "argument" is defined. Its crux consists not in a process of logical deduction but in an apprehension, namely the apprehension of finite beings as effect implying (or, better, manifesting) a transcendent cause; in this sense it might perhaps be better, with Mr. E. I. Watkin,

---

[1] I have nowhere seen this fact better expressed than in the following eloquent and militant words of Dr. Farrer:

"Everything else is in real relation to God but for whom it would not be. But in so far as Creation is an act which produces an expression of the Absolute in the inferior mode, it excludes any dependence of the Absolute on what is created or on the activity of creating. Neither can there be any conditionedness of an agent by what exists simply because he acts, and otherwise does not exist. Those who wish to make theology easier for the imagination by receding from this position, have removed every metaphysical reason for believing in God at all. There may be other reasons, and if there are men who have had particular experience of an eminent archangel, let them come forward and depose their testimony. God may condescend to the creature and make his activity wait on ours; that is another matter. He who condescends must be free and absolute in himself. The condescension of God does not belong to rational theology. Revealed theology is about little else". (*Finite and Infinite*, p. 58).

to speak of "monstrations" rather than of "demonstrations" of the existence of God. "The existence of God," he writes, "is not demonstrated, as demonstration is usually understood, namely as a process of cogent but non-intuitive reasoning. It is monstrated to contemplative intellection."[1] This does not, however, mean that argumentation has no place in the matter. Its function is, I believe, threefold; it can, if it is rightly conducted, do something to put us in the frame of mind in which the apprehension of finite beings in their dependence upon God is possible; it can convince us that such apprehension, when it has occurred, is not to be dismissed as an illusion, and it can elucidate its nature and content so far as that is possible. The apprehensive process is of a quite unique type, as from the nature of the case it must be, but it is, I am convinced, profoundly rational. However, it must be repeated that the positivist cannot be converted to theism on his own terms. If a man persists in limiting his gaze to the phenomenal surface of reality there is nothing that can be done about it on the purely human level, except to treat him kindly and to point out to him as gently as possible that by playing for safety in this way he is desperately impoverishing his experience. In our time this sort of metaphysical myopia has become a habit and almost a disease. In the last resort it can be cast out only by prayer and fasting.

There is one further point which must be added; it will provide a transition to the following chapter. I have alleged above that the cosmological approach declares God's existence without claiming to form a concept of him. This is strictly true, in the sense that we do not need to form a concept of God in order to assert that he exists. In St. Thomas's phrase, it tells us that God exists, but does not tell us what he is. It is nevertheless also true that natural theology, and not least the natural theology of St. Thomas, has had a great deal to tell us about the attributes of God. In declaring that God is the source of the existence of all his creatures, it has also asserted that he possesses in himself *formaliter et eminentius* all the perfections that they exemplify in their limited and splintered fashion. For all that they have and are derives from him. And

[1] *A Philosophy of Form*, p. 291.

this involves that, although the mere assertion of his existence does not require resource to concepts, any affirmation about his nature does. We cannot form a concept of God in order to know him; the only alternative is that, in some way, we know him in the concepts which we form of his creatures. To explain how such knowledge is possible and to investigate its nature is the province of the doctrine of analogy, a branch of natural theology which has undergone vast developments since the Angelic Doctor gave the first fully explicit statement of a fundamentally existential approach to theism. Its basis lies in the distinction which it makes between the perfection which we attribute to a being and the manner in which we attribute it, between the *perfectio significata* and the *modus significandi*. The point is one of quite vital importance, and its discussion will need a chapter to itself.

ADDITIONAL NOTE TO CHAPTER FOUR
(See page 81)

Hans Reichenbach in his book *Experience and Prediction*, which was published in 1938, goes so far as to write: "I cannot admit that impressions [i.e., sense data] have the character of observable facts. What I observe are things, not impressions. . . . I do not say that I doubt the existence of my impressions. I believe that there are impressions; but I have never *sensed* them" (p. 164). The realism of this is, however, very much weakened by his doctrine that sentences describing the world are never more than probable. In the last resort Reichenbach remains a positivist.

CHAPTER FIVE

THE DOCTRINE OF ANALOGY

'Εκ γὰρ μεγέθους καλλονῆς κτισμάτων ἀναλόγως ὁ γενεσιουργὸς
αὐτῶν θεωρεῖται.

Wisdom of Solomon, xiii, 5

I

ANY philosophical system which believes in a genuinely
transcendent God is bound sooner or later to find itself
faced with the question: How is it possible for men to talk
about God? This, as Dr. A. M. Farrer has remarked, is not a
problem only for those who believe in natural theology.
"There is a superstition among revelationists," he says, "that
by declaring themselves independent of any proof of God by
analogy from the finite world, they have escaped the necessity
of considering the analogy or relation of the finite to the
infinite altogether. They are completely mistaken; for all their
statements about God must be expressed and plainly are
expressed in language drawn from the finite world. No
revelationist supposes these statements to be perfectly literal;
God is not a man and human language requires to be read
with some tacit qualification before it applies to him. . . . The
problem of analogy is in principle prior to every particular
revelation. For the revelation has to be thought about to be
received, and can be thought about only by the aid of words
or finite images; and these cannot signify of God unless the
appropriate 'mode of signification' functions in our minds."[1]
This is undoubtedly true, however reluctant the revelationists
may be to admit it; nevertheless the doctrine of analogy may
be expected to play a far larger part among those who believe
in natural theology, for in their case it is not merely a question
of explaining how God can be spoken about in language

[1] *Finite and Infinite*, p. 2.

derived from our experience of a finite world or of explaining how some notion of God can be contained in finite minds. There is also the question how the infinite God can be seen to exist from the consideration of finite things, and what relation God can have towards them; for the cosmological theist analogy is not merely a matter of linguistics and of psychology but of metaphysics too. What Dr. Farrer calls "the 'cosmological idea'—the scheme of God and the creature in relation"[1] is fundamental.

This being so, it is surprising how extremely small a place the doctrine of analogy has been given in the thought of Anglican theologians, compared with that which it has received among Roman Catholics. In spite of its title, Bishop Butler's famous work on *The Analogy of Religion Natural and Revealed to the Constitution and Course of Nature* is concerned with it in only the remotest possible way. Bishop Berkeley devoted a few pages[2] to it, owing to his controversy with Dr. Peter Browne, and had apparently studied it in Suarez and Cajetan, but, as Mr. W. W. S. Marsh has remarked,[3] he failed to work out its applications. Dr. G. C. Joyce briefly outlined it in an article in the *Encyclopaedia of Religion and Ethics*,[4] but obviously did not think it to be of any very great importance; and Dr. Edwyn Bevan, while he devoted nearly half a chapter to it in his Gifford Lectures on *Symbolism and Belief*, confessed himself unable to make any sense of it[5] and found more satisfaction in the theories of Dean Mansel. Modern Roman Catholic theologians, however, under the stress of their controversy with symbolo-fideists and modernists of various kinds, have discussed the doctrine of analogy at great length; for the most part their work is little known in England, but some idea of its extent may be gained from the list of books and articles given in the Abbé Penido's treatise *Le Rôle de l'Analogie en Théologie Dogmatique*.[6] And it may well be that the neglect of this doctrine among English-speaking thinkers outside the Roman Communion is responsible for much of the unsatisfactoriness of Anglo-Saxon natural theology to-day, for their common failure to find any alternative to a transcendence which makes

---

[1] Ibid., p. 16.   [2] *Alciphron*, Dial. IV, xx, xxi.   [3] *Theology*, June 1942.
[4] Vol. I, pp. 416 f.   [5] p. 315.   [6] p. 12, *n*. 1.

God altogether unknowable other than an immanence which
makes him and the world necessary to each other, is precisely
what the doctrine of analogy was elaborated to avoid. It is
therefore a matter for satisfaction that quite recently two
works by Anglican philosophers have appeared which take it
thoroughly seriously, namely Dr. Farrer's *Finite and Infinite* and
Miss Dorothy Emmet's *Nature of Metaphysical Thinking*. I
intend to give a fairly thorough discussion of both these books
later on;[1] in the present chapter I shall deal with the doctrine
of analogy in its traditional form, which, like most scholastic
doctrines, derives its ultimate parentage from Aristotle, though
it received its full development, under the stimulus of the
Judaeo-Christian belief in a fully transcendent and yet genuinely
creative God, at the hands of the Angelic Doctor and the great
Thomist commentators, especially Cajetan and John of St.
Thomas.

One preliminary remark may be made before the discussion
is opened, namely that the function of the doctrine of analogy
is not to make it possible for us to talk about God in the future
but to explain how it is that we have been able to talk about
him all along. In spite of all that has been said by positivists,
logical and other, we do in fact find ourselves talking about
God, and talking about him in a way that is significant. It is,
I would maintain, transparently clear to anyone whose judgment is not shackled by a predetermined dogma that, if two
men respectively affirm and deny that God exists, they are in
fact disagreeing about the nature of reality, and not merely
expressing different emotional or aesthetic attitudes. There
is, unfortunately, a recurrent tendency among philosophers, in
analysing the mental activities of human beings in general, to
assume that until their analysis and criticism have been satisfactorily completed, nobody has the right to make any affirmations at all; so deeply has Cartesianism entered into our heritage.
The consequence is that the plain man laughs at the philosophers and goes on his own way without them. Against this
tendency we are, as I see it, bound to assert that the task of
any philosophical critique is to account for, to render precise
and, if necessary, to correct the body of doctrine that the

[1] Ch. vii *infra*.

human mind has acquired by the natural exercise of its own powers, but not, except in a purely relative and *ex post facto* way, to provide a justification for the activity of thought itself. To forget this is to doom oneself to a kind of intellectual suicide. For the critical philosopher is himself the heir of his past; before he was a philosopher at all he was a man, and before he was a man he was a child. To enter a second time into the womb and to be born again equipped with a fully developed critique of knowledge is a sheer impossibility. The fact is that, however fallible it may be, the human mind does acquire knowledge by the exercise of the powers which it possesses, and a sane philosophy will recognize this fact. To return, then, to the subject of our present discussion, the doctrine of analogy is not concerned to discover whether discourse about God is antecedently possible, or to endow it with a possibility that was originally absent, but to account for the fact that discourse about God has, as matter of experience, been taking place in spite of various considerations that might seem at first sight to rule its possibility out of court.

I would further add that the question of analogy does not arise at all in the mere proof of the existence of God; it arises only when, having satisfied ourselves that the existence of finite being declares its dependence upon self-existent being, we then apprehend that no predicate can be attributed to finite and to self-existent being univocally. Penido's remarks seem to me to be of the first importance here. "Formally," he writes, "the problem of analogy is a problem of nature, not of existence. We can arrive at the existence of God without *explicit* recourse to analogy, while it is impossible to think about the divine nature without conceiving it as equivocal, univocal or analogous to our own." And again: "It is quite true that the proofs of God are analogical *realities*, otherwise they would prove nothing. But they do not fall under the jurisdiction of the *method* of analogy, as theology employs it. Let us distinguish carefully—without separating them and still more without opposing them—the problem of analogical knowledge and the metaphysical problem of analogy. The former belongs in full right to the treatise on God, while it is only after the treatise on creation that we can approach the latter in its fullness. . . . Does this mean that analogy in no way depends on the *quinque viae*? By no means. Analogy begins at the precise point where the rational demonstration ends."[1] We had no need of any doctrine of analogy in the last chapter, in arguing from the existence of finite beings to the existence of God. When, however, the argument was complete, we saw that the God whose existence we were now asserting was a being of so radically different an order from everything else in our experience that it became a real question whether the word "God" in that context meant anything at all. There can be little satisfaction in demonstrating the existence of a being whom the very demonstration shows to be altogether inapprehensible. God would seem to have slipped from between our hands at the very moment when we had at last laid hold on him. It is at this point that the doctrine of analogy becomes altogether necessary, and it is for this reason that its full investigation only began among Christian philosophers who gave primacy of place to the existential approach to God.

The doctrine, as we find it in the Thomist tradition, appears in at least three distinct departments of philosophy, namely the metaphysical or ontological, the epistemological or psychological, and the logical or linguistic. This is only what we might expect in a fundamentally realist philosophy, which holds that words are not merely noises and that thought is not merely about ideas, but that speech with its words and thought with its ideas are ultimately about things.[2] It is well to make this point clear at the start or we shall find ourselves puzzled to know what precisely is the question with which analogy is concerned. Is it "How can we talk about God?" or "How can we think about God?" or "How are things related to God?"? In fact it is about all three, and we need not be worried by the way in which it slips from one to the other, so long as our

---

[1] *Rôle de l'Analogie*, pp. 85–7. The point, as I see it, of the assertion that, while the proofs of God are analogical realities, they do not fall under the jurisdiction of analogy is that, while any *mode of existing* can only be predicated analogically of God and creatures (since mode of existence is essence and falls under the concept), the act of existing, which is not conceptualizable, can be affirmed without any analogical reservation. There is thus no concession to the doctrine of univocity of being.

[2] "I am not yet so lost in lexicography," wrote Dr. Johnson in the Preface to his Dictionary, "as to forget that words are the daughters of earth, and that things are the sons of heaven."

attitude is confidently realist.[1] I shall, however, take the first question as my starting-point and consider the problem of analogical predication.

Is it possible, we therefore ask, for statements expressed in human language to mean anything when made about God—that is to say, are theological statements meaningful or meaningless? (The relevance of this discussion to the questions raised by the logical positivists will be immediately clear to those who have any acquaintance with their works.) Starting from a famous distinction made by Aristotle,[2] we remark that, even within the realm of discourse about finite beings, one and the same word, when applied to two things, sometimes bears the same sense in both applications and sometimes different ones. In the former case it is used *univocally* (συνονύμως), as when Carlo and Fido are both called dogs. Even if Carlo is a great Dane and Fido a Pomeranian, we mean the same thing about each of them when we call them both *dogs*; the characteristics in each that distinguish Carlo as a Dane from Fido as a Pomeranian, while they cannot be found in their totality except in dogs, are additional to caninity as such. But sometimes we use words purely equivocally (ὁμωνύμως), as when we apply the word "mug" both to a drinking utensil and to the victim of a fraud. (The neglect of this distinction can lead to unfortunate consequences, as the choirboys found who were starting a cricket team, when they asked the vicar for one of the bats which the verger had led them to believe were in the belfry.) But in addition to these two uses, it is alleged, a word is sometimes applied to two objects in senses that are neither wholly different nor yet wholly the same, as when we say that Mr. Jones and Skegness are both healthy, the former because he *enjoys*, and the latter because it *induces*, health; in this case we are said to use the term "healthy" *analogically* (ἀνάλογως).

---

[1] "Tripliciter quaelibet res, ad nos quantum attinet, considerari potest: ut est nempe *in se*, ut est *in intellectu nostro*, ut est *in nostro ore*, '*vox*, a postremo nunc incipiendo, *conceptus in anima*, et *res extra* seu conceptus objectivus', uti ad rem Cajetanus docet (*De Nom. Anal.*, cap. iv, no. 31). Triplex hinc exsurgit ordo: ordo videlicet *essendi*, ordo *cognoscendi*, ordo *significandi*" (S. Alvarez-Menendez, Introduction to Cajetan, *De Nominum Analogia* (1934), p. viii).

[2] *Categories*, I. It is true that in this text Aristotle mentions only univocity and equivocity, though elsewhere he makes considerable use of the notion of analogy. Cajetan remarks *à propos* of this text that logicians (in contrast to philosophers) call analogy of attribution equivocation (*De Nom. Anal.*, cap. ii, no. 19).

H

At first sight the introduction of this mode of predication might seem to be unnecessary and trivial, and certainly Aristotle did not accord to it anything like as much attention as the scholastics do. We might be tempted to suppose that analogy is only a dignified kind of univocity, and that it is quite sufficient to say that the healthiness of Mr. Jones and the healthiness of Skegness are merely two ways of being healthy, just as the Danishness of Carlo and the Pomeranianity of Fido are merely two ways of being canine. Or, alternatively, we might go to the other extreme and say that analogy is only equivocity in sheep's clothing, that to enjoy health and to induce health are two altogether different activities and that only for the sake of economy in words can there be any justification for using the same term "healthy" *tout court* to denote them both. Furthermore, it might be asked, even if we admit this *tertium quid* of analogy, can we ever be quite sure when it applies? When we say that Mr. Jones is alive and that an oyster is alive, is the difference between the life of Mr. Jones and the life of the oyster something additional to a quality, namely life, which is found univocally in both, as the Danishness of Carlo and the Pomeranianity of Fido are additional to their common caninity? Or, on the other hand, is the life which is attributed to Mr. Jones and to the oyster, as the scholastics would say, an analogical perfection, contracted to each subject not by external *differentiae* but by different internal modes of participation? Can one possibly settle this kind of question? Can we even give the distinction any real meaning?

Now, so long as we are merely considering qualities and properties of finite beings, the introduction of analogical discourse, in addition to univocal and equivocal, might well appear to be an unnecessary and artificial complication. There are, however, two instances in which it—or something like it —seems to be unavoidable, namely when we are discussing transcendentals and when we are discussing God. And it is worth noting that, in Christian thought, it is precisely the necessity of talking about God that has given rise to the great development which the doctrine of analogy has undergone. Let us consider these instances in order.

The transcendentals, in scholastic thought, are those six

primary notions—*ens, res, unum, aliquid, verum* and *bonum*—
which, because of their very universality, refuse to fall in any
of the Aristotelian categories, but cut across them all.[1] The
last five ultimately reduce to the first, so it will be sufficient to
consider that. What, then, is meant by the analogy of being?
Why is it denied that being is univocal? Simply because there
is nothing outside being by which it could be differentiated.
When we say that Carlo and Fido are both dogs, the word
"dog" means precisely the same when applied to each of
them; the differences that distinguish them as dogs are, as we
have seen, extrinsic to caninity as such. But when we say that
Carlo and Fido are both *beings*, the differences that distinguish
them as beings cannot be extrinsic to being as such, for being,
in its altogether universal reference, must embrace everything,
including differences; if differences were not instances of
being, they would be non-existent, and then no two things
could be distinct from each other. So the scholastics tell us,
being is not a genus,[2] since there is nothing outside it which
could act as a differentia to it, to subdivide it into species;
nevertheless everything is an instance of being, and being is
differentiated by its own inherent analogical variety. To be is
to be in a certain way, and the way is the very heart of the
being. So the whole order of beings, of *entia*, from the triune
Deity down to the speck of dust and the electron, consists of
nothing more and nothing less than analogical instances of
being: self-existent being and dependent being, actual being
and possible being, substantial being and accidental being,
real being and notional being, not in any pantheistic or monistic
sense, as if being were some kind of cosmic material, a metaphysical modelling-clay appearing now in this shape and now

---

[1] It should be noted that they are called transcendentals because they transcend
the categories. This is not the meaning which the word "transcendent" has
when applied to God to indicate that he transcends the realm of finite being. Nor
is it the meaning that "transcendental" has for Kant: "I apply," he says, "the
term *transcendental* to all knowledge which is not so much occupied with objects
as with the mode of our cognition of these objects, so far as this mode of cognition
is possible *a priori*" (*Critique of Pure Reason*, Introduction, ch. vii, trans. Meiklejohn).
Cf. Garrigou-Lagrange, *Dieu*, p. 200, *n*. 1.

[2] R. G. Collingwood surprisingly asserts that for the traditional metaphysics
being is the *summum genus* of which the ten Categories are species; in consequence
he has little difficulty in arguing that there cannot be a science of pure being
(*Essay in Metaphysics*, pp. 9, 10 f). What Aristotle actually thought will be found
in *Met*. B., 998b.

in that, but in the far more profound sense that every being must *be*, and must be in some determinate way, and—the theist will add—in the sense that the way in which it has being depends in the last resort upon its relation to the self-existent Being which is the prime analogate of all.

Now what is true about beings as such in their relation to one another must be true *a fortiori* about finite beings in their relation to the God who is self-existent Being. If being is not a genus, then the supreme Being transcends all genera, and the principle of analogy, which we have seen applies even between creatures when they are considered as they participate in the transcendentals, will apply with even greater force when creatures are brought into comparison with the altogether transcendent God and when God is spoken about in words whose meaning is derived from their application to finite things. Here, if anywhere, the distinction between the *perfectio significata* and the *modus significandi* will hold; here, if anywhere, will the classical definition of analogy apply, namely that it is the application of a concept to different beings in ways that are simply diverse from each other and are only the same in a certain respect, *simpliciter diversa et eadem secundum quid.*[1] It is noticeable that St. Thomas does not deny that analogues are equivocal but only that they are purely so.[2]

Let us now proceed to consider in more detail this classical doctrine of analogy. The precise classification of the various types of analogy that can be distinguished is to this day a matter of considerable controversy; the method that I shall adopt will, however, bring out the salient points.

---

[1] This is the Thomist definition of analogical discourse. For the Suarezians, however, with their conceptualist bias and the consequent sharp line drawn between thought and the extra-mental thing, an analogical concept applies to different beings in ways *simpliciter eadem et diversa secundum quid.*

[2] *Hoc modo aliqua dicuntur de Deo et creaturis analogice, et non aequivoce pure neque univoce* (*S. Theol.*, I, xiii, 5*c*). We may compare the well-known statement of the Fourth Lateran Council that "between the creator and the creature no likeness can be discerned without a greater unlikeness having to be discerned as well" (*inter creatorem et creaturam non potest tanta similitudo notari quin inter eos major sit dissimilitudo notanda,* cap. ii; Denzinger-Bannwart, *Enchiridion,* 11th ed., no. 432). It is easy to see what this means, but it would be difficult to defend it as a precise philosophical statement, as it appears to assume that likeness and unlikeness are two different species of a measurable genus. One can validly say that two objects are less alike in one respect than they are in another, but to say that they are less alike in one respect than they are *unlike* in another does not seem to be strictly intelligible.

II

In the first place, we may distinguish between analogy *duorum ad tertium* and analogy *unius ad alterum*; this is the fundamental distinction made by St. Thomas in both the *Summa Theologica* and the *Summa contra Gentiles*.[1] Analogy *duorum ad tertium* is the analogy that holds between two beings in consequence of the relation that each of them bears to a third (the analogy considered is, it must be noticed, between the *two*; the *tertium* only comes in as something in the background to which they are both related). For example, if the adjective "healthy" is applied both to Skegness and to the complexion of Mr. Jones who lives there, this double attribution of the adjective can only be seen to be legitimate if it is grasped that in its strict and primary application the adjective applies neither to Skegness nor to the complexion but to Mr. Jones. It is he who is (in the scholastic sense) *formally* healthy and is the *prime analogate*. His complexion is healthy only in the sense that it is a *sign* of health in him, Skegness is healthy only in the sense that it *induces* health in him (or in others like him); we cannot rationally justify the attribution of the same predicate "healthy" to things as diverse as a complexion and a seaside town except by referring them both to human beings to whom the predicate formally and properly belongs.

This type of analogy can, however, have little or no application to the case where we are attributing the same predicate to God and to a creature, for there is no being antecedent to God to whom the predicate can apply more formally and properly than it applies to him. We therefore pass to the other type of analogy, analogy *unius ad alterum*, which is founded not upon diverse relations which each of the analogates bears to a third, but upon a relation which one of them bears to the other. And this type of analogy itself subdivides into two.

The former of these sub-types is that which is known as analogy of *attribution* or of *proportion*, analogy *unius ad alterum* in the strict sense. In this case the predicate belongs formally

[1] *S. Theol.*, I, xiii, 5c; *S.c.G.*, I, xxxiv.

and properly to one of the analogates (which is thus not merely *an* analogate but is the *prime* analogate), and only relatively and derivatively to the other. Thus it is by an analogy of attribution or proportion that Mr. Jones and his complexion are both described as healthy; health is found formally and properly in Mr. Jones, and his complexion is described as healthy only because it bears a certain relation to his health, namely the relation of being a sign of it. In its theological application, where the analogates concerned are God and a creature, the relation upon which the analogy is based will be that of creative causality; creatures are related to God as his effects, by all those modes of participation by the creature in the perfection of its creator which are indicated, for example, by the Thomist Five Ways. Thus when we say that God and Mr. Jones are both good or that they are both beings, remembering that the content which the word "good" or "being" has for us is derived from our experience of the goodness and the being of creatures, we are, so far as analogy of attribution is concerned, saying no more than that God has goodness or being in whatever way is necessary if he is to be able to produce goodness and being in his creatures. This would not seem necessarily to indicate anything more than that the perfections which are found formally in various finite modes in creatures exist *virtually* in God, that is to say, that he is able to produce them in the creatures; it does not seem to necessitate that God possesses them formally himself. (In the case of Mr. Jones, of course, his complexion did indicate his formal possession of health, but there is, literally, all the difference in the world between the relation between two analogates in the finite realm and that between God and a creature.) Analogy of attribution certainly does not exclude the formal possession of the perfections by God, but it does not itself ascribe it to him. The mode in which the perfection which exists in the secondary analogate also exists in the prime analogate will depend on the relation between them; and if this relation is merely that the latter analogate is the *cause* of the former, the possession by the latter of a perfection that exists formally in the former will not, so far as the present mode of analogy is concerned, be necessarily anything more than a virtual one. Creatures are good (formally but finitely), God is the cause of them and of all that they have, therefore the word "good" applied to God need not mean any more than that he is able to produce goodness.[1] It is at this point that the second sub-type of analogy comes to the rescue.

This is analogy of proportionality, also called analogy *plurium ad plura*. In it there is a direct relation of the mode in which a perfection is participated to the being by which it is participated, independently of any relation to a prime analogate. (There may be a prime analogate, and indeed some would maintain that there must be,[2] but it does not come in at this stage.) A spurious, though sometimes useful, form of this type of analogy is *metaphor*, in which there is not a formal participation of the same characteristic in the different analogates but only a similarity of effects. Thus, to take a classic example, the lion is called the king of the beasts because he bears to savage animals a relation similar to that which a king bears to his subjects, but no one would assert that kingship is to be found formally in the lion. Again, God is described as being angry, because his relation to the punishments which he imposes is similar to that which an angry man has to the injuries which he inflicts, but no one (at least, no scholastic

[1] It is important to observe that we are not arguing that the formal possession of goodness by creatures does not *prove* that goodness is formally in God; the argument is not here on the metaphysical but merely on the linguistic and logical plane. All that is asserted is that if the only analogy between God and creatures was analogy of attribution then the word "good" applied to God would not necessarily *mean* any more than that goodness was in God virtually. *In fact* the metaphysical relation of the world to God implies analogy of proportionality as well, and it is at this latter stage that the formal attribution of goodness to God becomes clear.

[2] Thus Garrigou-Lagrange writes: "It is not necessary here to mention the principal analogate in the definition of the others, but there nevertheless always is a prime analogate. In metaphorical analogy of proportionality, it is the one to which the name of analogue belongs in the strict sense. In strict analogy of proportionality, the principal analogate is that which is the higher cause of the others: the analogical similitude that exists in this latter case is always based on causality; it exists either between the cause and the effect or between the effects of the same cause" (*Dieu*, p. 532, *n.* 3). This last remark seems to imply the assertion that will be made later on: that in its theological application analogy of proportionality needs to be reinforced by analogy of attribution; Garrigou-Lagrange does not, however, explicitly make the assertion. We may add here, as a point of terminology, that the word "analogue" (*analogum*) refers to the common predicate (or common quality or transcendental signified by it), while the word "analogate" (*analogatum*) refers to the various subjects to which it is attributed, or to its diverse modes in them. An alternative nomenclature refers to the analogue as *analogum analogans* and the analogate as *analogum analogatum*.

philosopher) would say that anger was to be found formally in God.[1] In the strict sense, an analogy of proportionality implies that the analogue under discussion is found formally in each of the analogates but in a mode that is determined by the nature of the analogate itself. Thus, assuming that life is an analogous and not a univocal concept, it is asserted that cabbages, elephants, men and God each possess life formally (that is each of them is, quite literally and unmetaphorically, *alive*), but that the cabbage possesses life in the mode proper to a cabbage, the elephant in that proper to an elephant, the man in that proper to a man, and finally God in that supreme, and by us unimaginable, mode proper to self-existent Being itself. This is commonly expressed in the following quasi-mathematical form, from which, in fact, the name "analogy of proportionality" is derived:[2]

$$\frac{\text{life of cabbage}}{\text{essence of cabbage}} = \frac{\text{life of elephant}}{\text{essence of elephant}}$$

$$= \frac{\text{life of man}}{\text{essence of man}} = \frac{\text{life of God}}{\text{essence of God}}$$

We must, however, beware of interpreting the equal sign too literally. For the point is not that the life of the cabbage is determined by the essence of the cabbage in the *same* way as that in which the life of the man is determined by the essence of the man, but that the way in which cabbage essence determines cabbage life is proper to cabbagehood, while the way in which the human essence determines human life is proper

[1] A further example of purely metaphorical proportionality is provided by Canning's celebrated epigram:
"Pitt is to Addington
As London is to Paddington."

[2] "Let magnitudes which have the same proportion (λόγος) be called proportional (ἀνάλογον)" (Euclid V, Def. 6). For the sake of clarity it may be useful to indicate by a diagram the classification of analogy which I have adopted:
I. Analogy *duorum ad tertium*.
II. Analogy *unius ad alterum*.
    (i) Analogy of attribution or proportion, strictly *unius ad alterum*.
    (ii) Analogy of proportionality, *plurium ad plura*
        (*a*) in loose sense (metaphor)
        (*b*) in strict sense.
Slightly different classifications may be found in Garrigou-Lagrange, *Dieu*, p. 351; Maquart, *Elem. Phil.*, III, ii, p. 36.

to manhood. But at this point various objections rapidly spring to the mind.

In the first place, it may be asked, has not the remark just made landed us in an infinite regress? We began by denying the univocity of the identity,

$$\text{life of cabbage} = \text{life of man,}$$

and substituted for it the proportionality:

$$\frac{\text{life of cabbage}}{\text{essence of cabbage}} = \frac{\text{life of man}}{\text{essence of man}}$$

But we now have denied that the equal sign in this latter equation really signifies equality and have substituted for it a proposition which, in quasi-mathematical form, can be written as follows:

$$\frac{\text{way in which life of cabbage is determined by essence of cabbage}}{\text{essence of cabbage}}$$

$$= \frac{\text{way in which life of man is determined by essence of man}}{\text{essence of man}}$$

And again we shall have to remember that the equal sign means not identity but similarity, and shall now have to write:

$$\frac{\text{way in which way-in-which-life-of-cabbage-is-determined-by-essence-of-cabbage is determined by essence of cabbage}}{\text{essence of cabbage}}$$

$$= \frac{\text{way in which way-in-which-life-of-man-is-determined-by-essence-of-man is determined by essence of man}}{\text{essence of man}}$$

and so *ad infinitum*.

To put this more briefly, if we write L for "life of" and E for "essence of," *c* for "cabbage" and *m* for "man," and use A/B to signify "determination of A by B," we began by denying $Lc = Lm$, and put in its place

$$Lc/Ec = Lm/Em \ ;$$

then we said that what we really meant was

$$(Lc/Ec)/Ec = (Lm/Em)/Em;$$

then we found that for this we should have to substitute

$$[(Lc/Ec)/Ec]/Ec = [(Lm/Em)/Em]/Em.$$

The next stage will be

$$\{[(Lc/Ec)/Ec]/Ec\}/Ec = \{[(Lm/Em)/Em]/Em\}/Em,$$

and so we shall go on for ever, at each successive stage denying progressively more complicated relationships between cabbages and men, and never managing to assert a relationship which we shall not immediately have to deny. And at the end of it we shall have nothing but a series of negations:

$$Lc \neq Lm,$$
$$Lc/Ec \neq Lm/Em,$$
$$(Lc/Ec)/Ec \neq (Lm/Em)/Em,$$
$$[(Lc/Ec)/Ec]/Ec \neq [(Lm/Em)/Em]/Em, \qquad \text{etc.}$$

Our proportionality has completely collapsed, and all we are left with is the fact that cabbages have nothing in common with men except the fact that, for no valid reason, men have described them both as being alive. In fact, the introduction of analogy as a *via media* between univocity and equivocity has turned out to be nothing more than an imposing piece of mystification. This is the first objection of which we must take account; it is obviously a serious one. It strikes, not in particular at the analogical application of terms to God, but to analogical predication as such. I shall not attempt a full reply until I have stated another objection which is concerned with the specifically theological case, but I shall offer a few observations in passing.

First, then, we may remark that the objection, while on the surface plausible, has something of the appearance of a conjuring trick. It brings to mind two somewhat similar feats of philosophical legerdemain. The first is Lewis Carroll's *What the Tortoise said to Achilles*.[1] In this problem, which its originator did not perhaps intend to be taken as seriously as it really demands, Achilles maintained that, if two premisses A and B logically implied a conclusion Z, then anybody who saw this and also accepted A and B as true would have to accept Z as

[1] *The Complete Works of Lewis Carroll*, pp. 1104 f.

true also. The tortoise objected that this would only be the case if he accepted a further proposition C, namely that if A and B are true then Z must be true. Achilles was thus forced to modify his original assertion, so that it now took the form "Anyone who accepts A, B and C as true must accept Z as true also." But again the tortoise objected that this involved the acceptance of another proposition D, which was that, if A and B and C are all true, Z must be true as well. And so on for ever! This corresponds, of course, to the well-known fact that the principle of inference is incapable of formal symbolic statement within the logical calculus to which it applies.[1] A logical system cannot, as it were, operate under its own steam, without help from outside; we shall derive from this fact a pointer towards the solution of our present problem. The other puzzle to which I wish to refer is one which its originator took much more seriously: I mean Mr. F. H. Bradley's famous argument that relations are illusions.[2] It is, he urged, of the essence of a relation to unite terms, but how is each term united to the relation? It can only be by another relation, but if so, what unites the term to this? To make the first relation intelligible we have to presuppose an infinite sequence of relations antecedent to it, and none of these is yet intelligible. Hence, Mr. Bradley concluded, relations are mere illusion. Lord Russell has caustically remarked that if Bradley's argument were valid it would prove that chains are impossible—and yet they exist.[3] Dr. C. D. Broad has dealt with Bradley's problem in some detail. He takes as an instance of it the fact that A is father of B. "Here," he writes, "we have a perfectly intelligible statement, involving the non-formal[4] relation of *fatherhood*. At the next stage we get the fact that A is referent to *fatherhood*, and the fact that B is relatum to *fatherhood*. The 'relations' introduced at this stage are purely formal. At the next stage we get the fact that A is referent to *referent to*, that *fatherhood* is relatum to *referent to*, that *fatherhood* is referent to

---

[1] Cf. B. Russell, *The Principles of Mathematics*, pp. 16, 35, where explicit reference is made to Lewis Carroll's puzzle.

[2] *Appearance and Reality*, I, ch. iii.   [3] *Outline of Philosophy*, p. 263.

[4] "Formal," for Broad and all the modern logicians, means "purely logical," "having no reference to particular concrete individual entities." This is very different from the scholastic use of the word.

referent to, and that B is relatum to *referent to.* Thus no new 'relations' are introduced at this or any subsequent stage. The fact that at every stage after the first the relating relations are purely formal and are merely repeated shows that we are now embarked on the self-evidently impossible task of explaining, by means of particular relational judgments, that general relational form which is presupposed by all relational judgments whatever."[1] We might, in fact, say that, while it is of the essence of relations to unite terms, they are not themselves terms in this context (though, of course, in another context they may become terms, as when we pick out two relations, or a relation and a term, and ask what is the relation between them). Similarly, in the case of analogy of proper proportionality, we might reply to our objector that we are simply concerned with the fact that essences determine their qualities, and that the truth of this is not in the least affected by the fact that they can only do this if they also determine the way in which they determine their qualities, and the way in which they determine the way in which they determine their qualities, and so on to the crack of doom. *Ce n'est que le premier pas qui coûte.*

Such a reply would, I think, go a very long way, though I am doubtful whether it is altogether sufficient. For the fact remains that we have denied that our equal signs really stand for equality and we have not indicated anything definite that they do stand for. Can we in some way re-establish this bond that we have broken? Clearly we cannot by analogy of proportionality, but I shall suggest that we can by analogy of attribution, and that the two types of analogy, while either in separation is insufficient, can in combination do what is required.[2] But this is an anticipation. I will pass on now to

---

[1] *Examination of McTaggart's Philosophy,* I, p. 86.

[2] It may be interesting to see how Dr. A. M. Farrer deals with this difficulty. For him "this proportionality claims to hold between four terms, and not two relations. We are not saying," he continues, "'The way in which the divine intelligence is related to the divine existence resembles the way in which the creaturely intelligence is related to the creaturely existence' for that is exactly what we have to deny. The way in which the several aspects of the divine being (e.g. intelligence) have their synthesis into one, itself differs from the way in which the several aspects of the creaturely being have their synthesis into one, *as* the divine being itself differs from the creaturely. What we are saying is completely different, viz. 'Divine intelligence is appropriate to divine existence as creaturely to creaturely'" (*Finite and Infinite,* p. 53, italics in original).

consider the second objection, which is specially concerned with analogical discourse about God.

III

Let us therefore see what happens when we attribute life both to a creature and to God; any other perfection which can be formally predicated of God would, of course, do as well. Analogy of proportionality asserts:

$$\frac{\text{life of man}}{\text{essence of man}} = \frac{\text{life of God}}{\text{essence of God}}$$

Now, the objector urges, even if the first objection has been successfully overcome, so that we have no longer to bother about the fact that the equal sign does not indicate an exact identity of relationship, our formula will not in fact tell us in

---

Dr. Farrer's first point seems to me to be valuable, at least as denying *equality* of relations; in this respect the older mathematical notation for proportionality,

$a : b :: c : d$, might be less misleading than the more modern $\frac{a}{b} = \frac{c}{d}$. But I do

not think any scholastic would deny that proportionality was *some* sort of relation between two relations or would reduce it simply to a polyadic relation uniting four terms. Dr. Farrer himself in the quotation above seems, by italicizing the word "*as,*" to admit the equal sign at a subsequent stage and, while denying

$$\frac{\text{divine intelligence}}{\text{divine existence}} = \frac{\text{human intelligence}}{\text{human existence}},$$

to be asserting

$$\frac{\text{synthesis of aspects in God}}{\text{being of God}} = \frac{\text{synthesis of aspects in creature}}{\text{being of creature}},$$

but I cannot think that this was his intention. He has previously said that the formula "presupposes that intelligence can be attributed to God, and declares how it is to be understood when it is attributed to him and not to the creature, viz. as differing from its creaturely mode with a difference analogous to that by which the divine existence differs from the creaturely. And so it presupposes also the 'proportion' between the two 'existences.'" He goes on to say: "Proportion logically underlies proportionality, but this need not mean that we originally entertain the notion of the proportion 'divine existence/creaturely existence except as the foundation for a proportionality; the two are distinguished by philosophical analysis only." The proportion now mentioned is, it will be noticed, not either of the proportions that form the two sides of the proportionality, but the proportion between a term on one side and a term on the other. This seems to be in line with my assertion that, in the relation of God to creatures, analogy of proportionality and of attribution (proportion) are interlocked. Dr. Farrer continues: "The natural use of the proportion is inseparable from that of the proportionality, as the apprehension of the very fact of the divine being is inseparable from some apprehension of its mode."

what sense life is to be predicated of God. For the essence
of God is as little known to us as is his life; indeed his life is,
formally considered, identical with it. Our equation has
therefore two unknowns and cannot be solved. Nor can we get
out of our difficulty by comparing essence with existence and
saying that the essence of a being will correspond to, and be
determined by, the act in virtue of which it exists:

$$\frac{\text{essence of man}}{\text{existential act of man}} = \frac{\text{essence of God}}{\text{existential act of God}}$$

Once again, both the terms on the right-hand side are unknown. Sheer agnosticism seems to be the outcome. What
reply can we make?

   Some scholastic philosophers, of whom Garrigou-Lagrange
is one, claim to answer this objection, while remaining in the
realm of analogy of proportionality, by denying that there are
two unknown terms on the right-hand side. This last-men-
tioned writer, for example, taking the analogy

$$\frac{\text{creature}}{\text{its being}} = \frac{\text{first cause}}{\text{its being}}$$

asserts that only the fourth term is in fact unknown. "We
have," he says, "(1) *the very confused concept of being in general*,
which a child possesses from the moment of its first intellectual
knowledge, (2) *the concept of finite being*, of which we know
positively the finite mode and which is nothing else than the
essence of the things that we see, stones, plants, animals, etc.,
(3) *the concept of analogous being*, imperfectly abstracted from
the finite mode . . . ; it is a precision of the first very confused
concept possessed by the child, and the metaphysician acquires
it by recognizing that the formal notion of being does not in
itself include the finite mode which accompanies it in the
creature, (4) *the concept of the divine being*, the cause of created
beings. These latter," he continues, "not having in their
essence the reason of their existence, require a cause which
exists of itself. In the concept of the divine being, the divine
mode is expressed only in a negative and relative way, e.g. as
non-finite or as supreme being. What is positive in this

analogical knowledge of God is what God has that is pro-
portionally common to him and the creature."[1] Again, he
writes, "*being* designates *that which* has relation to existence;
this relation is implied in the very nature of that which exists
and it is essentially varied according as it is necessary or contingent. The created essence in its inmost entity is altogether
relative to its contingent existence, which it can lose; the
uncreated essence is conceived only relatively to that necessary
existence with which it is identified. . . . Analogous perfections are thus not pure relations. They are perfections
which imply in the creature a composition of two correlative
elements, potentiality and act, but which in God are pure
act. Our intelligence conceives that they are realized more
fully according as they are purified of all potentiality; in
God they exist therefore in the pure state. We thus see that
there are not two unknowns in the proportionalities set up by
theology."[2]

For this distinguished French Dominican, therefore, the
third term in the formula is given us as that in which essence
and existence are identical, and this gives us a limited and
analogical, but nevertheless genuine, knowledge of the fourth
term, while remaining within the realm of analogy of proportionality.[3] We can transfer the notion of any perfection
from a finite being to God, remembering that the difference of
mode is that which corresponds to the difference between a
being whose essence involves merely a possibility of existence
and one whose essence involves existence of necessity. Of
course, we do not know positively what the mode of the per-

---

[1] *Dieu*, p. 541.   [2] Ibid., p. 542.

[3] Penido's answer to the objection (*Rôle de l'Analogie*, pp. 136 f.) rests upon his
assertion previously noticed (p. 96, n. 1, *supra*) that no use of analogy is necessary
in the mere demonstration of the *existence* of God. Thus, in the proportionality,

$$\frac{\text{essence of creature}}{\text{existential act of creature}} = \frac{\text{essence of God}}{\text{existential act of God}},$$

the fourth term is not unknown; it is already given to us as self-existence, *ipsum
esse subsistens*, existence not really distinct from essence. Thus, whereas for
Garrigou-Lagrange the *third* term is given to us *in* and *through* the analogy, for
Penido the *fourth* term is given to us *prior to* the analogy; thus he writes, "L'analogie
. . . n'apparait pas *explicitement* au début de notre marche vers Dieu, elle ne
s'occupe pas de la question 'an sit', elle n'entre en jeu que lorsqu'il s'agit du
'quomodo sit'" (*Rôle*, p. 138). I cannot help feeling that at this point Penido is
nearer the truth.

fection in God is; to demand that would be to demand a quidditative knowledge of the divine essence and to abolish analogy altogether in favour of univocity. We are given all that we have a right to ask for; the comparison of the finite and the infinite modes of perfection is based on a comparison of the relations to existence which are proper to finite essence and to the divine essence respectively.

Now all this seems very satisfactory so far as it goes, but does it go far enough? Is it sufficient simply to base the comparison of the finite and infinite modes of a perfection upon a comparison of the finite and infinite modes of the essence-existence relation, without bringing in an explicit reference to the concrete relation which the creature has to God? There are indeed traces in Garrigou-Lagrange's own discussion of an awareness of the need of this further step; the very form in which he writes the formula last quoted suggests this. For he does not describe the finite being as a being in whom essence does not necessarily involve existence, but as a "creature"; and he does not describe God as a being whose essence necessarily involves existence, but as the "first cause." "In these equations," he writes, "two created terms are known directly, one uncreated term is known indirectly *by way of causality* and we infer the fourth term which is known indirectly in a *positive* manner as regards what is analogically common with creatures and in a *negative* and relative manner as regards its proper divine mode."[1] And the first cause and the creature are directly related by the relation of creation, which thus, as it were, cuts horizontally across the analogy of proportionality with an analogy of attribution.[2] The equal sign does not, as we have seen earlier, express a mathematical identity, but, on the other hand, the two sides of the formula are not left in complete separation. They are bound together by an analogy of attribution *unius ad alterum*, of the creature to God in the case

[1] *Dieu*, p. 543 (first set of italics mine).
[2] Garrigou-Lagrange himself writes: "If the analogy of being is formally an analogy of proportionality it is virtually an analogy of attribution, in the sense that if, *per impossibile*, being did not belong intrinsically to the creature it could still be extrinsically attributed to it, in so far as the creature is an effect of the prime Being" (*Dieu*, p. 541, note). It is the word "virtually" in this passage from which I am disposed to dissent. Penido lays great stress upon the "mixed" nature of the analogy between God and the world (*Rôle de l'Analogie*, p. 134 *et al.*).

which we have just been considering. In the cases considered earlier, where the two sides of the formula both refer to finite beings, the linking analogy is an analogy *duorum ad tertium*, which holds in view of the fact that each of the analogates is in an analogy of attribution *unius ad alterum*, of itself to God. The figure below, Fig. 4, may help to make this plain.[1]

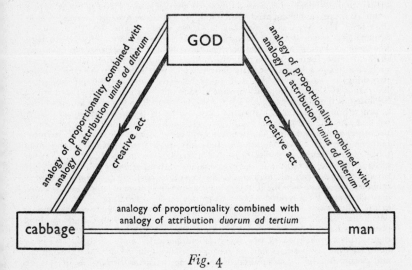

Fig. 4

The conclusion would thus seem to be that, in order to make the doctrine of analogy really satisfactory, we must see the analogical relation between God and the world as combining in a tightly interlocked union both analogy of attribution and analogy of proportionality. Without analogy of proportionality it is very doubtful whether the attributes which we predicate of God can be ascribed to him in more than a merely virtual sense; without analogy of attribution it hardly seems possible to avoid agnosticism. Which of the two forms of analogy is prior to the other has been, and still is, a hotly debated question among scholastic philosophers. Sylvester of Ferrara, in his great commentary on the *Summa contra Gentiles*, asserted the primacy of attribution and alleged that in this he was expressing

---

[1] It should here be noted that analogy *duorum ad tertium* is itself an instance of analogy of attribution.

I

the true thought of St. Thomas,[1] but the "prince of commentators" Cajetan, in his luminous little treatise *De Nominum
Analogia*, asserted that only proportionality was analogy in the
true and strict sense[2] and the majority of Thomists have

---

[1] *Comm. in S.c.G.*, I, xxxiv. In this place in *S.c.G.*, and in *S. Theol.*, I, xiii, 5c,
where (with purely verbal differences) he divides analogy into (a) *duorum ad
tertium*, and (b) *unius ad alterum* and asserts that only the latter of these applies
when creatures are compared with God, St. Thomas certainly seems to hold
this view. However, in *De Veritate*, ii, 11, he writes: "There are two kinds of
proportional association and so there are two kinds of community by analogy.
For there is a certain association between things which have a proportion between
them, because there is a determinate distance or other relation between them,
such as 2 has to 1 because it is its double, and there is another association when
two things are compared with each other between which there is no proportion
but rather a likeness of two proportions to each other, as when 6 associated with 4
because 6 is the double of 3 and 4 is the double of 2. The former is an association
of proportion, the latter of proportionality. So by the former mode of association
we find something analogously said of two things of which one has a relation to
the other, as substance and accident are both called beings because of the relation
between them. . . . But sometimes something is said analogically in the latter
mode of association, as bodily sight and understanding are both given the name
of sight, because as sight is to the eye so is understanding to the mind. Therefore
because in things said analogically in the former mode there must be some determinate relation between the things which have something in common analogically,
it is impossible for anything to be said in this mode of God and a creature. But
in the other mode of analogy no determinate relation holds between the things
which have something in common analogically, and so in this mode nothing
prevents a name from being analogically spoken of God and a creature. Nevertheless this can happen in two ways: [metaphorically and strictly]." We may
note: (i) that the passages can be reconciled if we take proportion (attribution)
and proportionality as a subdivision of analogy *unius ad alterum* (as in n. 2 on
p. 104), and see the passage in *De Ver.* as defining precisely the way in which
this type of analogy can validly be given a theological use, (ii) that the rejection
of proportion in *De Ver.* is made only on the assumption that proportion and
proportionality are mutually exclusive. It would be consistent with the passage
in question to hold that, whereas we should have to reject proportion if proportion
and proportionality were taken as being mutually exclusive, nevertheless proportionality needs to be combined with proportion (or even to be subordinated
to it) if the two are taken as mutually consistent. It must, of course, be admitted
that St. Thomas does not actually assert this, and it is in any case possible that he
changed his mind when he came to write the *Summae*. Cf. the quotation in the
next note from the Commentary on the Sentences, which is a still earlier work
than the *De Veritate*.
We may add that Suarez and his followers strongly hold to the primacy of
attribution, but in their case the matter is complicated by the conceptualist bias
of Suarezian epistemology.

[2] *De Nom. Anal.*, cap iii, no. 23. He says that the name of analogy is given only
improperly (*abusive*) to that "analogy of inequality" (not mentioned in my
discussion) in which the analogue is found in the various analogates in different
degrees but in the same precise sense in all, and which is therefore only a form of
univocity. St. Thomas makes this threefold distinction in his Commentary on
the Sentences of Peter Lombard: "Aliquid dicitur secundum analogiam tripliciter:
vel *secundum intentionem* et non secundum esse [*analogy of attribution*], et hoc est
quando una intentio refertur ad plura per prius et posterius quae tamen non
habet esse nisi in uno . . . ; vel *secundum esse* et non secundum intentionem [*analogy*

followed him, down to Garrigou-Lagrange,[1] Penido,[2] and Maritain[3] at the present day, though Descoqs is a notable exception[4].

IV

It is perhaps necessary at this point to make a clearer distinction than has yet been made in this discussion between the three orders of thought—the logical, the epistemological, and the ontological[5]—to which the notion of analogy applies. However anxious we are to maintain the realist position that words and concepts are both about things, the fact remains that words, concepts and things are not identical and that at some

---

of inequality] et hoc contingit quando plura parificantur in intentione alicujus communis, sed illud commune non habet esse unius rationis in omnibus . . . ; vel *secundum intentionem et secundum esse* [*analogy of proportionality*], et hoc est quando neque parificantur in intentione communi neque in esse" (*In I Sent.*, d. 19, q. 5 a. 2 *ad* 1).

[1] *Dieu*, pp. 530 f.   [2] *Le Rôle de l'Analogie en Théol. dogm.*, pp. 46, 145.

[3] *Distinguer pour unir*, app. II (not in E.T.). He stresses "the profound remark of John of St. Thomas that, in mixed cases (where analogy of attribution and of proportionality are joined together), the analogy of attribution is only virtual. When from the existence of created being we conclude that of its uncreated Cause, we are in fact (even if unconsciously) using analogy of strict proportionality, for this reasoning implies that the notion of *cause* is itself analogous with strict proportionality and also that the uncreated Being with which it ends and the created being from which it begins are both called by the same name 'being,' not only because the former is the cause of the latter but because what the concept of being signifies is found in both of them according to a similitude of proportions. From the fact that the relation of causality gives rise to an analogy of attribution between the effect and the cause, it does not follow that we formally use analogy of attribution whenever we follow the way of causality to establish the 'existence of the source' of the created perfections" (p. 826).

[4] See his *Praelectiones Theologiae Naturalis*, II, pp. 795 f., for his controversy on this point with Penido. Penido himself writes very reasonably: "From a certain point of view, it is perfectly true to say that proportionality is not primary, since it presupposes the causality which gives us the third term of all our proportions. Without the analogy of attribution which establishes the existence of a source, it is clear that proportionality would have no real support; we should remain enclosed in possibilities and conditional propositions. But is such an answer 'equivalent to putting all proportionality out of service'? By no means. It is simply equivalent to putting proportionality in its true place, which is the centre. As our opponent admits, causality demonstrates the *existence* of an X. But what is its *nature*? This is the proper domain of proportionality."

(*Rôle de l'Analogie*, p. 146. Note that what Penido here calls the *third* term is what he has previously called the *fourth*, i.e. the term which stands for the divine *existence*. He is here thinking of the proportion in the form:

$$\frac{\text{finite existence}}{\text{finite essence}} = \frac{\text{divine existence}}{\text{divine essence}}).$$

For my own reflections see the text.   [5] See p. 96 *supra*.

point the distinction must be made. (Cajetan himself remarks that for the logician analogy of attribution is merely a kind of equivocity, while for the philosopher it is a kind of analogy.[1]) And it is vital to the whole position which I have been maintaining to insist that in natural theology we are not merely instituting comparisons between two orders of concepts but considering created and uncreated being as the former actually exists in dependence on the latter. That is to say, we are not merely concerned with the question "How can an infinite, necessary and immutable Being be described in terms that are derived from the finite, contingent and mutable world?" but with a question that is anterior to this and without which this cannot be properly discussed at all, namely "How is the possibility of our applying to the infinite Being terms that are derived from the finite order conditioned by the fact that the finite order is dependent for its very existence on the fiat of the infinite and self-existent Being?" In the order of predication or of conceptualization it may well be the case that the two types of analogy are disconnected, that proportionality is prior to attribution, or that, as John of St. Thomas suggests,[2] the analogy of attribution between God and the creature is only virtual; but when we are concerned with the affirmation of God as the supreme existent, whose existence can nevertheless only be affirmed by us as a result of our prior recognition of the existence of finite existents, it would seem that our statements about God can hardly exclude all reference to the relation in which he stands to his creatures in existential fact.[3] M. Gilson has developed this line of thought in a most stimulating way in one of the sections which, in accordance with his enhanced recognition of the existentialism of St. Thomas, he has added to the revised edition of his book *Le Thomisme*.[4] He begins by commenting on the contrast between the paucity and restraint of St. Thomas's own treatment of the subject and the immense volume of the discussions that it has provoked

---

[1] *De Nom. Anal.*, cap. ii, no. 19, 20.
[2] *Cursus Phil.*, q. 14, a. 3. (Cf. Garrigou-Lagrange, *Dieu*, p. 541 *n*.)
[3] Thus St. Thomas writes: "We cannot grasp what God is, but only what he is not *and how other things are related to him*" (*Non enim de Deo capere possumus quid est, sed quid non est, et qualiter alia se habeant ad ipsum* (*S.c.G.*, I, xxx).)
[4] Part I, ch. v, sec. ii, "La connaissance de Dieu par voie d'analogie."

among his disciples.   He suggests that this is largely due to
"a secret desire to rescue from a too glaring lowliness the
knowledge of God which St. Thomas Aquinas allows us to
have.   People thus come," he says, "step by step to speak of
analogy as a source of almost positive knowledge which would
allow us to conceive more or less confusedly the essence of God.
But perhaps," he continues, "it is not necessary to force the
Thomist texts in order to obtain from this notion the services
desired.   It is enough to interpret them, as St. Thomas does
himself, not in the order of the concept but in that of the
judgment."[1]   For M. Gilson, then, the purpose of the doctrine
of analogy is not to allow us to form concepts of the divine
essence, but to allow us to affirm the divine existence; not to
compare God's features with those of finite beings, but to
allow us to assert that he exists when we can identify him only
by describing him in terms derived from the finite order.   As
we have seen,[2] the great problem for a radically transcendent
theism is how to keep God, as it were, from slipping out of
our grasp at the moment in which we affirm his existence.   The
world requires as its cause a being totally transcending it in
every respect; but how can we even affirm the existence of such
a being, if our experience of the world gives us no words by
which to define him?   There is no solution, says Gilson, in terms
of essences and concepts.   Referring to the perennial controversy between those who stress the element of agnosticism in
St. Thomas's theology and those who insist in contrast on the
positive value which it guarantees to our knowledge of God,
he writes as follows: "On the level of the concept there is no
middle way between the univocal and the equivocal.   At that
point the two interpretations are irreconcilable, but they
would surely cease to be so if we transferred them to the level
of the judgment.   We must observe, in fact, that in the case of
God, every judgment, even if it has the appearance of a judgment of attribution, is in reality a judgment of existence.
When we speak, with reference to him, of essence or substance
or goodness or wisdom, we are doing nothing more than
repeating about him: he is *esse*.   That is why his name *par
excellence* is *Qui est*.   If then we take the divine attributes one

---

[1] *Le Thomisme*, 5me éd., p. 153.   [2] See ch. iv *supra*.

by one and ask whether each of them is to be found in God, we must reply that it is not there, at least as such and as a distinct reality, and since we can in no way conceive an essence which is nothing but an act of existing, we cannot in any way conceive what God is, even with the help of such attributes. . . . On the other hand," he adds, "St. Thomas undoubtedly does allow us a certain knowledge of God, [and] unless we are to admit that St. Thomas has grossly contradicted himself, we must suppose that the knowledge of God which he grants us does not in any way bear upon his essence.[1] . . . Every effect of God is analogous to its cause. The concept which we form of this effect can in no case be transformed for us into the concept of God which we lack, but we can attribute to God, by our affirmative judgment, the name that denotes the perfection corresponding to this effect. To proceed in this way is not to posit God as similar to the creature, it is to ground oneself on the certitude that, since every effect resembles its cause, the creature from which we start certainly resembles God (*S.c.G.*, I, xxix)."[2]

This point is so important that I will try to make it in a slightly different way. So long as we are talking about finite beings we can make statements about their natures or essences without any assertion about their existence. I can say that a unicorn has a horn on its nose and that a rhinoceros has a horn on its nose without suggesting that any animals with horns on their noses exist; that rhinoceroses do exist and that unicorns do not is a purely empirical fact. But I cannot say that God is good without asserting the existence of a good being; for since God is by definition self-existent being, to affirm that God is good is to speak of self-existent goodness, that is to say of goodness that cannot but exist.[3] Again, in talking about finite beings, we can ascribe to them properties not necessarily included in their essences. If I say that the Cambridge buses

[1] He is referring, of course, to the knowledge of God that we can have by our natural powers and in this life. But even in the Beatific Vision, although the divine essence is known by the blessed, it is seen *totum sed non totaliter*.

[2] Op. cit., pp. 155 f.

[3] I am assuming here, of course, that God has been already shown to exist. Until that has been done, to assert that God is good does not ascribe to goodness existence *ut exercita*, but only *ut signata*; to hold otherwise would be to accept the ontological argument.

are red, I am not asserting that redness is necessarily inherent in the nature of a Cambridge bus; in fact there was a time when the Cambridge buses were green. When, however, I say that God is good or wise or just, I am inevitably asserting that goodness, wisdom and justice are inherent in the nature of God, for in God there are no accidents, no qualities that are not included in his essence.[1] It follows that all our statements about God have a directly existential reference, such as is possessed by none of our statements about finite beings except those in which existence is explicitly asserted. The only way in which I can assert that beings with horns on their noses exist is by affirming existence either of such beings in general or of some such being (for example, a unicorn or a rhinoceros) in particular; but I can assert that a good being exists simply by affirming that God is good. Since in God essence and existence are identical, any assertion about God's essence is at the same time an assertion about existence; anything which is affirmed to be included in God's nature is at the same time affirmed to exist, and indeed to be self-existent.

It is then, I suggest, in virtue of this inherently existential element in all our affirmations about God that the possibility of analogical knowledge of God and of analogical discourse about him can be maintained. If it were possible to make a statement about God that bore exclusively on the essential or conceptual order, that statement would collapse into sheer equivocity and agnosticism, for no concept of the essence of God can be formed by a finite mind.[2] Since, however, God's essence necessarily involves his existence, no statement about him can remain in the essential or conceptual order; it passes over immediately into the order of existence and the judgment. What begins as an attempt to conceive God's goodness—an

---

[1] The apparent exceptions to this statement, arising from God's action in the finite realm, are discussed elsewhere in this book. (Ch. vi *infra*.)

[2] On this ground one can, I think, justify Sertillanges' description of Thomism as "an agnosticism of definition" (*Le Christianisme et les Philosophies*, I, p. 270), for definition is concerned with the essence and the concept. One could not validly describe Thomism as "an agnosticism of the judgment." It is important to grasp that, whereas in the case of analogy between finite beings, the doctrine of analogy has merely to grapple with the distinction between the *perfectio significata* and the *modus significandi*, in the case of analogy between a finite being and God it has to grapple with the far greater difficulty of the gulf that separates the finite creature from the infinite Creator.

attempt which is doomed to failure—issues in an affirmation that self-existent goodness exists; but even this last statement needs careful interpretation if it is not to be taken as implying that we form a concept of "self-existent goodness."[1] It would perhaps be better to say that goodness exists self-existingly, for then the fundamental dependence of analogical predication upon the metaphysical analogy of being is made clear. We can then see how we must interpret the formula

$$\frac{\text{goodness of finite being}}{\text{finite being}} = \frac{\text{goodness of God}}{\text{God}}$$

as holding not merely in the order of essence but in that of existence, as expressing not a comparison of concepts but an existential judgment. The second term on the left-hand side of our formula ("finite being") expresses precisely that contingency of existence which arises from the fact that in finite beings essence and existence are really distinct; the second term on the right-hand side ("God") expresses that necessity of existence which arises from the fact that in God essence and existence are really identical. And the two sides of the formula are held together by that analogy of attribution which asserts, not merely in the conceptual but in the existential order, that finite being can exist only in dependence upon God. The goodness of God is thus declared to be self-existent goodness, and, as such, identical not merely with God's essence but with the act by which God exists. Analogy does not enable us to *conceive* God's goodness as identical with his essence but to *affirm* it as identical with his existence. Hence all our assertions about God are grossly inadequate in so far as they apply concepts to him, but they are thoroughly adequate in so far as they affirm perfections of him. Here the relevance of the distinction between the *perfectio significata* and the *modus significandi* can be seen at the full, as can also the reconciliation of the apparent contradiction between St. Thomas's "agnosticism" and his conviction that we can make genuine assertions about God. The names which we apply to God, he says,

---

[1] The tendency of the human mind to take refuge in concepts is as ineradicable as its tendency to turn to sensible images: *convertit se ad phantasmata*, indeed, but also *ad conceptus*! It is always trying to conceptualize existence instead of affirming it.

"designate the divine substance and are predicated of God substantially, but they fall short of representing him."[1] We cannot, in short, know God's essence by forming a concept of it, but we can know it analogically in our concepts of finite beings. I shall conclude at this point this already over-long discussion of the scholastic doctrine of analogy, and in doing so I will remind the reader again that its purpose has been, not to discover whether it is possible intelligibly to talk about God, but to explain how it is that we have been able to do so and to analyse what it is that we have in fact been doing. It is too much to hope that the explanation has been entirely adequate; it is perhaps sufficient if it has revealed some intelligibility in what by its very nature must be a mystery.[2]

---

[1] *Nomina significant substantiam divinam et praedicantur de Deo substantialiter sed deficiunt a repraesentatione ipsius (S. Theol.,* I, xiii, 2c).

[2] I have received much help in writing this chapter from an article on "God and Analogy," by Fr. Columba Ryan, O.P., in *Blackfriars,* April 1944.

CHAPTER SIX

GOD AND THE CREATURE

" Le problème de Dieu nour accule précisément à ceci: comprendre la nécessité de l'Incompréhensible; postuler par l'intelligence l'Inintelligible; connaître qu'il y a un Inconnaissable; expliquer par le mystère ce qui, sans le mystère, serait l'absurde, par conséquent le non-être, et qui cependant est. Sans Dieu, le monde, constitué par les relations d'êtres tous contingents et tous conditionnés pourrait se définir Un système de riens; le néant serait ainsi à la base du monde, alors que celui-ci se montre à nous distribuant l'être. Telle est la nécessité de Dieu."

A. D. SERTILLANGES, *Saint Thomas d'Aquin*, I, pp. 163-4

I

THE crucial moment for existential theism is that in which we apprehend finite being as what it really is, as existent and yet not self-existent, as effect-implying-cause. Its essence is really distinct from its existence, in the sense that there is nothing about the kind of thing that it is that necessitates that it exists. This does not, however, mean that its essence and its existence are two different *things*; as we have seen, any finite act of existence must, in view of its finitude, have some determinate character, and its essence is simply the particular determinate character that it has. The essence of a finite being therefore, just as much as its existence, is derived from the creative act of God. This is why it is that the apprehension of finite beings not only declares to us that God exists, but manifests to us his perfection; God not only gives them their existence but communicates to them their essence. They not only exist in virtue of his act but they also express his nature; to make this fact about them evident is the function of St. Thomas's Fourth Way. It must, of course, be immediately added that this participation in God's nature does not mean that finite beings are only parts or aspects or manifestations or modes of God; any form of pantheism is excluded, for the existential acts in which their identity subsists are numerically distinct from the existential act of God. Nevertheless in the order of essence, as distinct from the order of existence,[1] what each of them is is a reflection or "imitation" of what God is, contracted to the finitude of the creature's existential act. It follows from this that not only does the existence of creatures declare to us that God exists, but their nature manifests to us God's nature. If, *per impossibile*, they were related to him only in the order of existence, then the perfections which their natures imperfectly exemplify could only be alleged to exist *virtually* in God; God would *cause* the perfections in creatures but those perfections would not necessarily in any way resemble God. But the communication of existence to creatures is not one act and the communication of essence another. Finite essence is only the mode of finite existence, and in the order of essence, as in the order of existence, creatures are related to God by his one creative act which both makes them and makes them what they are. Creatures therefore manifest God's nature as well as declaring his existence, and we can thus assert with confidence that all the perfections that are found in creatures are also formally, though *eminentiori modo*, in God himself.

I must emphasize that in what I have just said I am not trying, by a process of logical or metaphysical gymnastics, to establish a truth previously unknown. If that were so, I might well be accused of the worst kind of verbal cobweb-spinning. I am simply trying to give a rational confirmation and elucidation of a fact already familiar. For the apprehension of God as the cause of finite beings upon which the whole existential approach is based, is not a mere apprehension of God's existence; it is a recognition of his nature as well. Strange as it may seem to anyone who has never made the experiment, the contemplation of finite beings does reveal that they both declare by their finitude that God in his self-existence is

---

[1] In God, of course, essence and existence are really identical. Nevertheless, in their contraction to the finite level essence and existence become distinct, even while each of them rests entirely upon the God in whom they coincide.

altogether other than they and at the same time that in their genuine but limited perfection they are like him.

As we have seen, their declaration of his existence does not raise any special problems; on the other hand the fact that God's essence or nature can be known through our experience of finite beings and can somehow be expressed in human thoughts and words raises very real problems, which the doctrine of analogy attempts to solve. It is, however, important to recall what the function of that doctrine is. It is not to furnish us with knowledge of God, but to explain how we have come to have it. The knowledge itself rests upon our apprehension of finite being in the cosmological relation. If the doctrine of analogy can explain how this is possible, so much the better; if it cannot, it is the doctrine of analogy that is discredited, not our knowledge of God. One can know much about God without even having heard of analogy; it is well for most of us that this is so. Otherwise the Christian preacher would have to deliver a lecture on analogy before he could assure his hearers that God is good.

Our discussion of the cosmological approach has so far been concerned with what it can tell us about God; I shall now go on to discuss what it can tell us about his relation to the world. And I shall remark in the first place, that while in one sense it postulates between God and the world a distinction than which none could be more ultimate and unconditional, in another sense it brings them into a relation more intimate than any other doctrine has ever postulated. In its unqualified assertion that God is self-existent and that every other being depends entirely upon him, it leaves no room for any semi-divine intermediaries between God and the world. No system of hierarchically graded aeons cascading down in a series of steadily diminishing divinity, no *Nous* or World-Soul neither fully divine nor yet exactly finite, no Arian Logos near enough to God to be able to make a world and yet far enough from God to demean himself to so lowly a work, nothing whatever to bridge the gulf between Being that is self-existent and being that is altogether dependent, except the sheer omnipotent fiat of God himself.

Ipse jussit et creata,
Dixit ipse et facta sunt.

But by this very fact the creature is brought into the closest relation to its creator, since everything that it is and has comes solely and entirely from him. It is this doctrine of a God who creates although he has no need to do so that is distinctive of the great Christian tradition, which, with its conviction that the fundamental question for cosmology is why there is a world at all, maintains that the very existence of finite, contingent, and imperfect beings demonstrates the existence of an infinite, self-existent and self-sufficient Being who has brought them into existence by an unconditioned act of sheer creative will. It does not claim to understand the mechanism by which the self-existent being exists; it does not claim to know how he is able to create or why he should wish to do so. It does claim to know why it cannot answer these questions, for the God whose existence it affirms is one that is *ex hypothesi* inscrutable by any finite mind. It alleges that a God who was anything less than infinite, self-existent and self-sufficient would be altogether inadequate to give the world its existence and would moreover require an explanation for his own. To posit a finite God as the ground of the world simply leaves us with two beings whose existence clamours for explanation instead of one; you cannot get necessity from contingency by multiplying contingency. The fundamental affirmation of traditional Christian theism can thus be stated in the following highly remarkable form: the existence of the world implies the existence of a God, and moreover the existence of a God whose existence does *not* imply the existence of a world. We cannot see *why* God exists or *how* he exists, or even how it is possible that he should exist; we can only see that if he did not exist nothing else could. We cannot see why he creates or how he creates; we can only see that unless he did create, the world would not be here. We can see why we cannot see all this, and that must suffice us.

We saw in the last chapter but one[1] that, from one point of view, the cosmological approach can be considered as an attempt to render the world intelligible. It does indeed claim to do this, but it is most important to realize in what this intelligibility consists. It does not claim that, in spite of first appearances, the world really explains itself; on the contrary

[1] p. 88 *supra*.

it asserts that the more fully we understand the world, the more clearly we can see that the world does not explain itself and that therefore its explanation must lie outside itself.   Considered as a closed system the world is unintelligible; given their atheist dogma, the Sartrians are quite right in asserting that existence is absurd, that the world does not make sense. It is perhaps on the whole healthier that an atheist should find the world nonsensical than that he should be under the delusion that it is a self-contained rational system. It may well be that the doctrine of the absurdity of the world is simply what the doctrine of the contingency of the world becomes when it is transposed from a theistic to an atheistic setting. Be this as it may, Christian theism asserts that the world proceeds from God, and that it proceeds from him not by any process of logical or physical necessity, but by an act of unconditioned creative will. The very contingency of the world declares that there is no necessity for its creation antecedent to the creative act itself. We can perhaps see that to create is not inconsistent with God's nature, for God is good, and *bonum est diffusivum sui*. Nevertheless, this does not make creation necessary. For the only being that *can* create is one that *need* not do so; only a God who is fulness of being, and whose own beatitude is therefore incapable of augmentation or diminution, can give existence to other beings.

But surely, it will be objected, all this scholastic word-chopping has led us into a contradiction. We said first that *bonum est diffusivum sui*, and then that goodness need not diffuse itself. Is it not the root weakness of the traditional Christian theism that it finds itself forced to assert that God could be perfectly good without having any object on which to bestow his goodness? And if we reply that God has always himself on whom to pour out his bounty and that, in his unqualified perfection, he is altogether worthy to receive it, are we not turning God's love into that self-love whose true name is selfishness? Is not our God in fact like a millionaire entirely wrapped up in the enjoyment of his riches, who may— or equally well may not—toss a penny, capriciously and more or less unconsciously, to a beggar in the gutter as he passes by? It is, I think, relevant to reply that, since the act of creation

does not confer any benefits upon beings who already exist
but gives them their very existence, if God had not created
finite beings there would be no finite beings to suffer from not
being created.[1] This is not however a complete answer, for
the objection arises not merely from the alleged unkindness
towards the creatures, but from a sense that not to have
created a world when he could have done so would argue
some sort of self-centredness and so an imperfection in the
nature of God. It must, I think, be admitted at this point that
if natural theology were left to its own devices it could not do
much more than say that there must be a solution to the
difficulty somewhere but it could not see where; it would no
doubt add that it had no right to expect to see it anyhow.
St. Thomas brings the point out clearly in two statements
which a hasty reader could easily take to be mutually contradictory. "It pertains," he writes, "to the nature of the will to
communicate to others the good possessed in so far as it is
possible; and specially does this pertain to the divine will, from
which all perfection is derived in some kind of likeness. Hence
if natural things, in so far as they are perfect, communicate
their good to others, much more does it appertain to the
divine will to communicate by likeness its good to others, as
much as is possible." Yet, he goes on to say, "since the goodness of God is perfect and can exist without other things, while
no perfection can accrue to him from them, it follows that his
willing things apart from himself is not necessary absolutely."[2]
The nearest thing that we get to a solution of this antinomy is
a brilliant reply which the Angelic Doctor gives to an opponent
who has urged that, since God's knowledge and will are both
identical with his essence and since whatever he knows he
knows necessarily, it must follow that whatever he wills he wills
necessarily too. The rejoinder points out an important difference between intellect and will. "As the divine existence is
necessary to itself, so is the divine will and the divine know-

[1] I remember a Roman Catholic priest once saying to me that of course no one
could expect him to think kindly of the Benedictines, because they had nearly
made a monk of his father! The remark was of course purely jocular, because,
as the priest in question pointed out, if he had never been begotten he would
not be there to grieve at his non-existence.
[2] S. Theol., I, xix, 2c, 3c. Cf. S.c.G., I, lxxvi, lxxxi.

ledge; but the divine knowledge has a necessary relation to the things known, not the divine will to the things willed. *The reason for this is that knowledge is of things as they exist in the knower; but the will is directed to things as they exist in themselves.* Since, then, all other things have necessary existence in so far as they exist in God [i.e. in the ideas which God possesses of them in the manifold imitability of the divine perfection] but no absolute necessity so as to be necessary in themselves, in so far as they exist in themselves it follows that God knows necessarily whatever he knows, but does not will necessarily whatever he wills."[1] In other words, although God's intellect and his will are really identical, for a creature to be an object of his knowledge and for it to be an object of his will are *not* identical, since these two characteristics arise from two different features of its creaturely being; its knowability from its necessary existence as an idea in the mind of God, and its willability from its contingent existence as an actual creature. This is, I think, as far as purely philosophical argumentation takes us; it is not so much a solution of the problem as an explanation why no solution is possible. And with such an explanation we have no right to be dissatisfied; *si enim comprehenderis, non est Deus.*[2] When, however, we see the question in the setting of the Christian revelation, a flood of light illuminates it. Yes, we reflect, *bonum est diffusivum sui,* and the divine goodness must pour itself forth. But just because its diffusiveness is infinite it cannot find an adequate expression in the production of any finite being. No possible world can, *pace Leibnitii,* exhaust the divine bounty; the perfect expression of the divine love means the generation of an Other who is himself divine, since he receives from God all that God himself is. Only God can be an adequate object of the love of God; and the *necessary* manifestation of the Father's goodness is the eternal generation of the Son. Yet the Son, though he is God, is not a second God, a *heteros theos.* For the Father communicates to the Son, in begetting him, not anything that he makes, not even anything that he has, but the very nature, the *ousia,* that he *is.* Just because, in begetting the Son, the Father imparts to him his own essence, the act of generation posits

---

[1] *S. Theol.,* I, xix, 3 *ad* 6.   [2] Augustine, *Serm. cxvii de Script. N.T.,* iii, 5.

the Son not outside the Father's being, but within it. I am not, of course, claiming to *deduce* the eternal generation of the Son from the fact that God is self-existent love, still less shall I attempt to demonstrate from natural theology that there are in the Godhead three Persons rather than two or four. But I do maintain that revelation confirms and illuminates reason in the conviction that the answer to the question why creation is not necessary to God is not that the divine love needs no exercise but, on the contrary, that no finite activity could provide a sufficiently ample sphere for it.

I am tempted here to draw a parallel. Dr. Leonard Hodgson has pointed out that the triumph at Nicaea of the Athanasian doctrine of the full godhead of the Son of God deprived the Logos-doctrine of what had been to many persons its most attractive feature, that of providing an intermediary between God and the world: "The Jewish belief in direct creation by the will of a personal God broke free from its entanglement with an alien and inconsistent metaphysic."[1] The point that I wish to make here is that this same recognition of the full godhead of the Son deprives the doctrine of creation of what is to many persons its most attractive feature at the present day, namely that of providing an outlet for the love of God. Thus while, as I have said above, in one respect revelation throws a flood of light upon the problem of the love of God, in another respect it leaves us as much in the dark as we were. Why in fact God creates remains unsolved, and I do not think that even such an elaborate and complicated discussion as that given by Fr. Johann Stufler in his valuable little book *Why God created the World* ultimately does anything much to help us. That there is an ultimate mystery in creation I have already emphasized; we can, I think, at least see that that is where the ultimate mystery ought to be. It is just because there is no necessity for creation that we have to postulate the will of God as its cause. And the reason why God's will itself has no cause is that, being identical with God's essence, it needs none. Creation cannot be *necessary* for God's self-expression and self-fulfilment just because it is not *sufficient* for them; what is both necessary and sufficient is the mutual intercourse of self-giving

---

[1] *The Doctrine of the Trinity*, p. 122.

K

and self-receiving of the three Persons in the one Godhead, the life in which the Three are One in essence because each of them gives to and receives from the others all that he himself is. Here at least I think we must agree with the Vatican Council: that God creates *non ad augendum suam beatitudinem nec ad acquirendam, sed ad manifestandam perfectionem suam.*

II

But here we come to the heart of our problem. If the life of God is expressed in its fulness within the interior of the divine being, so that his beatitude is neither increased nor diminished by the vicissitudes of the created world, must we not agree with Aristotle (at least as many of his commentators understand him) that God is altogether unconcerned with the affairs of the world? St. Thomas himself tells us that the relation of creation, while real in the world, is only logical in God,[1] and he adds the warning that our mind "is unable to conceive one thing as related to another without on the other hand conceiving that relation as reciprocal."[2] Such a statement, however, tends to increase our misgivings rather than to allay them, for the example always given by the scholastics to illustrate a relation that is real in one term and logical in the other is that of knowledge, which makes a real difference in the knower but none in the thing known.[3] Are we then to suppose that the creation of the world means no more to God than my thinking about Stalin means to Stalin or my thought of Sirius to Sirius? And does not St. Thomas in fact contradict himself by admitting that God knows things other than himself, and indeed knows each separate thing in its individuality?[4] For, since knowledge implies a real modification in the knower, God would seem at any rate to be modified by his knowledge of the world, even if not by his creation of it.

I will put this last point in another way, following substantially Dr. Evgeny Lampert's recent work *The Divine Realm.* We are told by St. Thomas that God does not necessarily will

---

[1] *S. Theol.*, I, xii, 7 *ad* 4; xlv, 3 *ad* 1. [2] *De Pot.*, I, i, 1 *ad* 10.
[3] Cf. *S.c.G.*, II, xii. [4] *S. Theol.*, I, xiv, 5, 11; *S.c.G.*, I, lxxv.

anything other than himself and yet that, in willing himself, he wills, by the one act of his will, both himself and all other beings.[1] Now we can perhaps admit that the ideas of all possible things are included in the idea which God has of himself in the manifold and infinite imitability of his all-embracing unity; but how, in the simplicity of the one necessary act by which God knows and wills himself, is there found the distinction between those possibilities on which God (unnecessarily) confers actual existence and those other possibilities which are never actualized? Dr. Lampert's own reply is that in fact everything possible *is* actualized and that God necessarily wills its actualization. This seems to me to cut away the very ground of rational theism, namely the contingency of the finite world; it leaves us only the *character* of the world from which to infer God's existence and, if carried through consistently, will tend, in the way upon which I have commented elsewhere,[2] to a doctrine of unbalanced immanence. I hope I shall not be suspected of bigoted Latinism if I say that I discern in Dr. Lampert's book traces of the pantheizing tendency which much Eastern Christian theology has manifested. The position I am criticizing seems also to imply that the actualization of one possible being can never exclude the actualization of another; in other words that all things that are possible of actualization separately are possible of actualization together. In effect the distinction between the possible and the actual vanishes. This world becomes not only the best of all possible worlds but the only possible world. It seems impossible any longer to maintain even a notional distinction between God's unnecessary willing of the world and his necessary willing of himself. But if this is not maintained we shall be landed quite openly in either pantheism or absolutist monism. The fundamental question remains, how the unnecessitated willing of the created world is included in the necessary act by which God wills himself. Does the willing and knowing of the finite world by God add anything to God's willing and knowing of himself? If we answer No, we have apparently denied that the world is really distinct from God. But if we answer Yes, we have apparently denied the divine

[1] *S. Theol.*, I, xix, 1–4.   [2] *He Who Is*, p. 177.

self-sufficiency. That is the dilemma with which we are faced. Can we do anything to ease it?

The simplest way of circumventing the difficulty is to point out that the objection itself rests upon the assumption that God's concern with himself and his concern with the world can be added together, and that a significant statement can be made about their sum. This assumption could be justified only if God and the world were of the same order of being, whereas the fundamental conviction of Christian theism is that they are not. If we denote God's willing (or knowing) of himself by G and his willing (or knowing) of the world by W, the question which has been raised is whether $G+W$ is greater than G. But to talk about $G+W$ at all is to assume that G and W can be added together. And they can be so added only if they are of the same order of being, and this is manifestly false. $G+W$ is what the logicians would call an illicit totality; no significant statement can be made about the sum, because the sum cannot be formed.

This answer is, I believe, fundamentally correct, but it is important to go a little further and see in precisely what way $G+W$ is an illicit totality, for illicit totalities are of various kinds. The simplest form is that which arises when one of the terms, instead of being of the same type as the other, is a class of individuals of that type; there is a well-known story of a Chinese philosopher who contended that if there were a cow and a horse in a field, the field actually contained three things, namely a cow, a horse and a pair of animals. A less straightforward instance would be exemplified if we tried to make a statement about the class of objects consisting of the Albert Memorial, the virtue of prudence, the square-root of minus one, and a pain in the stomach. In the case with which we are concerned the terms G and W are analogically related by an analogy of proportionality. God's willing of himself (G) related to his nature analogously to the way in which his willing of the world (W) is related to the world's nature. Because of this proportionality we are able to make statements about G on the basis of our knowledge of W. We can significantly say that God wills himself, although we know nothing about the mode in which he wills himself, except that it is proportionate to the object willed. This does not however imply that there is any common element in G and W such that they can be taken as forming a sum; that would imply between them a relation of univocity, not of analogy. Any problem, therefore, that arises from the assumption that we can form such a sum is only a pseudo-problem. The objection simply falls to the ground.[1] But there is one point involved which we can hardly stress too strongly.

The analogical passage from finite being to God must always be understood as exalting our notion of God, not as depressing our notion of finite being. It is because finite beings have perfections which, however limited, are real that, on the basis of our knowledge of finite beings, we can affirm their perfections *altiori modo* of God. If, having done this, we then used God's supereminence as a ground for asserting that the finite perfections were not after all as real as we had thought, we should be kicking away from under us the very ladder by which we had climbed. To apply this consideration to our present instance, when we assert that the act by which God wills and knows the world does not augment the act by which he wills and knows himself, we do not imply that his willing and knowing of the world is illusory or fictitious; just the reverse. To establish this fact is of fundamental importance to our whole position, for it enables us to answer what is perhaps the most weighty objection that is commonly brought at the present day against traditional Christian theism; I mean the objection that it is inconsistent with any real belief in the compassion of God. To this particular question I shall now turn.

---

[1] In my book *He Who Is* (pp. 102, 104), I illustrated the point from the case of infinite and finite quantities in mathematics. I still think that the illustration may be useful, but it is purely an illustration and nothing more. And I am less convinced of its usefulness than I was. In any case, *theologia symbolica non est argumentativa*.

I fear that even the late Dr. William Temple failed really to grasp the point which is here at issue. He did indeed sum up the cosmological relation in the two equations:

$$\text{God} - \text{the World} = \text{God}$$
$$\text{The World} - \text{God} = 0.$$

(*Nature, Man and God*, p. 435.)

But he also wrote: "If [God] did not create he would still exist, for he is not dependent for his existence on creation. But *if he did not create, he would not be what he is*, for he is Creator" (ibid., p. 493, italics mine). To say this surely is to say that creation adds something to God.

III

There are few doctrines that can claim in their support so long and consistent a witness in the tradition of Christian theology as the doctrine of the impassibility of God; the very full discussion given by Dr. J. K. Mozley in his work on the subject makes this strikingly clear. "The material brought together . . .," he writes, "shows the existence of a steady and continuous, if not quite unbroken, tradition in Christian theology as to the freedom of the divine nature from all suffering and from any potentiality of suffering." But he added (writing in 1926) that "of this tradition the truth is not unchallenged to-day."[1]

And indeed it has been very widely asserted in recent years that the doctrine can no longer be held by a sensitive and intelligent Christian. I will give two examples to illustrate this; it would be easy to add to them. Dr. W. R. Matthews has asserted that the doctrine as held by the scholastics "is surely very near to a rejection of the belief that God loves the world or human persons at all," and that "the love of God, if we interpret it after the scholastic fashion, falls short of the best human devotion."[2] Dr. H. M. Relton writes that "the revelation of God in Christ was for ever a refutation of his 'impassibility,' since it was a revelation of Love himself incarnate"; he insists that, "if the Heart of God thus revealed is a heart of mercy and compassion, redemptive love and consequent suffering are not alien to him, and the doctrine of his impassibility . . . will have to be modified."[3] Elsewhere he writes as follows: "God for the Christian is . . . known to be no exalted Impassible Deity, separated by an unbridgeable gulf from the world; no impersonal Absolute, untouched and untouchable by the world's pain, but One whose Love necessitates his willingness to share our infirmities, to work in us for our redemption, to achieve through us man's conquest of the many ills that flesh is heir to."[4]

[1] *The Impassibility of God*, p. 127.
[2] *God in Christian Thought and Experience*, pp. 227–8.
[3] *A Study in Christology*, pp. 57, 160.
[4] *Some Postulates of a Christian Philosophy*, p. 26.

Nor is it only from the standpoint of a certain type of modern theology that the divine impassibility might seem to be put in question. There is throughout the history of Christendom an emphasis upon the tenderness and compassion of God for his creatures which has been an essential element in the Church's proclamation of the Gospel of the divine mercy and love, and it is far from obvious that such compassion can be reconciled with impassibility. It is not, I think, sufficient to say that this compassion is to be located simply in the human nature of Christ (which orthodox theology has readily admitted to be passible, at least before its glorification in the Resurrection and Ascension) and that neither Christ's divine nature nor the Person of the Father has any share in it. The language of Christian doctrine has never been satisfied with this restriction. The assertion that

> "There is no place where earth's sorrows
> Are more felt than up in heaven"

was made by a writer whom no one could accuse of having been unduly under the influence of liberal theology. It is thus, I think, well worth while to investigate the relation of divine impassibility to divine compassion, in the hope that, even if we cannot see in every respect how the two are to be reconciled, we may at least do something to clarify the issue.

Dr. Prestige has pointed out[1] that, when the Greek fathers describe God as "impassible" ($\dot{a}\pi a\theta\dot{\eta}s$), the primary connotation is one of moral transcendence: God is "incapable of being diverted or overborne by forces and passions such as commonly hold sway in the creation and among mankind." "It is clear," he adds, "that impassibility means not that God is inactive or uninterested, not that he surveys existence with Epicurean impassivity from the shelter of a metaphysical insulation, but that his will is determined from within instead of being swayed from without."[2] Hence much of the anthropomorphic language of the Old Testament had to be interpreted metaphorically. It is, however, impossible to restrict impassibility to the moral sphere, as if it had no metaphysical significance. "Impassibility . . . ," Dr. Prestige remarks, "is a

---

[1] *God in Patristic Thought*, p. 6.   [2] Ibid., p. 7.

department of the larger question of self-consistency. God is, in the fullest sense, the same yesterday, to-day and for ever. As the ground and unifying principle of the multiplicity of experience must, on the Greek view, itself be conceived as single, so must it also be regarded as possessing a changeless identity."[1]

It is perhaps well to emphasize that whatever difficulties are raised by the doctrine of divine impassibility do not arise merely in connection with the Incarnation, though they do appear most clearly in the *Verbum supernum, prodiens nec linquens Patris dexteram*, in the "great Creator" who "makes himself a house of clay." They arise out of the very notion of creation itself, as it is understood by Christian theism in relation to the divine providence: the notion, that is, that, although God is altogether infinite and self-sufficient and the world is altogether finite and dependent upon him, nevertheless this self-sufficient God has the most intimate and loving concern with the finite world which is his creature. God, says St. Thomas, loves all existing things.[2] Traditional theism has not failed to recognize the compassion of God; the only question is whether it is consistent in affirming at the same time his impassibility. For, it may be urged, does not his compassion mean that God is genuinely affected by what goes on in this world, while his impassibility means that he is entirely unaffected by it? The problem is obviously closely related to the problem which we have already discussed, whether, if God is one whose nature and whose name is Love, it is possible to hold that creation is unnecessary to God's own self-fulfilment. Nevertheless, the two problems, though related, are not absolutely identical. For, when the traditionalist has alleged that creation is shown to be an exercise of love precisely by the fact that God gains nothing by it, it might still be objected that, when God *has* created the world as an object of his love, the interest in its existence and its history that he is thereby shown to have argues a certain enlargement of his own experience. If God sorrows for our sins, rejoices at our repentance and feels for us in our sufferings, in any other than a purely metaphorical sense, is not this sympathy an addition to his activity, even if he was

---

[1] *God in Patristic Thought*, p. 11.   [2] *S. Theol.*, I, xx, 2c.

under no impulsion to create us? It should be noted that this difficulty cannot be avoided by the assertion, true though it is, that, considered *ex parte Dei*, creation is an act performed outside or above time by a Being whose own mode of existence and operation is timeless and eternal.[1] It can still be maintained that for God to be interested in the world as well as in himself is something more than for him to be interested in himself alone.

I have already remarked upon the widespread abandonment of the doctrine of divine impassibility at the present day. It is not, however, always sufficiently recognized that this abandonment rests not merely upon moral considerations, but also upon a particular metaphysical attitude which denies that God is, in the traditional sense, genuinely transcendent to, and independent of, the finite world. The most extreme expression of this tendency with which I am acquainted occurs in a book by an American writer, who maintains that "the worst thing that could happen to God would be to remain an autocrat while the world is moving to democracy. . . . It is not enough," he continues, "for theology to eliminate this or that autocratic trait. Its God must join the social movement."[2] I do not suggest that anything quite so crude as this could be found in the work of a serious philosopher. But when

> "Lord Gifford, deep beneath the ground,
> Heard Alexander's bugle sound"

in the stimulating notes of *Space, Time and Deity*, or Whitehead weaving his not less elaborate music in *Process and Reality*, or even James Ward magnificently refuting naturalism and agnosticism in the name of what is, I am afraid, in the last issue only a pluralistic substitute for a genuine theism, in each

---

[1] This is a convenient point at which to reply to the objection that, in asserting that creation is not merely the act by which the world receives its temporal beginning, we are defending something other than the belief of the "plain man," to whom creation means "the beginning of the world." It is true that the plain man normally uses the word "creation" in this latter sense, but it is also true that, if he is an instructed Christian and not a deist, he also believes that God perpetually preserves his creatures in existence; and this is simply a description, from the standpoint of the creature, of the extra-temporal act which is "creation" in the strict philosophical sense. The objection is thus a purely verbal one.

[2] W. Rauschenbusch, *A Theology for the Social Gospel*, p. 178.

case the great benefactor of natural theology might have observed the assumption that, whatever God might be like and in whatever sense he might be said to exist, he was certainly not metaphysically transcendent to his creation. I have argued elsewhere,[1] taking such typical representatives of modern philosophy as Ward, Whitehead and Tennant, that the main reason for this is that the fundamental question of cosmology is assumed to be concerned not, as for traditional theism, with the world's existence but with its nature. The question for which an answer has been sought is "Why is the world the sort of thing it is?" rather than "Why is there a world at all?"; indeed this latter question has frequently been openly rejected as altogether illegitimate. Such an attitude is, of course, quite in line with the generally positivist and anti-metaphysical tendency of modern philosophy as a whole. Just as Dr. Karl Barth maintained in his Gifford Lectures that in arguing that there was no such thing as natural theology he was at least talking about it, so modern metaphysics has all too frequently seen one of its chief functions to be the demonstration that metaphysics cannot exist. I do not believe, however, that the Science of Being is condemned to commit hara-kiri on its own doorstep or to empty itself out of the Cartesian bath with the Humian water; I should claim that such a profoundly impressive work as Dr. Farrer's *Finite and Infinite* has shown that the question why there is a world at all can still be significantly asked and that it demands (and can receive) an answer. The rehabilitation of the notion of existence[2] and of the doctrine of analogy is of quite outstanding importance for the reorientation of metaphysics and cosmology. When Dr. Tennant provides us with a God who is less than the God of traditional theism in that, while in a certain sense the universe depends upon God for its existence, he is nevertheless bound to create it and, having created it, is limited by it, this is only to be expected in view of the starting-point that has been adopted. For if we restrict ourselves merely to asking questions about the way in which the universe behaves, we can

---

[1] *He Who Is*, ch. viii (additional note), xi, xii, esp. pp. 177–8.
[2] I would remind the reader again that I do not intend in such a phrase as this to suggest that existence can be included in a concept. See p. 50, *n.* 5 *supra*.

never arrive at the affirmation of a genuinely transcendent cause. Whitehead, who is far more consistent than Tennant in this procedure, cogently remarks that "any proof which commences with the character of the actual world cannot rise about the actuality of this world. . . . It may discover an immanent God, but not a God wholly transcendent."[1] Unfortunately Whitehead never seriously considers the possibility that a proof might commence not with the character which the world exemplifies but with the fact that it exists. It is not surprising, therefore, that his final description of God is "the great companion—the fellow sufferer who understands";[2] he has, I suggest, mistaken God's reflection in his dealings with the world for God himself. And Dr. Matthews, while he affirms that "there can be no evil, which, in the end, will frustrate the divine redeeming will" and that "the suffering of God is transfigured by the vision of the travail of his soul in which is his satisfaction," also insists that "succession is real for God" and that "the experience of change which enters into the divine Life must obviously be that of the changes of the created order."[3]

To return to the point from which we digressed, I believe that while, as I said, the moral problem of the divine impassibility is not absolutely identical with the metaphysical problem of the unnecessity of creation, its solution, so far as a solution can be found, is to be sought along the same lines. It will be remembered that I stressed that the analogical passage from finite being to God must not be understood as depressing our notion of finite being but as exalting our notion of God. There is, it seems to me, an all too common assumption in present-day theology that, if X is greater than Y, the necessary consequence is that Y must be very small. I will, in passing, give two instances of this from the sphere not of natural but of dogmatic theology. The first is the neo-Calvinist insistence that, in order to extol the order of grace and redemption, we must depress the order of nature and creation, as if, however exalted a view of nature we take (even of fallen nature), there were not unlimited room for grace above it. The truth surely is that,

---

[1] *Religion in the Making*, p. 71.
[2] *Process and Reality*, p. 497.   [3] Op. cit. sup., pp. 248, 262.

provided we are fully aware that the order of grace incalculably
exceeds the order of nature—that *bonum gratiae unius majus est
quam bonum naturae totius universi*[1]—then any goodness which we
discern in the order of nature will *a fortiori* redound to the
superexceeding honour of grace. My second instance will be
that of the Protestant refusal to give honour to the saints for
fear of treating them as if they were greater than God. Here
again, the truth surely is that the full recognition of the created
glory of the saints enhances rather than diminishes our recognition of the uncreated glory of their Creator, provided—and
this is altogether essential—that we clearly apprehend that
God infinitely surpasses even the greatest of them.

> "If Mary is so beautiful,
> What must her Maker be?"

For he that built the house hath more honour than the house,
even if the house be the house of God himself.

In practice, I am afraid, both Protestants and Catholics
have, in their thought, sometimes substituted for the infinite
God a being who is great but nevertheless finite; and if our
conception of God is only—shall we say?—that of a magnified
municipal official, we shall either (with some Protestants)
refuse to the saints their due honour for fear of making them
greater than God or else (with some Catholics) give them their
due honour at the expense of making them greater than God
as we have conceived him. I suggest, in fact, that when the
veneration of the saints has lost its due proportion in the life
of Christian devotion, either by excess or by defect, it is not so
much because Catholics have had an exaggerated notion of
the worthiness of the saints as because Catholics and Protestants
have only too often had a much impoverished notion of the
splendour of God. The right course surely is to admit in their
fulness, without fear or grudging, the glories that God manifests
in his creatures, in both the natural and the supernatural order,
and then to reflect, "If even this is infinitely exceeded by God's
own perfection, how much more glorious must he be than in
our wildest dreams we could have supposed!" To quote
Faber's hymn for the last time:

[1] *S. Theol.*, II I, cxiii, 9 *ad* 2.

"How wonderful creation is,
The work which thou didst bless,
And O! what then must thou be like,
Eternal loveliness."

It is, I suggest, then, this use of the *Quo majus* which we need when we pass from the consideration of the finite world to the consideration of its Maker. The more we are able to discern of the reality of God's concern with the finite order, the less obscurely shall we recognize the supreme reality and inner beatitude of him upon whom it depends for all that it has and is. In the words of Osuña, "the greater a creature is, the more it has need of God."[1] For what has it that it has not received?

Applying this method, then, to the problem of the divine compassion, we must not say "Because God's interior beatitude can be neither increased nor decreased, therefore the events of the finite world are of no real concern to him." Rather we should say "If even the concern which God has with the things of this world—a concern far more penetrating and intimate than any that we ourselves experience—can neither increase nor diminish the beatitude and felicity of God's own triune life, how unimaginably rich and glorious must that beatitude and felicity be." This is a true analogical passage from the finite to the infinite,[2] which uses the finite to deepen our knowledge of the infinite, and not the infinite to deprive the finite of the true, though limited, reality that it has. As we have seen earlier in our discussion, analogy gives us a knowledge of God in the concept which we form of the finite being, though we cannot form a concept of God; still less can we form a concept of God and the finite together. It is for this last reason that we cannot validly assert that the finite either adds to or detracts from God.

---

[1] Quoted by Bremond, *Lit. Hist. of Rel. Thought in France*, I, p. 11.

[2] It may be noted that the analogical passage here is not simply from a finite being to God, but from God's concern with finite being to his concern with himself. It is important to recognize that analogy is not a genus of which the different examples of analogy are species; analogy is itself not a univocal but an analogical notion. So deeply does the principle of analogy penetrate the whole realm of being. In the present instance it occurs in two stages, first when we pass from our concern with finites to God's concern with finites and then when we pass from God's concern with finites to his concern with himself.

But here the plain man will impatiently break in upon the detachment of the professional philosopher. You have admitted, he protests, that God "feels for us" (though you would probably be not too happy with so crude a phrase as this) in our sufferings as intensely as, and indeed more intensely than, we feel for ourselves. But in swamping his compassion with his interior beatitude you have deprived the admission of all its value. Is this really of any help to people like me who have to put up with the sufferings without enjoying the beatitude? If I am plagued with a raging toothache it will not comfort me much to be told that someone whose tooth is equally bad is finding it quite bearable because he has just been left an immense fortune. The protest is understandable, but I think there are two considerations which help to rebut it. The first consists in pointing out that when we are in trouble what really helps us is not sympathy, in the sense of an imaginative or even an actual participation in our sufferings, but concrete practical help.[1] And from this point of view there is real consolation in the knowledge that God is *au dessus de la mêlée* and is not entangled in our predicament. This is, I think, the real point of St. Thomas's startling remark that "to bewail (*tristari de*) the misery of others belongs not to God, but it does most properly belong to him to dispel that misery."[2] So, I would suggest, when we reflect upon the fragility and tenuosity of the beings that compose this finite world of ours and upon the ephemerality of all in it that we hold most dear, we shall see that the God who can meet our deepest needs will not be one who is himself entangled in its contingencies—not merely "the great companion—the fellow sufferer who understands"—but one who, while his loving care extends even to the least of his creatures and while he knows them in their weakness and need better than they know themselves, is himself unchanged and unchangeable, the strength and stay upholding all creation who ever doth himself unmoved abide, a God in whom compassion and impassibility are reconciled in the union of omnipotence and love. "I the Lord change not;

---

[1] I am, of course, excluding here any consideration of the sense in which God may be said to suffer in the personal assumption of human nature in the Incarnation, with its sequel in the Passion of Christ.   [2] *S. Theol.*, I, xxi, 3c.

therefore ye, O sons of Jacob, are not consumed."[1] But there is a further and more profound consideration than this.

The Christian revelation assures us that the end for which God has made us is nothing less than the sharing of his own life in the beatific vision; we are, to put it in quite plain terms, to *enjoy God*. It follows that God's unruffled beatitude is not something in which he luxuriates in self-centred detachment; it is something which he intends to confer on us. If suffering were, strictly and formally, contained in God, then either our ultimate destiny would have to be something less than real union with him or our eternity would be an eternity of suffering. Only a religion which views the beatific vision in purely extrinsic terms could hold that the impassibility of God implied any ultimate defect in his compassion.[2]

IV

The act of creation, being entirely unique and, moreover, being profoundly mysterious, we are more than usually liable to fall into error by thinking of it in terms of finite operations which are more tractable to our limited and sense-bound intellects. The most obvious of such tendencies is the tendency to view creation as a kind of manufacture or manipulation. Finite agents can make things out of material already pro-

---

[1] Mal., iii, 6.

[2] It is perhaps interesting to see how St. Thomas deals with the question whether sorrow (*tristitia*) can be predicated of God. In *S.c.G.*, I, xci, he tells us that love and joy are properly, and not merely metaphorically, in God, though the important caution is added that even these emotions (*affectiones*) are not in God, as they are in us, by way of passions. Other emotions, such as anger and sorrow, which by their very nature are inconsistent with the divine perfection, are predicated of God in Holy Writ only metaphorically. But within this metaphorical attribution St. Thomas draws a distinction. Some attributes, he says, are applied metaphorically "on account of a likeness of effects." Anger is one of these; it exists in God only virtually, in the sense that God produces on occasion effects similar to those produced by an angry man, but this does not mean that God is angry *formaliter*. Sorrow, on the other hand, although it is predicated of God metaphorically, is so predicated "on account of likeness to a preceding emotion"; "God is said to sorrow (*tristari*) in as much as certain things occur contrary to those he himself loves and approves, even as we sorrow for those things which happen to us against our will" (cap. cit. *ad fin.*). We are thus, I think, not contradicting St. Thomas if we say that there is formally in God something that appears to us as sorrow, but it appears to us in this guise not because it is formally such but because certain creatures act contrary to God's will. For a very interesting discussion of the relation of all this to God's timelessness, see Fr. Gerald Vann's profound little Aquinas Paper on *The Sorrow of God*.

vided; God, being infinitely powerful, can make things out of nothing. "Nothing" thus comes to be imagined as a kind of stuff on which God works, and God himself is reduced in our thought to the status of a demiurge.[1] Even when we have recognized that the creative act is, *a parte Dei*, non-temporal, we are still in danger of this tendency to hypostatize non-existence. Few things are more difficult than to grasp consistently the fact that, just because it is the provision of the act by which finite beings *exist*, creation demands no material cause whatever. Nor must we be beguiled into the equally tempting snare of imagining creation as the ejection by God from himself of material initially contained within him; in whatever form such an opinion is held it ultimately leads to pantheism.[2] There is a passage in St. Thomas which is very instructive in this connection. "Changes (*mutationes*)," he writes, "acquire their nature and their importance not from their *terminus a quo* but from their *terminus ad quem*. Therefore a change is more perfect and primary according as its *terminus ad quem* is more noble and primary, although the *terminus a quo* which stands over against the *terminus ad quem* may be more imperfect. Thus generation is simply more noble and primary than mere alteration, because a substantial form is nobler than an accidental form; nevertheless the *terminus a quo* of generation, namely the absence of the substantial form, is more imperfect than the *terminus a quo* of alteration, which is the contrary accident (*contrarium*). And thus creation is more perfect and primary than either generation or alteration,

---

[1] I am afraid that even Mr. F. J. Sheed in his useful book *Theology and Sanity* does not seem to be quite clear that to say that God used no material in making the world is not quite the same as to say that nothing is the material which he used in order to make it. (Op. cit., p. 5.)

[2] Reference may be made to St. Thomas's very interesting discussion whether God enters into the composition of other things (*S. Theol.*, I, iii, 8): "On this point there have been three errors: Some have affirmed that God is the world-soul, as is clear from Augustine (*De Civ.*, vii, 6), and this is practically the same as the view of those who hold that God is the soul of the first heaven. Again others have said that God is the formal principle of all things; this is said to have been the view of the Almaricians. And the third error is that of David of Dinant, who most absurdly (*stultissime*) held that God is prime matter." Elsewhere (*S.c.G.*, I, xvii) St. Thomas refers to the "frenzy" (*insania*) of David of Dinant. A similar view is found to-day among those who use God as a name for the evolutionary process. St. Thomas does of course occasionally speak of the "emanation" of creatures from God (*S. Theol.*, I, xlv) but in an entirely different sense from that of the "emanationists."

because its *terminus ad quem* is the whole substance of the thing. But what we think of as its *terminus a quo* simply does not exist (*id autem quod intelligitur ut terminus a quo, est simpliciter non ens*)."[1] It is in fact almost impossible for us not to envisage a hypostatized non-being as the material cause of creation. Nevertheless in reality creation has no material cause whatever, and it is only in a highly qualified sense that we can describe it as a "change" at all. Creation does indeed "make a difference" to the creature, and the most radical of all differences, since were it not for creation there would be no creature at all; nevertheless, were it not for creation there would be no creature to which this difference could be made. Thus creation is, to use the phrase of Père Sertillanges, "a unilateral relation of dependence, and nothing else." "From the side of God," he says, "no effect arises from the fact that the world exists. God does not change. From the side of the creature too, no effect arises, except the creature itself and the relation of dependence which it has with its primary Source. Now," he goes on, "see what follows. In order for the creature to be in relation with God it must first of all exist. If creation is this relation, creation comes into the order of being after the creature. This is indeed turning the world upside down! Nevertheless, it is so; it cannot but be so, once it is admitted that absolutely nothing is interposed between God, who is the world's cause, and the world as it begins; that the world is prior in time, with its quality of being a dependent thing, and that this attribute, which is creation itself, is necessarily subsequent, both for our minds and in the nature of things (*intellectu et natura*, as St. Thomas says), to the subject which it relates to its creator."[2]

Père Sertillanges adds that, in the logical or notional order, creation comes first and the world second; we think first of God, then of his creative action, then of the created world. But in the real order there is first of all God, and then the creature which depends entirely upon him. "In creation," writes St. Thomas, "it is not non-being that receives the divine action, but the thing which has been created."[3]

---

[1] *S. Theol.*, I, xlv, 1 *ad* 2.   [2] *L'Idée de création*, p. 46.
[3] *In creatione, non ens non se habet ut recipiens divinam actionem, sed id quod creatum est* (*De Pot.*, iii, 3 *ad* 1).

L

It is, I think, interesting to note how the Old Testament, in spite of its use of metaphorical and anthropomorphic language, is able successfully to guard against any notion of creation as simply a manipulative process. In the first chapter of Genesis the work of the six days of creation is represented as brought about by nothing more than a series of uttered commands. "God said, Let there be light. *And light was* . . . God said, Let the earth bring forth the living creature after its kind. *And it was so.*" Nothing could be in sharper contrast with the general run of creation-stories in the ancient world. There is no manipulation, no emission of substance, no medium between God and the world, nothing but the omnipotent fiat by which the creatures receive their very existence together with their natures.

I have said, a little further back, that the act of creation is unique and mysterious, and this is true. It is not, however, in the least degree unfamiliar, since everything that we perceive is a creature and we are creatures ourselves. Perhaps the main difficulty in speaking about it arises from its very universality; for we cannot call attention to it by remarking on the difference between objects of our experience which exemplify it and those which do not. The same difficulty arises in the case of such notions as those of substance and causality. We cannot *see* what the difference is by looking at a being which does not exemplify it, because there are no such beings.

> "No birds were flying overhead,
> There were no birds to fly."

To be a creature is simply to exist, but to exist with a received existence. It is sometimes asserted that the basic fact about a creature is that, left to itself, it is nothing. This is no doubt true, but it can easily be taken as if it meant that nothing is the sort of thing that, if it was left to itself, it would be, and then we are falling again into the fallacy of hypostatizing non-existence. The really basic fact about a creature is that God does not leave it to itself and therefore that, as the object of his creative act, it is the very thing that it is. There is a passage in Sertillanges that is very illuminating in this connection.

"That beings tend to non-being," he writes, "taken literally has no meaning; for non-being, not being anything, cannot be the object of a tendency. Anything that is tends to *being*, and not only to being but to the perfection of its being. This is intelligible, because it participates God,[1] to whom belongs being in its fulness, so that anything that participates God can have no other law than to tend to the perfection of this participation, that is to say to the perfection of itself. To realize the creative thought is indeed our whole ideal.

"For this reason some thinkers, well-meaning but nevertheless misguided, have said that a being when once created could cease to be only by a positive act of God aimed at its destruction. This is a recognition of the creature's autonomy, but it goes too far; for, while God can quite well grant his creatures the power to be and to be autonomous, he cannot grant them the power to get on without him. . . .

"The tendency of every creature to persevere in being is a reality, but this tendency does not come from its own sole power, it comes from the Cause from which it derives its being; as, on the other hand, if we say that it tends to non-being, this is not because of its nature but because of its deficiency. Subtly perhaps but none the less truly, St. Thomas writes: 'Non-being has no power against the being of creatures, but also it has no power to preserve them.'[2]

"Let us repeat once for all, with careful attention to every word: creatures, as soon as they exist, tend to exist and not to collapse. But first of all they must exist. Now they do not exist of themselves. And thus the power that they need is not one which would prevent them from collapsing when they existed, but one which makes them exist. The point of application of this power is not between the creatures and an alleged non-being, thought of as a kind of chasm; Henri Bergson has once for all exorcized this image in a famous piece of analysis. The point of application of the sustaining power is between the creatures and God, in order that the contact shall not be broken and that the creature shall continue to flow from its source."[3]

What being a creature really means has, I think, nowhere

---

[1] "Participe de Dieu"; there is no suggestion of pantheism.

[2] *De Pot.*, v, 1 *ad* 8.

[3] Op. cit., p. 68. Bergson's criticism of *le néant* (*Creative Evolution*, ch. iv) has received an interesting discussion in Maritain's essay on "The Metaphysics of Bergson" (*Redeeming the Time*, p. 61).

been more admirably expressed than in these words of Père Sertillanges. No more radical distinction could be found than that between God and his creatures, nor (at least if we restrict ourselves to the realm of natural theology) any more intimate relation than that in which they are united to him in their creation. And these two facts—the fact of the distinction and the fact of the relation—are only two aspects of the one fundamental cosmological truth, the truth of finite being as genuinely existing and yet existing with an existence that is altogether derived.

V

I shall conclude this chapter with some remarks upon an approach to theism which claims to be fully in agreement with the demands of Christianity and which, at least on first examination, appears to differ very profoundly from the view which I have been expounding. I mean the approach which is common among philosophers and theologians of the Eastern Orthodox Church and to which expression has recently been given by M. Vladimir Lossky in his fascinating *Essai sur la Théologie mystique de l'Église d'Orient*. This outlook pays immense respect to the writings of the fifth-century Syrian who adopted as his pseudonym the name of Dionysius the Areopagite, the disciple of St. Paul, and it makes use of them without any of those hesitations and reinterpretations which have been so marked a feature of their rather uneasy adoption in the West. In spite of the neo-Platonic background and flavour of these works, M. Lossky denies categorically that the pseudo-Areopagite was importing into the Christian tradition an element that was really incompatible with it. He sees the proof of this in the radically negative or apophatic character of the Dionysian system.

"If Plotinus," he writes, "rejects the attributions proper to being in seeking to attain God, it is not, as with Dionysius, because of the absolute unknowability of God clouded by everything that can be known in beings; it is because the domain of being, even at its highest, is necessarily multiple and has not the absolute simplicity of the 'One.' The God of Plotinus is not unknowable by nature; if we cannot under-

stand the One either by knowledge or by an intellectual intuition, it is because the soul, when it seizes an object by
knowledge departs from unity and is not absolutely one. . . .
This is why Plotinus designates his ecstasy by a quite characteristic name, that of 'simplification' (ἅπλωσις). It is a way of
reducing to simplicity the object of contemplation which can
be defined positively as the One—ἕν—and which, in this
quality, is not distinct from the subject who contemplates.
In spite of all the external resemblances, which are due mainly
to the common vocabulary, we are here far from the negative
theology of the *Areopagitica*. The God of Dionysius, unknowable by nature, the God of the Psalms 'who makes the shadows
his hiding-place,' is not the primordial unity which is the
God of the neo-Platonists. If he is unknowable, it is not in
virtue of a simplicity which would be unable to accommodate
itself to the multiplicity infecting all our knowledge relative
to beings; it is, so to speak, a more fundamental, an absolute
unknowability."[1]

God, therefore, from this point of view, is in his essence
entirely unknowable and incommunicable. Yet we know that
he manifests and communicates himself in the act of creation,
and, if we are Christians, we believe that to us he reveals and
communicates himself in an even higher way. How is this to
be explained? At this point recourse is had to a discrimination
which is made in the *Areopagitica* between the "unions"
(ἐνώσεις) and the "distinctions" (διακρίσεις) in God. The
"unions" are altogether interior to the superessential nature
of God and have no external manifestation, while the
"distinctions" are "processions" (πρόοδοι), "manifestations"
(ἐκφάνσεις) or "powers" (δυνάμεις) in which everything that
exists participates, making God known through creatures. This
doctrine was developed by subsequent theologians and received
a fully systematic presentation from the fourteenth-century
Archbishop of Thessalonica, St. Gregory Palamas,[2] by whom

[1] Op. cit., pp. 28–9.
[2] A full, though unsympathetic, discussion of Palamism may be found in
the two articles s.v. "Palamas, Grégoire" and "Palamite (Controverse)" by
Père M. Jugie in *Dict. de Théol. Cath.*, XI, cols. 1736, 1777. Reference may also
be made to the article by Fr. Basil Krivoshein in *Eastern Churches Quarterly*, January–
October 1938, on "The Ascetic and Theological Teaching of Gregory Palamas,"
and to the sympathetic, though critical, article by Dom Clément Lialine in the
same periodical, January–March 1946, on "The Theological Teaching of Gregory
Palamas on the Divine Simplicity."

an explicit contrast is made between the "essence" of God and his "energies."

"The presence of God in his energies," writes M. Lossky, "must be understood in a realist sense. It is not an operative presence of a cause in its effects; the energies are not effects of the divine cause, as are creatures; they are not created, produced from nothing, but flow eternally from the one essence of the Trinity. They are overflowings of the divine nature, which cannot limit itself and is more than the essence. We can say that the energies denote a mode of existence of the Trinity outside its inaccessible essence. God exists, then, at once in his essence and outside his essence. . . . If we denied the real distinction between essence and energy, we should be unable to draw a clear line between the procession of the divine Persons and the creation of the world; both would be equally acts of the nature. . . . We must therefore distinguish in God the one nature, the three Persons, and the uncreated energy which proceeds from the nature without being separated from it in this procession of manifestation."[1]

M. Lossky adds that we must avoid two false views about the divine energies. In the first place, "the energy is not a divine function in relation to creatures, although God creates and operates by his energies which penetrate everything that exists. Creatures might not exist, but God would still manifest himself outside his essence." Secondly, "the created world does not become infinite and coeternal with God from the fact that the natural processions or the divine energies are such. The energies imply no necessity of creation, which is a free act effectuated by the divine energy but determined by a decision of will common to the three Persons."[2]

The full bearing of this doctrine is seen when we consider not merely God's operation in the natural order in creation but also his operation in the supernatural order by grace. Indeed, the very distinction between an order of nature and an order of supernature lacks altogether the sharpness which it has in the West. For Western theology, in Mersch's words, "the infinite Being has two ways of communicating himself to finite beings; the first is that by which he gives himself to them

---

[1] Op. cit., p. 71. [2] Ibid., p. 72.

in their way and makes them themselves, the second is that by which he gives himself to them in his way and makes them one with him."[1] The nature and possibility of this second donation of God to his creatures has, of course, been the subject of much discussion among scholastic theologians. But in the Palamite theory, God gives himself in only one way, in both nature and grace; he gives himself in his energies.[2] For the Thomist, supernatural grace means a communication of God himself to the creature in the created mode under which a creature can receive him; for the Palamite, it means a communication of the uncreated energy of God though not of his incommunicable essence. It is easy to see the kind of argument to which this can give rise. The Palamite says to the Thomist, "You make no distinction between the essence of God and his energy, and you say God gives himself to the creature in a finite mode. But that must mean that the divine essence is given in a finite mode, and this is impossible. Either what is given is finite and therefore is not God, or what is given is God and therefore cannot be given finitely. In the former case there is no real divinization of man, in the latter case man ceases to be a creature. Neither alternative is tenable." The Thomist replies, "Of course the whole question is highly mysterious, but you have not been fair to my words. I did not say that God-in-a-finite-mode was given to the creature, but that the creature participated God in a finite mode. The finitude is in the mode of participation, not in the object participated. And here is a dilemma for you, to match that in which you tried to catch me. You say that the creature participates in the divine energy though not in the divine essence. Now listen. Either the energy and the essence are identical, or else in participating the energy the creature does not really participate in God. In the former case you have abandoned your own theory, in the latter case it fails to provide for a real divinization of man." "No," the Palamite rejoins, "now it is you who have been unfair to me. The energy is divine, and therefore in participating the divine energy the creature participates

---

[1] "Filii in Filio," in *Nouv. Rév. théol.*, 1938, p. 820.
[2] Lossky, p. 85. Eastern theology, he says, "knows no other distinction, or rather division, than that between the created and the uncreated. For it, the created supernatural does not exist" (ibid.).

God. God is present, really present, in his energy as much as in his essence. Thus God is really communicated in his energy, though he remains incommunicable in his essence." "Really," protests the Thomist, "this is intolerable. God and his essence cannot be separated. If the energy communicates God it communicates his essence. And then you need my theory to explain how the creature can participate God without losing its creatureliness." And so the debate goes on, and there seems no prospect of its ceasing. I think myself that the Thomist has the better of it, but it is perhaps hardly fair to claim the last word. I have made this excursus outside the sphere of natural theology because I think it brings out fairly clearly the point at issue. Let us now return to the question of creation.

The point of view which I have been expounding in this book postulates no intermediary whatever between God and the creature. The creature indeed has its archetype in the divine ideas, but these ideas are not differentiations within the divine being; they are simply the modes under which the divine being is imitable by finite beings.[1] Except in relation to the finite beings they have no distinguishing characteristics. Just as the creative act, while it is the efficient cause of the existence of creatures, comes, in the order of being, after the creatures and not before, so the ideas, in their multiplicity and distinction, while they are the formal cause of the creatures, come in the order of being after the creatures, and not before. Unless God was multiply *imitable* on the finite level there could be no finite beings, but the multiple modes in which God is *imitated* are not antecedent to the finite existents but consequent upon them. In the last resort it is not the creative act or the ideas that give existence to the creature, but God, who operates according to the ideas by the creative act. Nothing is ejected from within God's being by creation; God wills that there shall be a world, and the world exists. In the theory which M. Lossky expounds, on the contrary, the divine ideas are dynamically pre-existent in the divine energies. He writes as follows:

"The term θελητικὴ ἔννοια [taken from St. John of Damascus], which I have translated 'will-thought,' and which it

[1] See the additional note at the end of this chapter.

would perhaps be more exact to call 'volitive thought,' is
very significant. It expresses perfectly the Eastern doctrine of
the divine ideas, and the place which the theology of the
Eastern Church assigns to the ideas of created things in God.
The ideas are not, according to this conception, eternal
notions of creatures contained in the very Being of God,
determinations of the essence to which created things are
related as their exemplar cause, as they are in St. Augustine's
thought, which later became a common teaching of the whole
Western tradition and a sharply formulated doctrine in St.
Thomas Aquinas. In the thought of the Greek fathers the
divine ideas have a more dynamic and intentional character.
Their place is not in the essence, but in 'that which is after
the essence,' in the divine energies; for the ideas are identified
with the will or the wills ($\theta\epsilon\lambda\dot{\eta}\mu\alpha\tau\alpha$) which determine the
different modes in which created beings participate in the
creative energies. . . . If the divine ideas are not the very
essence of God, if they are, so to speak, separated from the
essence by the will, then not only the act of creation but also
the thought of God is no longer a necessary determination of
the nature, the intelligible content of the divine Being. Thus
the created universe will not be presented, as in Platonic or
Platonizing thought, under the pale and puny aspect of a bad
copy of God, but will appear as an absolutely new being, as a
creation newly come from the hands of the God of Genesis
'who saw that it was good,' a created universe willed by God
which was the joy of his Wisdom."[1]

The essential features of M. Lossky's view will, I think, now
be clear. It forms the most attractive alternative which I have
yet seen to the traditional doctrine of the West. Nevertheless
I cannot feel that it is satisfactory. The whole debate turns
upon two questions: (1) Can we accept the distinction made
by the Eastern tradition, as M. Lossky interprets it, between
the essence and the energy in the divine being? (2) Can we
accept the account of creation which it offers? I feel obliged
to reply in the negative in each case. But let us do the theory
full justice. It cannot with fairness be accused of simply
importing neo-Platonism into the Christian Troy in a wooden
horse bearing the name of St. Paul's Athenian convert. And
it voices a fully justified protest against materialized and

[1] Op. cit., pp. 90–1.

pedestrian versions of Thomism which view creation as the manipulation by God of a non-existent material exterior to himself, in accordance with certain neatly chiselled models laid up in a divine repository. But I do not think that the protest holds against such a doctrine as I have tried to expound in this book, a doctrine in which existence is sheer actuality and act and in which creatures possess a real, though imparted, vigour and novelty. It may be the case that, if one gets beneath the differences of philosophical terminology and outlook, the divergence is not as great as at first sight it appears. We are moving in the realm of the highest mysteries, and we are, in the last resort, believers in the same God. A really adequate exploration of the matter would require a much more extended discussion than can be attempted here. It would, for example, be necessary to investigate how far the doctrine of the divine energy can be assimilated to the Thomist doctrine of analogy.[1] I have, however, thought it worth while to give this brief outline of M. Lossky's views, partly because of their intrinsic interest and partly because the contrast which they offer may help to throw into higher relief the lineaments of the doctrine which I have been expounding throughout this book.[2]

ADDITIONAL NOTE TO CHAPTER SIX
(See page 152)

I am glad to have the opportunity at this point to draw the reader's attention to a very striking discussion of St. Thomas's doctrine of the divine ideas by Anton C. Pegis. It is entitled "The Dilemma of Being and Unity. A Platonic Incident in Christian Thought," and is printed in the volume *Essays in Thomism*, edited by R. E. Brennan, O.P.

Pegis points out that in Platonic thought there is a radical opposition between *being* and *unity*. "Being in its ultimate nature is an organized whole of distinct and hierarchically arranged

---

[1] Cf. Lossky, p. 24.

[2] It is perhaps well to note that, in spite of some similarities, M. Lossky rejects the "sophiology" of certain of his fellow-Orthodox, such as Bulgakov and van der Mensbrugghe, in which the divine essence and energy are identified with each other and with the divine wisdom (*sophia*). A note on the subject will be found in my book *He Who Is*, p. 140. (Lossky, pp. 61, 78.)

Forms. . . . By nature, being is, therefore, a system of determinate essences. By nature being is possessed of what may be called the principle of interior diversification or otherness" (pp. 156–7). But the doctrine of the Forms is elaborated in order to give intelligibility to the world of beings. Hence, for Platonism, the intelligible is the diverse, and we can proceed from diversity to unity only at the expense of losing intelligibility. "It is the very meaning of the One of Plotinus that it is above being in order to save itself from this plural determinateness of being; but it is the misfortune of the Plotinian One that the same indeterminateness which saves it from plurality also empties it of intelligibility" (p. 158). The problem for Christian Platonism therefore was how the Platonic theory of being could operate in a world in which God is perfect being and *therefore* one. "The perplexing mystery of the Platonic Forms is that in a Christian world they can be neither God nor creatures. They cannot be creatures because they are immutable and eternal; and they cannot be God because they are a real plurality of distinct and distinctly determined essences. And yet they rose before the minds of Christian thinkers again and again, and they hovered somewhere on the horizon between God and creatures, strange aliens both from heaven and from earth, and yet aliens whose message proved so enduringly dear to Christian thinkers that, rather than forget it, they exhausted their energies in pursuing it. . . . How could [the Forms] introduce their plurality into God? And yet how could creatures bear their immutability and their eternity?" (pp. 158–9).

Following the line thus introduced, Pegis argues that the nominalism of Ockham, while it was an open attack on Platonic realism, managed to get its results only by adopting the fundamentally Platonic doctrine of the antithesis between intelligibility and unity. "For Ockham, as for Plato and Plotinus, there is one standing paradox which reality offers and . . . it is the conflict between essence and individuality, intelligibility and unity. In the presence of this paradox, we can maintain a world of singulars only by suppressing essences from being; which means also that our notion of what a singular is includes within itself, *as a constitutive principle*, such a suppression" (p. 168). So again, for Ockham, the unity of God means that he is altogether silent and opaque. Ideas become simply creatures; they are in no way identical with the divine essence. Thus creation becomes altogether unintelligible: "it is a mystery why the world which proceeds from the will of the Ockhamist God contains more than the stability of a pure *fiat*, and why the divine will itself can contain the wisdom, the independence and the necessity of an infinite being" (p. 171). Plotinus and Ockham are, indeed, in opposition: "Contingency, as a vehicle of autonomous activity, is as unknown to Plotinus as necessity is unknown to Ockham. Such is the opposition: Plotinian necessity, which excludes autonomy and liberty, versus Ockhamist omnipotence which excludes necessity in order to retain liberty, but in which autonomy has surrendered to radical contingency" (ibid.). Nevertheless Ockham and Plotinus agree in their fundamental assumption of an antithesis between intelligible being and unity. And there is no way out along this road. "Ockham's manner of avoiding Platonism consists in closing his eyes in a Platonic heaven, whereas the manner of St. Thomas Aquinas consists in laying the ghost of Platonism" (p. 159). And St. Thomas laid the ghost by the doctrine of creation, which could identify intelligible being with unity in God and at the same time maintain the radical distinction between God and the world.

For St. Thomas there is a plurality of divine ideas, yet it does not violate the simplicity of the divine essence; this is the doctrine of the divine imitability. "God knows his own essence perfectly, and this must mean that he knows it in all the ways in which it is knowable. But the divine essence can be known not only as it is in itself, but also as it can be participated according to a particular manner of likeness by creatures. . . . Therefore, inasmuch as God knows his own essence as thus imitable by a given creature, he knows that essence as the proper expression (*rationem*) and idea of that creature" (p. 177). If we ask how it is that God's knowledge of singular beings does not conflict with his own simplicity, the answer is that his essence is compared with created essences not as the general to the particular, but as perfect act to imperfect acts: "through a perfect *act* imperfect *acts* can be known with a proper knowledge" (p. 178). There is no need for such a theory as the Avicennianism of Henry of Ghent, in which there is first a production of the *essential* being of creatures in the divine intellect and then a production of their *existential* being in the external realm (p. 175). "*Only if we begin with a God who is infinite Being can we solve the problem of how the divine self-knowledge can include within itself a proper knowledge of all other beings*" (p. 179). Plato and Aristotle did indeed discern in a dim and hesitant fashion that the world could not be explained simply in terms of *generation*, but they never clearly grasped the notion of *creation*. "Hence it is true to say both that they arrived, and that they did not arrive, at a doctrine of creation. They did not arrive, for they never asserted it; they did arrive, but they never knew it" (p. 180). In St. Thomas's thought, Pegis concludes, "we are in principle beyond the Platonic conflict between unity and intelligibility. We have reached a notion of being in which being and unity are reconcilable in the order of creatures because they are identified in God" (p. 183).

Pegis's essay, as a whole, strikes me as one of the most impressive exhibitions that I have seen of the fundamentally existential character of St. Thomas's teaching, and also of his extraordinary originality and intellectual courage. It may be compared with Dr. A. H. Armstrong's very interesting Aquinas Paper (No. 4) on *Aristotle, Plotinus and St. Thomas*, in which great stress is laid on the importance of Plotinus. "It was Plotinus who more than anyone else brought Hellenic philosophy to a point where it could meet Christian doctrine to produce the new synthesis of the *philosophia perennis*. St. Thomas's Aristotelianism is the application of the great Aristotelian principles which his genius was able to liberate and purify from the unacceptable elements in Aristotle's system to the completion or correction of the Christian-Plotinian tradition (with its large Aristotelian element) which he received from his predecessors, above all from St. Augustine" (p. 11). Armstrong emphasizes that "the decisive difference between the Christian and Plotinian conceptions of God arises from the Jewish-Christian doctrine of free creation instead of the necessary emanation or procession of the created universe" (p. 8).

CHAPTER SEVEN

TWO RECENT DISCUSSIONS OF THEISM

I

I COMMENTED, at the beginning of the last chapter but one, on the almost complete lack of any serious attention to the doctrine of analogy on the part of English-speaking philosophers and theologians outside the Roman Catholic Church. Quite recently, however, this silence has been broken by the appearance of two books of first-rank importance; I mean Dr. A. M. Farrer's *Finite and Infinite* and Miss Dorothy M. Emmet's *Nature of Metaphysical Thinking*. I shall therefore devote this concluding chapter to a consideration of these two works. And I shall begin with *Finite and Infinite*, which was published in 1943.

It must be admitted that Dr. Farrer's book does not make for altogether easy reading, especially for anyone whose background is provided by scholasticism rather than by the Oxford Greats School. And it is interesting to note that Roman Catholic reviewers, while almost unanimously acclaiming the work with enthusiasm, have found it very difficult to assess its precise nature; while one of them, for example, declared, with a few minor reservations, that it was "Thomist *pur sang*,"[1] another wrote that "it would be quite misleading to describe the author as Thomist."[2] Perhaps this antinomy is resolved by Professor A. E. Taylor's judgment that, although Dr. Farrer "shows himself to be thoroughly steeped in Thomism" and "indeed, his argument is couched all through in Thomist technical language, . . . the main reason for this is the simple one that it is appropriate to discuss the issues of rational theology, so far as possible, in the traditional language in which it has been historically delivered to us" and that "he

---

[1] Vincent Turner, S.J., in *Theology*, May 1944, p. 104.
[2] Gervase Mathew, O.P., in *Blackfriars*, January 1944, p. 33.

is no blind devotee of Thomist formulae."[1] With these preliminaries, then, we may pass on to consider the work in some
detail.

In the first part of the book, under the heading "Analysis
of Rational Theology," the author confines himself deliberately within the logical and linguistic realm, for he is clear
that it is simply courting disaster to commit oneself to argumentation for the existence of God without first investigating
what God and his existence mean. He begins by remarking,
in words which I have already quoted,[2] that even the most
extreme theological revelationists must, in spite of their own
passionate protestations, accept rational theology in some
sense; for even if truths about God are altogether beyond the
powers of the human mind to discover, they have at least to be
apprehended by the human mind when God has revealed
them, and to be stated in human language. He asks as his first
question, not whether God exists, but what sort of thing a
proof of God's existence would be; he is concerned with the
morphology of theistic argumentation. And it is vital to the
whole outlook that this preliminary investigation should be
made. For if God exists, he is unique; and if other beings are
related to him, that relation is also unique. How, then, could
we hope to prove his existence? God and his activity cannot
be made the instance of a class or the case of a rule; and if we
argue from his effects and activities, "to know that they are
effects in the relevant sense is to know the nature of the activity,
. . . and again, to know the activity is, in this case, to know
the Agent."[3] The question will have been begged from the
start. Whatever Thomists may say, God's existence cannot
merely not be demonstrable *a priori*; it cannot be demonstrable
a posteriori either. How then can it possibly be known? Well,
at least God's activity will be there for the mind, if God does
in fact exist, however wrong Descartes may have been in some
of the things that he said about it. Can we hope to bring it
into view? That is the basic problem for rational theology.
But before we can do this we must analyse more fully. What
do we mean by the "Cosmological Idea," the scheme of God-
and-the-creature-in-relation?

[1] *J.T.S.*, 1943, XLV, p. 239.   [2] p. 92 *supra*.   [3] Op. cit., p. 7.

The one thing we must not do, says Dr. Farrer, is what most modern philosophers have done, namely to treat the finite-infinite relation as if it were one special case of inter-finite relations; that would queer the pitch before the game began. "About that which is simply unique there can be no discourse."[1] We can, however, make significant comparisons with various types of inter-finite relations, stating in each case where they do not apply. And when we do this, our attention may in consequence be led to direct itself to the unique relation between God and finite being which, if God does exist, is in fact waiting in every finite being for us to recognize it. Such inter-finite relations are those between substance and constituent, between a phase of active process and the phase to which it gives rise, and between an active process and the affectedness of other processes by it.

From the relation itself we turn to the terms which it unites, namely God and the creature. God is absolute existent, and *esse est operari*. What do we mean by degrees of *esse* considered as *operari*? And what do we mean by an absolute degree of it?[2] Again we make comparisons with the finite, indicating where each fails to apply, and we take first the relation of a higher mode to a lower, then that of the perfect expression of a species to its incomplete and perverted examples, then that of finite substance to constituent.[3]

The ground thus being cleared, the question is next asked by what ladder we can hope to ascend from finite beings to God. The scale of nature, which sees created beings ranged in order from lifeless matter at the bottom to man at the top, although it was dear to the Middle Ages and has been given a modern evolutionary form by Fr. L. S. Thornton,[4] is asserted to be very precarious, though not entirely useless.[5] Since spirituality occurs at the top of the scale, it points to God as absolute spirit. But with the *mode* of God's spirituality "we are not and cannot be acquainted. All we can do is (a) barely to assert that his spirituality is absolute, i.e. such as is proportionate to absolute being, (b) to strike out those aspects of our own spirituality which plainly belong to its lowly degree, and so will

---

[1] Op. cit., p. 23.   [2] Ibid., pp. 26 f.
[3] Ibid., pp. 34 f.   [4] In *The Incarnate Lord*.   [5] *Finite and Infinite*, pp. 41 f.

have no counterpart in God."[1] "Now," says Dr. Farrer, "it does not seem plausible that the way to God goes round by such a by-pass as is the construction of the *scala naturae*. It would, on the other hand, seem plausible (*a*) that men should be aware of a relation between their own existence and God, and (*b*) should feel bound to interpret this as the instance of a relation between finite existence as such, and God, and so universalize the analogy, recognizing God wherever they recognized existence."[2] Our attention is therefore now directed to the "interior scale" of our own mental life, that is, the gradation, in degree of spirituality, of the acts that make it up. This interior scale, being a real unity and not an artificial construction, and being the actual indicator through which aspiration reaches God, will be adopted.[3] But how are we to utilize it? This leads to a consideration of analogy of proportionality,[4] and it is argued that the three negative criteria by which we may hope to specify the mode in which our concepts are to be applied to God are simplicity, self-sufficiency and universality.[5] This concludes the first part of the work; we now know what sort of thing a proof of God's existence would be. "Here, then," the author writes, "we leave our sketch of the cosmological idea, i.e. of the direct content of rational theology, and turn to that investigation of substance in which the validity of its assumptions is to be examined."[6]

This examination of finite substance occupies the whole of Part Two of the book. From the point of view of refuting the atheism or agnosticism of most modern systems of philosophy, everything turns upon it; for the notion of substance is the indispensable basis of any theistic metaphysic, in spite of the fact that it has been almost universally rejected since the time of Berkeley and Hume.[7]

This second part is subdivided into three sections. The first examines the idea of substance from a logical and linguistic

---

[1] Ibid., p. 43.   [2] Ibid., p. 44.   [3] Ibid., pp. 46 f.
[4] See p. 108, *n. 2 supra.*   [5] Ibid., pp. 55 f.   [6] Ibid., p. 62.
[7] Berkeley, of course, thought that he could dispense with substance and still keep God; in this he was, as events proved, mistaken. It is important, however, to note that what he demolished in fact was Locke's doctrine of substance, not St. Thomas's. In the Third Dialogue, Hylas could have blown Philonous sky-high had he not unwittingly been lured into accepting a sensationalist doctrine of perception.

M

standpoint, to establish the validity of the use of the notion of substance in speech. The positivists, logical and otherwise, are refuted, and substance-language is vindicated. The notion of substance, it is concluded, is indeed obscure, but we cannot do without it.

The second section of Part Two begins with the observation that if everything in our analogical dialectic is to depend on our ability to describe or indicate substance, we had better start with the most accessible instance of it. This is obviously the self, and our determination to start with it will be reinforced by our previous identification of substance with activity. We are, however, committed to a bold undertaking, in view of what modern psychologists and philosophers have reduced the self to! Hence this section is devoted to re-establishing the validity of the concept of the self; it does it in two stages. In the first, the reality of the will is shown to follow from the failure, which is argued at length, of any attempt to reduce it to a merely fictitious or logical class of mental states or acts; in the second, with equal thoroughness, the reality of the self is vindicated against the attempt to reduce it to a merely fictitious or logical class of acts of will. This part of the work, which has been rightly described by Professor Hodgson as "a book within a book,"[1] merits examination on its own by experts in that particular realm. I have neither the space nor the personal equipment to enter on that task here; I shall only remark that Professor A. E. Taylor found it convincing and commended it warmly.[2] Dr. Farrer sums up his results in the following passage:

"We have two structures of unity. *The* unity of the self is neither the focusing of the many acts in the single act, nor is it the continuity of activity from one act to the next. Both belong to the unity of the self, which is neither. It is itself indescribable; it is not a structure or pattern but that which has these. A good reason is found for its elusiveness in the very form of thought. The unity of the self and its structural complication cannot be grasped in one; yet they imply and support one another. The unity is best seen when the self is opposed to

---

[1] In a review in the *Guardian*, November 12th, 1943.
[2] *J.T.S.*, art. cit., p. 245.

external things, not to its own constituents. . . . The self is a
continuous intellective and creative activity which proceeds by
concentration into successive particular acts. It is the substantial connexion provided by activity as such and studied
under the name of will, which holds together the self as well as
the act. For the act is not even as an act self-sufficient; its
boundaries extend to embrace the totality of a self, which is thus
metaphysically, and not just phenomenally or logically, one."[1]

All that has been described above is, whatever its intrinsic
importance, merely preliminary to Part Three of the work,
in which the demonstration of theism or, as the author calls it,
"the dialectic of rational theology" is undertaken. Dr. Farrer
first of all makes it plain what his method is. "Every argument
for God's existence," he writes, "must start from the world of
finites, or from the nature of finite substances as such. And it
must proceed from a distinction taken within the finite. . . .
We must take some distinction within the finite and then claim
to show that the co-existence of the elements distinguished, in
the way in which they do co-exist, is intelligible only if God
exists as the ground of such a co-existence."[2] We must exhibit
the co-existence in the finite, and then argue from it to the
divine existence. But how can we make this jump? If, for
example, we treat divine causality as an instance of universal
causality and argue from finite causality to divine causality
tout court, we shall fall straight into univocity. (This, as I have
already remarked, is what is done by most modern theistic
philosophers—Ward, Tennant and Whitehead, to name but
three—who arrive at a finite or merely immanent God.) To
do this would be "formal paralogism, for all analogical
syllogisms have *quaternio terminorum* and are invalid. But we
avoid the charge of paralogizing, if we abandon the pretension
of syllogizing at all and allow that the 'syllogism' is not the
simple application of a rule to an instance, but a challenge to
us to recognize a genuine analogy and in doing so to arrive
at the cosmological idea. Consequently there are two ways of
presenting the theological dialectic. We may state the arguments as syllogisms and refute them—a procedure neither

---

[1] *Finite and Infinite*, p. 229. It is clear that in this passage the word "creative"
is not to be taken in the strict theological sense.   [2] Ibid., p. 262.

useful nor edifying. Or we may state the manner in which the given distinction in the finite acts as a splintered image of God and treat the quasi-syllogism as analogical illustration. And this is the method we shall use."[1]

Having stated the method in principle, Dr. Farrer goes on to display, in an analytic and dialectic presentation, how the mind can actually pass from the finite to the infinite. He observes first of all that the arguments will differ according to the finite distinctions upon which they are based, but that there is a secondary distinction that cuts right across these. For, if we denote the two distinguishable elements by A and B, we may either (1) take A for granted and show that the addition of B to it is the effect of divine action, or vice versa (this is the *immanental* form, attractive to the mind but philosophically absurd), or we may (2) take neither A nor B for granted but exhibit AB as forming a nature so "composite" that it must derive from what is "simple" (the *transcendental* form). Less important than these is (3) the *experiential* form, which appeals to men to recognize that in particular instances of this complex AB they have seen or habitually see the work of God.[2] Whichever of these we adopt—and it is the second which is the really philosophical one—we can divide the types of finite distinction available as the basis for our analogical dialectic into two great classes, in accordance with the argument of the earlier part of the book: namely, the *usiological*, which are found in finite beings in general, and the *anthropological*, which are found in the particular kind of finite beings that we are—that is, man. Both are needed, for God must be exhibited as the creator of all finite being, while "we have no direct knowledge of any particular mode of existence except our own." "Without anthropology we should not start, and without usiology we should not arrive."[3]

Usiological arguments are of two classes: (A) based on the *finitude* of finite being, and this includes the two contrasts of (I) essence-existence and (II) actual-possible; (B) based on substantial relations, subdividing into (I) operation and interior effect, (II) continuous ingredience, (III) discontinuous ingredience: formality and informality, (IV) discon-

---

[1] *Finite and Infinite*, p. 263.   [2] Ibid., p. 263.   [3] Ibid., p. 264.

tinuous ingredience: condition and action, (V) generation, (VI) generation and decay. The last five of these are all concerned with different aspects of the contrast between the self-unity of an operation and the affectedness of other operations by it. Anthropological arguments (C) subdivide as follows: (I) intellect as such and its human impurities, (II) will as such and its human limitations, (III) intellectual and voluntary activity, (IV) moral obligation, (V) the pursuit of perfection.[1]

In all these thirteen cases, the procedure is, in its broad outlines, the same. Having discerned in the finite datum a complex of two distinguishable elements A and B, we ask, so far as the nature of the particular complex renders it possible, each of the three following questions: (1*a*) Assuming A, why B?; (1*b*) Assuming B, why A?; (2) Assuming AB, why the combination? (We may also call attention to (3) the experience of the complex in question as exhibiting God's activity.) In each case we get an answer about the infinite cause which is expressed in terms proper to finite being and is strictly absurd if applied *tout simplement* to infinite being, but is none the less valuable as ruling out some opposite misconception. As a result of this we arrive at a whole set of notions which, as it were, approach the infinite being which theology calls God from a large number of different directions while all falling short of their goal. What they all designate is God, but each of them designates him in a different and an imperfect way. The supereminent mode in which each applies to him is beyond our grasp; we are in the realm of analogy, not of univocity. This is of course nothing that need worry a Christian; have we not always known that we cannot, at least in this life, *comprehend* God? Here we see *per speculum in aenigmate*, not as yet *facie ad faciem*. We can sum up the conclusion in Dr. Farrer's own words:

"The knowledge of God to which rational theology leads us—the knowledge of him which is bound up with an apprehension of the universal aspects of finite existence or of human

[1] Ibid., Part III, *passim*. For the details of these arguments I must refer the reader to Dr. Farrer's book. It is impossible to outline them adequately in the space at our disposal.

existence—is the knowledge of existent perfection conceived through the analogy of spirit, and the knowledge that this Being is the creator of all finite existence. But that is all. We learn from it that all finites, in being themselves and expressing their natures in their acts, are expressing also the creativity of God who creates through them."[1]

The conclusion, therefore, is strictly limited. Not only, with the Thomists, does Dr. Farrer deny that rational theology can give us any knowledge of the order of grace; he will not even go so far as to assert that it can give us any knowledge of divine providence. On the other hand, neither providence nor grace is excluded. Rational theology thus provides the basis upon which a full Christian theism, deriving not merely from reason but predominantly from revelation, can be reared. "For any convincing proof that God acts by providence or grace either within this world or by calling into being a new to redress the balance of the old, we must turn to the field of particular 'contingent' events, and see whether he habitually so acts, or whether in one or more revealing events he has given the promise of so acting."[2] The final paragraph of the book deserves to be quoted in full:

"As I wrote this, the German armies were occupying Paris, after a campaign prodigal of blood and human distress. Rational theology will not tell us whether this has or has not been an unqualified and irretrievable disaster to mankind and especially to the men who died. It is another matter, if we believe that God Incarnate also died, and rose from the dead. But rational theology knows only that whether Paris stands or falls, whether men die or live, God is God, and so long as any spiritual creature survives, God is to be adored."[3]

II

It will, I hope, be evident from this summary of Dr. Farrer's argument that he has presented the theological and philosophical public with an apologia for theism of great originality and importance. To attempt to rehabilitate the traditional doctrine of a strictly infinite God, to whom the world is

---

[1] *Finite and Infinite*, p. 299.   [2] Ibid., p. 300.   [3] Ibid., p. 300.

altogether unnecessary and who is nevertheless its creator and preserver, is a daring exploit at the present day, but to do it from the starting-point not of medieval scholasticism but of modern philosophy and psychology (as Dr. Farrer does in Part Two of his book) is enough to cause a scandal; in many quarters it will be felt as adding injury to insult. How far Dr. Farrer's work will in fact revolutionize modern philosophy it is not for me to say; that will depend, among other factors, on how many modern philosophers are prepared to study it seriously. In itself, so impressive a vindication of the notions of analogy, substance, the will, the self and (in the strictest traditional sense) God can, one would imagine, hardly be passed by in silence. My own judgment is that this is one of the most important philosophical works of the present century. Dr. Farrer has, however, no need of my commendation, and I shall now turn to a task which is more germane to our immediate concern and make a few brief observations on the general character of his approach from the standpoint which I have adopted in the present work.

In the first place we may notice how radically existential is Dr. Farrer's whole attitude. Fr. Vincent Turner sees this as one of its chief merits. Dr. Farrer's book, he writes, "is both extremely traditional and extremely 'philosophical' precisely because its metaphysics is through and through an existential metaphysics. Herein, perhaps, lies its greatest originality, for with a wealth of fresh insight the old problems of analogy and the cosmological *schema* are thought out again in the context of the immanent activity of finite selves." He adds that "the existential character of [Dr.] Farrer's careful and impressive argument has another very considerable virtue. Outside scholastic circles most recent natural theology, it is perhaps not too much to say, has been of a Kantian and Idealistic flavour, and has presupposed the habitual reduction of the notion of substance to the notion of subject. But from any presuppositions such as these [Dr.] Farrer breaks away, and that without a single nostalgic backward glance."[1]

In line with this fundamental existentialism is Dr. Farrer's conviction that any finite being whatever, if we know how to

[1] Art. cit., p. 100.

look at it, declares the existence of God. I have argued in the present work that the primary datum for rational theology is the real distinction of essence and existence in all finite beings. And, as Professor A. E. Taylor pointed out, this is central in Dr. Farrer's argument. "I wholly agree," he wrote, "with what I take to be [Dr.] Farrer's opinion that the characteristic of the 'creatures' at large which most imperatively imposes on us the attempt to ascend to God is the manifest divorce in them between *essentia* and *existentia*. . . . So long as we are rational beings at all, we cannot be content to sit down with an 'ultimate inexplicability'; we do and we must ask, But why? And to ask why is already to be conceiving of a Supreme Being in which existence and *essentia* coincide, a Being who, as the schoolmen said, *est sua existentia*."[1] And in Dr. Farrer's exposition the function of the arguments derived from the particular kind of finite being which is man (the "anthropological" arguments) is not ultimately to call our attention to characteristics which are possessed by man alone among finite beings, but, by putting before us the type of finite being with which we are most familiar (namely ourselves), to call our attention to a universal character of finite being as such. In explaining his preference for the "interior scale" over the *scala naturae*, Dr. Farrer, as we have already seen, maintains that it is "plausible (*a*) that men should be aware of a relation between their own existence and God, and (*b*) should feel bound to interpret this as the instance of a relation between finite existence as such, and God, and so universalize the analogy, recognizing God wherever they recognized existence."[2] This is certainly very close to my own point of view; I am not, however, convinced that it is absolutely the same. In arguing for the ontological and transcendental validity of the notions of substance, existence and causality, I affirmed, against the widely held view that our attribution of such notions to the external world is merely a projection from our own subjective experience, my conviction that we objectively apprehend the world as possessing these characteristics, although, from the nature of the case, it is only as they occur in us that we can

---

[1] Art. cit., p. 246. St. Thomas, I am sure, preferred to say *est suum esse*. Cf. p. 49 *supra*.   [2] *Finite and Infinite*, p. 44.

subjectively experience them.[1] And I should say the same
about the exemplification in finite beings of the real distinction
between essence and existence, with its concomitant of a radical
dependence upon self-existent being. It seems to me that Dr.
Farrer admits that there *is* a projection, although it is a valid
one;[2] my position is that there is no *projection* at all, but rather
a discovery. Dr. Farrer seems to be asserting that we subjectively experience our own dependence and then validly
affirm it of finite being as a whole; my assertion is that we
objectively apprehend it in all the finite beings which we
perceive and then turn to ourselves in order to experience it
subjectively. But I may very well be making too sharp an
antithesis; the important point is that, for both of us, the
character of dependence can validly be affirmed of finite being
as a whole, although it is only as it occurs in ourselves that we
can know what dependence "feels like." And perhaps in this
era of subjectivity there may be a real strategic advantage in
pointing to the one finite being—namely himself—to whose
nature the modern man is most likely to pay attention.

To turn to another point, it will be remembered that, in
discussing the Thomist Five Ways, I made the assertion that
their real function is not to provide five independent ways of
proving that God exists, but to point to five different features
of finite being in which the one fundamental character of it
which points to God—namely the real distinction within it of
essence and existence—could be seen as exemplified.[3] In Dr.
Farrer's system the place of the Five Ways is held by the eight
usiological and the five anthropological arguments. Now, we
may inquire, are these thirteen ways themselves thirteen different arguments for the existence of God or are they thirteen
different ways of bringing us to apprehend some fundamental
characteristic of finite being or of man from which God's
existence may be recognized? I think that, as long as we are
concerned simply with the affirmation of God's *existence*, in

---

[1] See p. 83 *supra*.

[2] Thus he says, in a passage on which Fr. Turner comments: "The premiss of
St. Thomas's *Via Prima* is not 'constat quaedam moveri in hoc mundo' but is the
habit men have of *reading into* the system of events an absolute agency which can
find its ultimate agent in God alone" (p. 10, italics mine).

[3] See p. 71 *supra*.

abstraction from anything that we may come to assert about his *nature*, the second alternative gives the true interpretation. For, in the first part of the book, all the emphasis is laid upon the fact that what is meant by God is an "Absolute Degree of Existence," and in the second part the whole purpose of the highly elaborate discussion is to vindicate the validity of substances and selves as beings that really *exist*. But in so far as the arguments tell us analogically something about God's *nature*, they do tell us different things about it; to say that God is supreme intelligence, for example, is not the same as to say that he is supreme will. This does not, however, mean that we can perform the whole process twice over, first in relation to existence and then in relation to essence; if that were the case we should find ourselves being led, first to affirm the existence of a being of which we knew nothing, and then to acquire various transcendental notions which had no necessary relation to existence. Each of the arguments leads simultaneously to an affirmation of God's existence as self-existent being and to an analogical knowledge of some one of his attributes. The argument's function is to describe some feature of finite being in such a way as to exhibit the fundamental character of finite being as consisting in the real distinction of essence and existence, and thus to convince us of its dependence upon a Supreme Being in whom essence and existence are really identical and in whom, *formaliter et eminentius*, there is found the archetype of that feature of finite being from which the argument began. (In consequence it would seem that, for Dr. Farrer, the first usiological argument, which starts from the essence-existence distinction itself, must be the *prima et manifestior via*; indeed he himself suggests this.[1]) The arguments, if I am not mistaken, move in the order of existence and of essence at once, though their primary character is existential, in the sense that they take their beginning in the existence of finites and end by affirming the existence of God. I think, therefore, that in the last resort Dr. Farrer is doing in his thirteen arguments what St. Thomas did (or meant to do) in his Five Ways; and just as St. Thomas chose as his five starting-points five features of finite being that were readily

----

[1] Op. cit., p. 265.

recognizable by men of the thirteenth century, so Dr. Farrer singles out thirteen features of the finite world which are, it is to be hoped, not less readily recognizable by philosophers of the present day.

But now we come to a point which, I must confess, I find it very difficult to decide. It concerns the actual way in which Dr. Farrer makes the transition from finite being to God. Is his method of analogy fundamentally identical with analogy as the classical theology of Christendom has envisaged it? I do not find myself as scandalized as some of Dr. Farrer's Thomist reviewers have been, by his assertions that God's existence cannot be demonstrated *a posteriori*[1] and that all analogical syllogisms are invalid by *quaternio terminorum*,[2] though I should not myself have used just those words. I think he only means to assert, as arrestingly as possible, that the proof of God's existence is not a syllogistic demonstration in the ordinary sense of the term; and with this, as will be clear from the present work as a whole, I agree. What does, however, seem to me somewhat doubtful is whether Dr. Farrer's own account of analogy is quite sufficient to justify the use which he makes of it. *"Positive analogical argument,"* he writes, "takes place when we use an analogical relation already admitted in order to conclude from better known analogue to less known analogate. Let it be granted that the subjectivity of a dog bears some analogy to our own. From this unsupported and unchecked analogical premise nothing can be concluded: we should never know but that the unstated difference belonging to the dog's mode of subjectivity might not be precisely such as to exclude the aspect of our own which we proposed to transfer. But in the phenomena of the dog's behaviour we have a certain check. Comparing these with the phenomena of our own, we are able to analogize as to his consciousness not, heaven knows, within a mile of accuracy, but not wildly or senselessly either." Passing from this to *theological analogizing*, that is the use of analogical discourse about God, Dr. Farrer inquires what in this latter case plays the part of check to the general analogical premiss. "Not," he replies, "behaviour phenomenally evidenced, but the notion of an absolute degree or mode of activity. But this in turn is defined by a most exhausting and difficult process of 'negative dialectic,' i.e. the distinction of absolute activity, causality, etc., from all the analogies through which we arrive at our thought of it." He adds an important warning. "The application of our negative dialectic in theology is not the *via negativa, remotiva*, etc., of tradition. What we call the negative dialectic negates all analogues *on the basis of some obscure apprehension of the object we are attempting to distinguish*, and its purpose is to grasp the mere notion of absolute being. Whereas 'via negativa' is traditionally used of the negative aspect of the proportionality argument in which absolute being is already presupposed; when starting with existence or activity in the full-blooded finite mode we simply strike out (negate, remove) the aspects that can have no archetype in that absolute. The purpose of our negative dialectic is *to distinguish the analogate from all analogues, however precise*; that of the traditional *via negativa* is *to make the analogues as precise as possible by distinguishing their applicable aspects from their inapplicable*. It is then essentially the negative precision inseparable from what we call positive analogical argument. We are really concerned with the positive analogical movement which transfers characters found in the finite to the infinite; but the transference is made possible by negation of what will not go across."[1]

The passage just quoted is of first importance if we are not to do Dr. Farrer an injustice. For, it may be objected, Dr. Farrer's procedure, as developed in his third part, appears to provide nothing more than a sequence of negations. It takes, one by one, a sequence of characters exemplified by finite beings and then denies that these can exist in their finite modes in God. But it never shows that the existence of these characters in any other than finite modes is possible. This may tell us quite a lot about what God is not, but it tells us nothing about him; and if it tells us literally *nothing* about him, how do we know of whom we are talking when we say that God exists? This may be the *via negativa*; it is certainly not the *via analogica*.

---

[1] Op. cit., pp. 95–6 (italics, except of Latin words, mine). It will be seen that Dr. Farrer uses "analogate" and "analogue" for what in the usage of chap. v *supra* would be called "prime analogate" and "secondary analogate" respectively.

There is nothing analogical in saying that God is *not* this, that and the other; analogy says he *is* this, that and the other, *perfectissime*. You may perhaps try to get out of this (the objection will continue) by saying that, when you denied that the characters applied to God, you only meant to exclude certain elements in them which were proper to finite beings alone; the remainder of the content applies without difficulty to God. But in what mode does that remainder apply? If analogically, then you have got no further, you have merely reduced analogy to negation *plus* a fresh analogy. But if univocally, then you have turned analogy into a mere conjunction of negation *plus* univocation, and whatever analogy is it must be something more than that. These objections would, I think, be plausible if the purpose of Dr. Farrer's dialectic was simply to talk about finite things in a way which would also be talking about God. But this, as I see it, is not the case. His purpose is to talk about finite beings in such a way as to help us to see them as themselves dependent upon God. The function of the dialectic is to turn us from dialectic to reality. In the words of Dr. Farrer just quoted, it is not to distinguish the applicable aspect from the inapplicable, but to distinguish the analogate from all analogues, however precise. Although the dialectic moves by analogical statements, the recognition of God is not given us in the analogical statements but in the act of apprehending finite being. The cosmological idea—"the knowledge of [God] which is bound up with an apprehension of the universal aspects of finite existence or of human existence"[1]—is given as a unity to those who see things as they really are, and it is on this direct understanding of finite beings, not upon analogical statements derived from usiological or anthropological arguments, that our affirmation "God exists" is based. The function of the arguments is primarily instrumental. "The argument," writes Dr. Farrer, "exhibits a distinction of elements within the creature in order to make us jump to the cosmological intuition, i.e. to the apprehension of God as the being in whom this distinction is, in its finite form, transcended—who is the 'coincidence' of these 'opposites.' But how does the argument lead us to make

[1] Ibid., p. 299.

this intuitive jump? It may be sometimes enough to state the distinction and its transcendence in God, for the hearer or reader to see the conclusion. But the further removed he is from theistic ways of thought, the less likely is this to succeed; for he will not see what is meant by the notion of this transcendence, and so it will be necessary to help him out with analogies."[1]

I am inclined to think that Dr. Farrer's discussion would be even more impressive than it is if he had given rather greater weight to the doctrine of analogy in its classical form; his discussion of proportionality, for example, seems to me somewhat cavalier.[2] But I am fully in agreement with what I take to be his fundamental conviction, that it is not necessary for us to construct a watertight theory of how knowledge of God is possible before we can allow ourselves the luxury of knowing him. That would be like forbidding anyone who had not been trained in physiology from making use of his legs. For Dr. Farrer, if I understand him, the arguments have two main functions: they can help us to apprehend God in his creatures, and they can rebut the assertion that this apprehension was a delusion; the apprehension itself does not, however, rest simply upon the arguments. If we are going to get further than this, we shall, I think, have to show less readiness than Dr. Farrer to make concessions to post-scholastic epistemology. I suspect that the extremely restricted nature of his conclusions, compared for example with those of St. Thomas, is chiefly due to this cause. Nevertheless, in the last resort it is, I think, clear that he is committed, with whatever qualifications, to a realist

---

[1] Op. cit., p. 262. I will add a brief comment on what seems to me to be the function of the "scale" (whether "exterior" or "interior") in Dr. Farrer's discussion. It is not, as I see it, to argue that there must be a maximum member of the scale, and that this maximum member is God; for, in the first place, such a God would himself be finite and, secondly, there is no need that an infinite sequence should have a maximum member at all (e.g. the ordered sequence of the natural integers). What the scale does, by contrasting the members with one another, is to exhibit as clearly as possible their finitude, and to safeguard us against the error of supposing that any or all of them are self-explanatory or self-subsistent. In principle, two members of the scale are all that are needed for this purpose, since the fact that two items can be compared with each other is sufficient to exhibit their common finitude, but the construction of a more extensive sequence may assist the human mind to disengage the character of finitude to which its attention is being invited. God himself is then apprehended as transcending the scale and conferring existence upon all its members.   [2] Ibid., pp. 52 f.

doctrine of knowledge. If thoughts were about ideas and words were mere labels for them, then the validity of argument would be altogether dependent upon our power to shuffle the labels correctly; words would do our thinking for us if we made them behave properly. But if, on the other hand, words and ideas are instruments which the intellect utilizes in order to accomplish its own inherent function of grasping, however imperfectly, finite beings in their real but derived intelligibility, understanding the world will not be precisely the same as talking about it. Dr. Farrer's development of the doctrine of analogy may be, and indeed obviously is, very different from that of the scholastics. It might perhaps have benefited by more attention to them; it certainly grapples with questions with which they were never faced. But in the last resort, I think those reviewers were right who, with whatever reservations, pronounced his book to be in the tradition of the *philosophia perennis*.

III

I shall discuss Miss Emmet's book more shortly than Dr. Farrer's, for the only alternative would be to discuss it at very much greater length. As its title indicates, it is not primarily a work on rational theology, but on the nature of metaphysics as such; nevertheless the theological implications stand out plainly, and it is to these that I shall mainly confine myself.

For Miss Emmet "metaphysics is an analogical way of thinking." It takes concepts drawn from some form of experience or some relation within experience and extends them analogically, not only in order to co-ordinate experiences of different types but also in order to say something about the "reality" transcending experience.[1] The theistic issue is thus immediately raised, and Miss Emmet throws her own approach to it into relief by a penetrating discussion of two other present-day outlooks, namely the extreme "revelationism" of Kierkegaard, Barth, Brunner and their disciples, and the Thomist *analogia entis*. Her discussion of the former of these is admirable; it combines real sympathy with quite drastic criticism. If the revelationists are right, she says, "we must face the result; it

---

[1] *The Nature of Metaphysical Thinking*, p. 5.

must mean that there can be no real communication on ultimate questions between theologians and the historians, philosophers and scientists who are pursuing their own methods of inquiry, unless the historians, philosophers and scientists are prepared to adopt a purely positivist attitude towards their own inquiries and deny that they are in any way concerned with metaphysical questions."[1] She sees significance in the contemporaneity of revelationism in theology with logical positivism in philosophy. For, "if we are not allowed to say anything significantly about the transcendent, it would appear that the only escape from complete agnosticism would be for the transcendent itself to declare itself to us in some way recognizably distinct from our own forms of thought."[2] She expounds the Thomist doctrine accurately and understandingly, though she makes the rather startling remark that the proper Thomist term for God is *ens realissimum*;[3] *ens ipse subsistens* would, I think, be more correct. Her main criticism of Thomism is directed against the rash use which, in her opinion, it makes of the notion of causality.

> "There may," says Miss Emmet, "yet be some fundamental relation or relations of finite actuality to absolute reality transcending it. But to describe this relation as that of things to a 'First Cause' will not do, unless more explicit recognition than we find in St. Thomas's Five Ways is given to the fact that the word 'cause' can here only be used analogically. And if the word 'cause' is here only used analogically, can it define the relation in virtue of which we draw analogies?"[4]

I must admit that I sympathize with Miss Emmet in her difficulty about the Five Ways; as I have argued in a previous chapter,[5] they do not seem to me to express the real nature of St. Thomas's own thought. The divergence lies, however, deeper than this. Miss Emmet herself writes:

> "Our main divergences from the Thomist philosophy follow from an epistemological difference of a deep-seated kind. We have allowed to mind a spontaneity in the creation of symbolic forms which makes the problem of the objective reference of ideas more difficult for us to answer."[6]

[1] *The Nature of Metaphysical Thinking*, p. 130.   [2] Ibid., p.131.   [3] Ibid., p. 172.
[4] Ibid., p. 188.   [5] Ch. iv *supra*.   [6] Op. cit., p. 188.

This being so, it seems to me a real misfortune that in the chapters[1] in which she discusses epistemology Miss Emmet makes no reference to the epistemology of Thomism; in consequence her exposition and criticism of the Thomist use of analogy[2] is left altogether hanging in the air. The three epistemological doctrines which she examines before expounding her own are direct realism, idealism and phenomenalism. All that she has to say about these is admirable, and she is particularly happy in arguing, from the results of physiological research, against the view that either the events in the brain which, in the last stage of the physiological chain, give rise to sensation, or the ideas that are finally experienced, can be assumed as having a spatio-temporal pattern whose structure is identical with that of the external world. She nowhere considers, however, the Thomist doctrine that the ultimate object of perception, the *objectum quod*, is a being of the intelligible order, grasped by the intellect through a sense-datum which is only the *objectum quo* of the whole process.[3] This doctrine may not be exempt from criticism, but her failure to criticize it, or even to state it, introduces a serious gap into Miss Emmet's argument. Her own theory of perception is based upon a somewhat modified form of A. N. Whitehead's "philosophy of organism."

"The 'direct' mode of perception," she writes, "will be . . . a responsive state of the organism in *rapport* with, or receiving shocks from its environment. . . . And where there is response some 'transmutation' takes place, as Whitehead would say, so that we have not mere conformity of pattern, but some novel experience created out of *how* the organism responds. But when we come to the level of conscious mental activity, something different in kind is happening. Mental activity . . . seeks to understand a thing by expressing or seeing it simplified in terms of another. The world as grasped in sense perception is a highly simplified and selective perspective. Its function in the first instance is practical, to provide the organism with clues for its orientation to its environment. Mental activity takes these patterns, built out of the practical responses of the

---

[1] Ch. ii, iii.   [2] Ch. viii.
[3] For a fuller exposition of the Thomist doctrine, reference may be made to ch. iii, § III *supra*.

N

organism, and uses them for *theoretical* ends. It first reintegrates them through judgments of meaning into a world of objects. But this world of objects remains a simplified and distorted appearance. Mental activity then treats it as a 'projection' [in the sense of the map-maker rather than that of the psychologist] in which it can study clues concerning objective relations in the external real world. Such conclusions as it reaches can only be indirect and inferential constructions from the perspectives of sense experience. If we consider sense experiences as symbols, in this particular way, namely as able to be treated for theoretical ends as projections in which real relations are cast, they are symbols behind which we cannot go, in the way of directly intuiting the contents into which they should be translated. . . . *This means that the relation of our perceptual experience to nature should be thought of neither in terms of direct apprehension nor of likeness, but as a highly simplified and abstract 'projection' which nevertheless bears some relation of systematic concomitant variation to the things projected.*"[1]

Elsewhere Miss Emmet writes, concerning the *rapport* between our intellectual processes and nature beyond them:

"It may not go so far as an identity of structure. It looks rather as though certain structures within certain processes in nature may be projected in a systematically distorted way in our sensory experience and in the intellectual constructions based upon it. *Distorted*, since we are responding to environing processes and not reproducing them. . . . But that the distortion is *systematic* is borne out by the way in which we find that, if we act as if we could assume some sort of concomitant variation between our most carefully controlled observations and their differential conditions in nature beyond us, we are able to predict accurately and bring coherence into further ranges of otherwise disconnected observations."[2]

These quotations, I think, are sufficient to show Miss Emmet's doctrine of the relation of the contents of the mind to extra-mental reality. It is difficult to criticize it directly, but it is perhaps valid to suggest that it is difficult to see how the truth of this doctrine is compatible with knowledge of its truth. If all our perception is inevitably distorted, how can we become aware of this distortion? And can we be confident

[1] Op. cit., pp. 61–2 (italics mine).   [2] Ibid., p. 91 (italics in original).

about the "concomitant variation" to which Miss Emmet refers?[1] This criticism bears weight, I believe, against the philosophy of organism as a whole, but to go further into this question would involve writing a book on the subject.[2] I will only add at this point that, as I see it, perhaps the chief weakness in Miss Emmet's very profound discussion of epistemology lies in the fact that she so concentrates on the part which she believes the mind to play in the construction of its object that she pays little attention to the question how the mind knows its object when it has acquired it. As the scholastics were well aware, the real problem about knowledge is how such a remarkable activity should occur at all. For it *is* queer that we should be able to get other things inside ourselves. There may be a better description of knowledge than is given in such Thomist tags as "The mind is able in some way to become everything," "The mind abstracts from the sensible object its intelligible essence," "The thing is in the mind by intentional being," and so on, but Miss Emmet seems never to look for it and so fails to find it. Yet how near she comes to this can be seen from such a statement as the following:

> "The framing of the epistemological problem which starts from conscious mental states, and then asks how you can prove the existence of anything beyond them, is a question *mal posée*. If put in this form, there is no escape from phenomenalism, or subjective idealism, since 'experience' has been defined in terms of subjective states, and the idea of an object transcending them can only be a pure act of faith or the result of an animistic projection."[3]

In her concluding chapters, Miss Emmet works out a doctrine of analogy in accordance with her epistemology. In this she makes great use of the notion of "importance," and her handling of this notion was estimated by the late Professor A. E. Taylor[4] as one of the most profitable features of her book. "What the metaphysician does, therefore, is to construct a theoretic model drawn from analogy from some form of intellectual or spiritual relationship which he judges to be

---

[1] See, on this point, Mr. R. I. Aaron's review in *Philosophy*, 1946, XXI, p. 81.
[2] I may perhaps refer to my remarks on Whitehead in *He Who Is*, ch. xi.
[3] Op. cit., p. 64. "Projection" here is, of course, used in the psychologist's sense.   [4] *J.T.S.*, 1946, XLVII, p. 122.

especially significant or important. . . . I do not believe,"
Miss Emmet tells us, "that any of the great metaphysicians
have cast round looking for some interesting idea in terms of
which they might be able to construct a theory. They have
been charged with the sense of importance and significance in
some spiritual or intellectual experience, and the excitement
of this has driven them on to attempt to give intelligible form
to other vague reaches of experience with reference to this
basic insight."[1] Such an urge can only be justified "if it can
be maintained that experience is not only a spontaneous
process of form creation, but arises out of a relation to that
which transcends the subject."[2] This is the answer to the
Barthians, for if they were right our metaphysical analogies
could in no sense give insight into the nature of reality; they
could only tell us something about the nature of the human
mind.[3] "The transcendent," writes Miss Emmet, "may be
outside our categories; but that does not mean that it is entirely
outside our experience. It is the environment in which we live
and move and have our being."[4] The ultimate question is
what analogies are "important"; to decide this we must get
outside the realm of analogy. "There is no direct apprehension
of the intrinsic nature of transcendent reality. We only know
it through relationships interpreted in the symbolic forms of
our thinking."[5] Miss Emmet finds great significance in Martin
Buber's doctrine of the "I-Thou" relationship, but she refuses
to confine it to the exclusively personal; "such moments of
rapport may arise in any context."[6] She shows marked restraint
in refusing to push her argument any further than it can
legitimately go, but it is clear that, for her at least, this awareness provides the key to the ultimate meaning of the world.
"The appropriateness of form and analogy," she says, "may
be controlled by the basic experience of awareness. We have
suggested that religious analogies take their rise from such
moments of awareness. But they may also sometimes be the
hidden sources of the judgments of 'importance' from which
metaphysical analogies spring."[7] Miss Emmet deliberately
refuses to give a definitive answer to the problems of contem-

[1] Op. cit., pp. 197–8.   [2] Ibid., p. 205.   [3] Ibid.
[4] Ibid.   [5] Ibid., p. 207.   [6] Ibid., p. 213.   [7] Ibid., p. 213.

porary philosophy. The time, she considers, is not ripe for
that yet; the present task is to face responsibly together the
tensions of our time. From that, rather than from an over-
hasty improvisation of "agreed formulae," significant thinking
may come.[1] "A metaphysical thinker may try to see life
steadily; he cannot see it as a whole."[2]

It would be absurd to attempt in a few lines to pass a com-
prehensive judgment on Miss Emmet's discussion. It has,
however, I think, been well worth while, from the point of
view of our immediate interests, to see what kind of use can be
made of the principle of analogy by a Christian philosopher
whose approach is very different from that which I have
adopted in the present work. I have, I hope, indicated sufficiently clearly what seem to me to be the main points on which
her discussion can be criticized; the reader will no doubt be
more conscious than I can be of the weaknesses in my own.
That her arguments are penetrating and impressive is not, I
think, open to doubt; they would, I believe, be even more so
if she had paid more attention to Thomist epistemology than
she has. I have already ventured to criticize Dr. Farrer on this
point, but any force that there may be in that criticism will
bear far more strongly against Miss Emmet. An epistemological
doctrine must not, of course, be judged simply by its power to
provide an apodictic demonstration of the existence of God; to
maintain that would be to put the cart before the horse. But
when a certain doctrine has led to inconclusive results, it is
relevant to point out that the results were bound to be inconclusive by the very nature of the doctrine. And if there is an
alternative doctrine whose results would not be inconclusive
it is at least worth while to see whether that doctrine may not
have something to be said for it. Briefly, my complaint against
Miss Emmet is that she has neglected to give serious attention
to the one approach which might really solve our problem.
For what it is worth, my own judgment is that she has failed,
but only just failed, to write the book that is needed to restore
metaphysics to its rightful place in philosophy. However, to
have only just failed in such a task is to have achieved a
remarkable measure of success.

[1] Ibid., p. 226.   [2] Ibid., p. 227.

CONCLUSION

"IT is better," St. Athanasius tells us, "to incur the blame of redundancy than to omit anything which ought to be written."[1] And the number of things which "ought to be written" about natural theology is very great indeed. Nevertheless, every book must end somewhere, and this seems as good a point as any at which to bring the present discussion to a close. For, with whatever deficiencies, I have, I hope, not altogether failed in the task which I set before myself when I began, namely to exhibit the importance for rational theism of the doctrines of existence and analogy. I can only hope that others may be led to take up the subject where I have left it and to pursue it more tenaciously and successfully. I shall only add in conclusion a few brief remarks on the relevance of my main theme to the straightforward practice of religion.

If my argument has been substantially correct, it will follow that we are surrounded by, and are in intimate intercourse with, a world of active beings which, by their very existence, declare their dependence upon God who is Pure Act. A number of recent writers, and in particular the followers of Martin Buber, have attacked the traditional system of Western Catholic theism on the ground that it postulates as the realm of our experience a world of passive and inactive objects in which the possibility of any direct responsible confrontation of human persons with a personal God is to all intents and purposes absent; for the "I-it" attitude of an arid scholasticism we must, we are told, substitute the "I-Thou" attitude of an immediate existential relation to God. Such a criticism would, I think, be perfectly valid of a Cartesian universe, in which the direct object of human experience is simply a realm of intramental ideas and in which any possibility of knowing other existents than ourselves arises simply from the accuracy with which our ideas copy them. It would hold with almost as much force against a doctrine which asserted that we have a direct

[1] *De Incarn.*, xx, 3.

apprehension of extra-mental beings, if those beings were conceived as purely passive and inactive lumps, lying about the
world in a meaningless fashion or merely strewn before our eyes
by God. But it does not hold, I would maintain, against a
view such as I have endeavoured to expound in this book and
which I believe to be that of the scholastic tradition in its full
vigour, according to which existence is an activity and indeed
the most fundamental of all activities, and which claims that
in our experience of the objects of perception we are entering
into a living relationship with fellow creatures whose very
existence declares the incessant creative energizing act of God.
I do not think it is altogether adequate to describe this as
simply an "I-Thou," as contrasted with an "I-it," relation;
such a form of words would tend to suggest either that we are
confronted only with beings (whether God or creatures) that
are alive and personal, or else that we ought to react to every
being in our environment as if it were alive and personal,
whether in fact it is so or not. It is not, I think, necessary either
to deny or to personify lifeless matter in order to get what we
need; it is sufficient to realize that even the lifeless "it" is the
subject of an activity which enables it to be the object of, and
to contribute to, our own experience. In existing it is not just
passive, but is performing, on its own level of being, an activity
—the activity of existing—which, on a vastly higher level and
in the analogical mode proper to rational beings composed
of soul and body, we too perform. If the radically analogical
character of the act of existing is fully understood, we shall be
able, without falling into the fallacy of personifying the lower
creation, to recognize sub-human creatures, whether animate
or inanimate, as partners with us in the activity of existing and
as combining with us in the hierarchical order of the universe
to praise and glorify God. And while recognizing that in this
hierarchical order the lower creatures are subordinated to us
for our welfare and can indeed achieve their own perfection
only in ministering to it, we shall be warned against that
ruthless exploitation of them which has been so calamitous a
feature of the modern world and which, in the last resort,
derives from a refusal to admit that they in their mode, as we
in ours, are stamped with an inherent and inalienable dignity

as fellow creatures of the same God. In understanding the "I-it" relation to sub-human creatures in this way we shall at the same time be brought into the "I-Thou" relation to God whose creative activity is manifested to us as the ground of every finite existence.

In every finite being, then, its existence is a real, though a received, activity, communicated by the creative act of the God who himself is absolute existence, who "is all that he has." *Esse* is *esse a Deo* but it is also *esse ad Deum*, for the final end of every creature, the purpose for which it exists, is to glorify God, by manifesting in its operations, *in actu secundo*, the nature which it possesses *in actu primo* as the sheer gift of God. Sub-rational beings glorify God involuntarily and necessarily, and this is something not to be despised; but rational beings have the even greater privilege of glorifying him by the free and loving offering of their service. This is an offering that they are free to make or to withhold; therein lie both the greatness and the wretchedness of man.

"Man was created to praise, reverence, and serve God our Lord, and by this means to save his soul,"[1] but the Christian Church has never held that man was made merely for an extrinsic service of his Creator. The vision of God, union with God, assimilation to God—in such terms Christianity, basing itself on the Bible itself, has consistently described man's ultimate end and beatitude. Yet it is by no means easy to see how such a destiny is consistent with the maintenance of the radical distinction between God and the creature. To be a creature is to exist with a derived existence; to exist with an underived existence is to be God; there can be no half-way house. How then can a creature be *deified*?—for this is the term which Christian theology has dared to use. It is to meet this difficulty that Western Catholic theology has distinguished between the two orders of nature and supernature, between living with our own life and living with the life of God. A full discussion of this question would lead us beyond the boundaries of natural theology; I have discussed it elsewhere at some length.[2] It is, however, relevant to notice that the

---

[1] St. Ignatius Loyola, *Spiritual Exercises*, First Week, Principle and Foundation.
[2] *Christ, the Christian and the Church*, ch. v, vi, xii.

problem itself can only arise in a system which combines a quite uncompromising emphasis on the absolute distinction between God and creatures with an equally firm conviction that we can literally become "partakers of the divine nature."[1] It is significant that opposition to the Catholic doctrine of nature and supernature has come from two main sources: from Protestants who have denied the possibility of a real deification of man, and from Eastern Orthodox who have tended in the direction of pantheism. Some of the objections rest upon a sheer misunderstanding of what the doctrine is, a misunderstanding which is largely due to the superficiality with which its supporters have sometimes expounded it. It does not, for example, assert that supernature is a mere second storey superimposed upon the order of nature and having a purely extrinsic relation to it; on the contrary it asserts that nature is the material in which the supernatural works and that in consequence nature's own powers are released and enhanced and vivified. Nor does it claim that man can attain his ultimate fulfilment on the purely natural level; a remarkable amount of discussion has taken place in recent years on the question of the natural desire of man for the vision of God.[2] To go into the matter in any detail would take us far beyond the limits of our present subject, but the fact that Catholic thinkers have come to a general acceptance of the view that, in spite of the fundamentally gratuitous character of the supernatural order, man has by nature some kind of desire for it, is, I think, profoundly relevant to natural theology. For it is surely directly connected with the fact that the natural order is inherently incomplete and relative. The root fact about created being is that, while its reality is not an illusion, the basis for it is not to be found in the creature. Earlier in this book I laid stress upon the fact that Christian theism repudiates any suggestion that the created realm is intelligible in the sense of explaining itself. Its very essence is that it is dependent; its existence can only be explained as communicated to it from outside itself.

---

[1] 2 Pet. i, 4.
[2] The discussion has recently been summarized in Dr. P. K. Bastable's book *Desire for God*. The most thorough discussion in English is *The Desire of God in the Philosophy of St. Thomas Aquinas* by Dr. J. E. O'Mahony (Fr. James, O.S.F.C.). Reference should also be made to Fr. de Lubac's more recent book *Surnature*.

It must be understood in relation to God or it cannot be understood at all. This being so, it is hardly a matter for wonder if created being has at its roots a yearning for the God in whom alone its own meaning is to be found, a yearning which reaches consciousness only on the level of rational beings. And even on that level it cannot be more than obscure and confused; we know our own finitude, we know our dependence upon God, our *esse* is *esse ad Deum*, but what *esse ad Deum* means in the providence of God we cannot by nature discern. What in the providence of God it does mean is the subject of revelation, not of the natural reason. But the dim and conditional yearning for union with God which is so striking a feature of human religion shows that in man the essential incompleteness and insufficiency of created being has at last reached a conscious awareness. "As a whole, or in miniature," writes Dr. O'Mahony, "the universe is full of a divine discontent. . . . God is, as it were, the anonymous object of all desire."[1] "Natural theology," wrote Dr. William Temple, "ends in a hunger which it cannot satisfy."[2] And here on this note of incompleteness I shall leave my subject. Natural theology, by its very essence, cannot be a neatly rounded whole, for finite being, which is its subject-matter, is not a neatly rounded whole. "I asked the earth, and it answered me, 'I am not He'; and whatsoever are in it confessed the same. I asked the sea and the deeps and the living creeping things, and they answered, 'We are not thy God, seek above us.' I asked the moving air; and the whole air with his inhabitants answered, 'Anaximenes was deceived, I am not God.' I asked the heavens, sun, moon, stars; 'Nor (say they) are we the God whom thou seekest.' And I replied unto all the things which encompass the door of my flesh: 'Ye have told me of my God, that ye are not He; tell me something of Him.' And they cried out with a loud voice, 'He made us.' . . . I asked the whole frame of the world about my God; and it answered me, 'I am not He, but He made me.'"[3]

What he did in addition to this is not the subject of natural theology.

[1] *The Desire of God* . . ., pp. 79, 93.
[2] *Nature, Man and God*, p. 519.   [3] Aug., *Conf.*, X, vi, 9.

INDEX TO PROPER NAMES

(Derivatives are included under their originals; e.g. *Plato* includes *Platonic,
Platonism* and *Platonist*.)